IDENTIFYING THE BIBLICAL PATRIARCHS FROM NON-BIBLICAL SOURCES

Locating the names and placing the proper times of the Biblical Patriarchs in non-biblical records of the 30th to 20th centuries BC

STEVEN NORRIS

Published in the United States of America

Brilliant Books Literary
137 Forest Park Lane Thomasville
North Carolina 27360 USA

ISBN:
Paperback: 979-8-88945-368-0
Ebook: 979-8-88945-369-7

Contents

Prologue

There is a dichotomy among scholars that appears when dealing with the Bible as a source as opposed to any other source outside the Bible. The dichotomy is really quite simple, yet it has never, as far as I am aware, been properly defined. The issue revolves around the longevity of the Patriarchs.

When dealing with the mythology of the Greeks, no one talks about the fact that Zeus, for instance, had relationships with young maidens who had to have lived hundreds of years after he was born. He was, after all, a god. However, ancient historians weren't ignorant. They knew that behind the "myths" of the gods there were real people. Jupiter, the Roman king of the gods, but also the god of the sky and thunder, was also the same as Zeus of the Greek pantheon. Although not the subject of this book, ancient historians have equated Iapetos (Jupiter) with Japheth, the son of Noah. But was he a man? Let's allow the historians who existed over 2000 years before us answer that question. That would place us 2000 years closer to the "myth".

Japheth was literally the progenitor of many nations, including all the Indo-European peoples. In fact, it would be surprising indeed if his name had gone unremembered among them. As it is, we find that the early Greeks worshipped him as Iapetos, or Iapetus, whom they regarded as the son of heaven and earth, and the father of many nations. Likewise, in the ancient Sanskrit vedas of India, he is remembered as Pra-Japati, the sun and ostensible Lord of Creation.

His name was further corrupted and assimilated into the Roman pantheon as Iupater, which eventually became that of Jupiter. None of these names are recognized as being of Greek, Indian or Latin origin; but are rather mere corruptions of the Hebrew name of Japheth. Similarly, the early Saxon races perpetuated his name as Sceaf, and recorded his name in their early genealogies as the son of Noah, the forebear of their various peoples.

On the other hand, in Greek mythology Iapetus, or Iapetos, was a Titan, the son of Uranus and Gaia, and father (by an Oceanid named Clymene or Asia) of Atlas, Prometheus, Epimetheus, and Menoetius and through Prometheus and Epimetheus and Atlas an ancestor of the human race.

Pausanias (8.27.15) writes:

> "As I have already related, the boundary between Megalopolis and Heraea is at the source of the river Buphagus. The river got its name, they say, from a hero called Buphagus, the son of Iapetus and Thornax. This is what they call her in Laconia also. They also say that Artemis shot Buphagus on Mount Pholoe because he attempted an unholy sin against her godhead."

Lactantius in the "*Epitome of the Divine Institutes*" writes:

> "But let us leave the poets; let us come to history, which is supported both by the credibility of the facts and by the antiquity of the times. Euhemerus was a Messenian, a very ancient writer, who gave an account of the origin of Jupiter, and his exploits, and all his posterity, gathered from the sacred inscriptions of ancient temples; he also traced out the parents of the other gods, their countries, actions, commands,

and deaths, and even their sepulchres. And this history Ennius translated into Latin, whose words are these: 'As these things are written, so is the origin and kindred of Jupiter and his brothers; after this manner it is handed down to us in the sacred writing."

The same Euhemerus, therefore, relates that Jupiter, when he had five times gone round the world, and had distributed governments to his friends and relatives, and had given laws to men, and had wrought many other benefits, being endowed with immortal glory and everlasting remembrance, ended his life in Crete, and departed to the gods, and that *his sepulchre is in Crete* (emphasis mine), in the town of Gnossus [Knossos], and that upon it is engraved in ancient Greek letters Zankronou, which is Jupiter the son of Saturnus. It is plain, therefore, from the things which I have related, that he was a man, and reigned on the earth.[1]

"Let us pass on to former things, that we may discover the origin of the whole error. Saturnus is said to have been born of Coelus and Terra. This is plainly incredible; but there is a certain reason why it is thus related, and he who is ignorant of this rejects it as a fable. That Uranus was the father of Saturnus, both Hermes affirms, and sacred history teaches. When Trismegistus said that there were very few men of perfect learning, he enumerated among them Iris' relatives, Uranus, Saturnus and Mercurius. Euhemerus relates that the same Uranus was the first who reigned on earth, using these words: "In the beginning Coelus first had the chief power on earth: he instituted and prepared that kingdom for himself together with his brothers.[2]"

From this we see not only that the ancients realized that Jupiter [Japheth] was a man, but that he also was the son of Uranus [Noah], who was the first king after the Great Flood. Therefore, we can see that Greek mythology matches with the biblical record.

We now must get back to the dichotomy which dealt with the longevity of man. It seems clear to me that the issue of the longevity of man was solved by making the earliest men, after the Flood, into gods. Doing so solves some problems, both for the ancient people who may have known these god/men who lived long lives, and also for us. For us, the problem can easily be solved by calling all of this mythology. With one simple word, history is eliminated as a viable answer to the stories about which we are about to deal.

Yet the dichotomy is that we still have "history" running into "mythology." This occurred in Troy, the scene of the Homer's "*Iliad*" and the "*Odyssey*".

These works, which were written about 850 BC, or 2870 years ago, speak of an interaction of "gods" and men in a battle over a city, named Troy. It was termed "mythology" for 2870 years, give or take. Then, in 1868, a German archaeologist, Heinrich Schliemann, claimed to have found the actual ruins of the ancient city of Troy, the site of the Trojan War, which was the setting for the books of Homer. Actually the site had been identified as early as 1822 and was worked by a certain Frank Calvert, but the credit eventually went to Schliemann. The point here is that the ancient city of Troy was actually discovered. Furthermore, other places that were mentioned in the books were also discovered, including the actual home of Menelaus, for instance. Troy was found to have actually existed. My point is simple: myths are only myths until they become history.

Now, moving to the Bible we begin to deal with a very similar scenario as that which existed with Homer's work. It was considered "mythology" until the mid 1800's when, all of a sudden, archaeologists began discovering things that proved that in fact the Bible was largely historical. Furthermore, the discoveries were showing that, where evidence exists, it confirms the historicity of the Bible. I am aware of the fact that the Bible contains proverbs, poetry, hymns, and parables. After all, it consists of 66 books written over a period of 2000 years by some 40 authors on 3 continents in at least three original languages. Therefore, it is not all history. However, it contains history, and where that history has been verified, it has been shown to be true history, which has taken it out of the mythology category.

We now move to the book of Genesis, the theme of this book. The question is simple: is this history or is this mythology (I use the term to mean "not history" here). The remainder of this book will allow the reader to decide the answer to this question. However, before entering into this effort of truth search, it will be important to dispel one more myth. That myth is that men cannot live over 100 years, or so. This myth clearly exists, both in the Bible and in other ancient literature. However, we are back to the dichotomy I referred to earlier, namely that somehow it is not a problem in Greek mythology, while it is a definite problem in Biblical mythology.

Why is that? The answer, to me, is obvious. There is a prejudice that exists when dealing with Biblical studies that does not exist outside of those studies. It is really that simple. There is no way that I can overcome prejudice. This was taught to me by my father a long time ago. In jest he said to me the following: "don't confuse me with the facts; my mind is already made up[3]!"

In this work my emphasis will be on the persons from Noah's son Shem down to Abraham. The work will include non-biblical but important personages as well. It will show the familial relationships of these persons, both within and without the Bible, and how their interactions formed the world after the Great Flood. I trust that the reader will have a fuller understanding of just how our world after the Great Flood came to be the way it is today.

Chapter One

Identifying the Patriarchs
from Non-Biblical Sources

A s Biblical Archaeology has improved during the last several decades, there have been an amazing number of finds that corroborate statements made in the Bible, verifying with each decade that passes that the book contains a great deal of accurate history. This is not to say that the Bible does not contain poetry, proverbs, and parables. Obviously, it does. However, the historical books are being shown to be among the best records for the times that they cover.

According to the dominant theory called Greek primacy, the New Testament was originally written in Greek, of which 5,650 handwritten copies have survived in Greek, and over 10,000 in Latin. When other languages are included, the total of ancient copies approaches 25,000. The next ancient text to come close to rivaling that number is Homer's Iliad, which has survived in 643 ancient copies.[4] While arguments of "volume" don't prove accuracy, it is the case that there is more accuracy, in terms of similarity, among the earliest copies of the Bible than there is of any other non-Biblical books from the time in which these Biblical records exist.

Today many scholars of ancient literature would consider the Bible to be among the most accurate of history books. It also has the best preserved attested history of any other history of its era. For instance, among the copies of Julius Caesar's *War Memories* there are about 20% differences in currently outstanding copies of his work, none of which is the original. Yet the Bible, after 2000 years, has over 99% consistency in the content of the work. This is true in spite of the fact that it has been translated into hundreds of languages with numerous "versions" within each language. In fact, up until the Dead Sea scrolls were found in 1947, the oldest manuscripts of the Bible were dated from the 12th century, and held in the Vatican (*Codex Vaticanus* and *Codex Sinaiticus*). Then, older books of the Bible were found in these caves. The only Old Testament book not in those caves was the Book of Ruth from the Bible. Surprisingly, the content of each book agreed with the otherwise earliest manuscripts to 99% accuracy, in spite of the fact that they were over 1300 years separated in time.

Clearly this is a testament to the accuracy of the witness of the Bible. Arguments that it has been changed fall by the wayside. At the very least we may state that the witness in the Bible has been more accurately transmitted to us today than any other ancient document. However, the fact that the record itself is accurately presented does not mean that the stories within it are historical. That will be the subject of this book, in which I will show that the characters were not only real, but that they also interacted with other real non-biblical persons who are accepted as historical. Furthermore, I will place these persons in their right time frame in history as we know it today.

The Dead Sea caves revealed other non-biblical books that talk about the same subject of this book, namely, the Patriarchs. To ignore them would be foolish. After all, they precede us by over 2000 years. Perhaps they reveal more of the truth than current scholars have found about this subject. The Torah consists of the first five books of the Old Testament of the Bible. It claims to have been compiled by Moses, who lived in the 15th century BC At the end of the second book, Exodus, however, Moses' own death is described. This has led some scholars to conclude that Moses could not have written this book. However, the tradition does not state that he wrote the five books. Instead it says that he compiled the five books. The fact that his death is described at the end of the second book may be explained in that someone who succeeded him, such as Joshua, added a few sentences to the end of this book to complete it.

In any case, the fact that the Torah existed before Moses compiled it can be very easily shown to be the case. The book of Genesis refers to Akkad, called Agade in the Bible. In the days that Moses lived, that city-state did not exist. Furthermore, in the days that more liberal theologians claim that the Bible was written, about 650 BC, Agade had been in the dust for nearly 1700 years! The precise archaeological site of the city of Akkad has, at present, not been found.[5] The convergence of the Tigris and Euphrates was called Ancient Babylonia and it had two parts: Akkad to the north and Sumer in the south.[6]

Since Moses didn't know where it was, and since the "priests" of the period of the Kings of Israel didn't know where it was, and since we today don't know where it is, how could it show up in Genesis? The reality is that the King of Akkad, Sargon the Great, has been shown to be a real king. He is among the best attested kings of ancient history, as I will show. Yet his city-state disappeared. Furthermore, it disappeared around 2200 BC, over 7 centuries before Moses and 14 centuries before the "priests" were said by some current scholars to have written the book of Genesis, for political reasons!

The case is made: Genesis purports to speak of things that happened a long time ago, and it had to have been created when those things happened, or shortly thereafter. It had to have been put on paper while the memories were still real. Therefore, Genesis had to have been written at least 4400 years ago, or before 2200 BC, when

Akkad was destroyed. Joseph died in 1806 BC His name is the last mentioned in the book of Genesis. By the time of Moses, Akkad was not even a memory. Yet it exists in the book. Someone must have been keeping a record relatively close to the actual events. The book of Genesis purports to tell of the first 30 generations of man, from Adam to the end of the life of Jacob, grandson of Abraham. The next book begins with Moses, about 300 years and several generations later after Joseph.

My research has been focused on a simple premise: if the Bible is good history, we should be able to identify the characters of Genesis outside the Bible in other contemporary works. After years of research I am now able to show that the characters of the Bible were not only real, but that they were also interactive in the world as it was known then, holding the positions of power that would have evolved naturally if they were the survivors of the Great Flood.

In the process, I will develop a more accurate timeline of the lives of these personages. By accurate dating we will be able to place them in context one to another. This will allow us to explore the why and how the various interactions with which these early rulers had to deal came about. The majority of this work is, therefore, genealogical in nature. This happens to be a passion of mine and it is the genealogical search that has led me to identify, outside the Bible, these key Patriarchal figures. I hope to be able to show the reader relationships that will explain the movements of the Patriarchs throughout the Bible lands. I will also draw on extra-biblical sources that will confirm that the biblical records are accurate.

When I began this research, I became aware that proper dating is imperative if one wishes to get an accurate picture of the players in their correct time frame. It is essential to be in the correct *sitz im leben*, or "place in life," as Rudolph Bultmann, the pre-eminent theologian of the last century has rightly shown. Therefore, we must first find some dates that are undeniable, or at least nearly universally accepted. From that starting point we can move backward in time based upon the biblical records themselves, supplemented by non-biblical but datable materials. In this way, we will avoid the tempting process of shoving a given person into a time frame or culture that is not relevant to the person or his time.

The earliest definite date that exists in the Bible is the beginning of the reign of King Solomon of Jerusalem. King Solomon was the son of King David, the first King of Jerusalem. Some scholars have claimed that there is no evidence that King Solomon even existed. In fact, that is not the case. One clear example is sufficient to prove this point. The Bible indicates that King Solomon made King Hiram of Phoenicia an ally and formed a treaty with him. We have, from extra-biblical records, the fact that Hiram of Phoenicia reigned from 980 BC to 947 BC. Therefore we should expect to find that King Solomon, if he existed, had a reign at least roughly similar to that of King Hiram. Hiram's beginning date is derived from the statement of Josephus, citing both Tyrian court records and the writings of Menander.[7]

During Hiram's reign, Tyre grew from a satellite of Sidon into the most important of Phoenician cities, and the holder of a large trading empire. He suppressed the rebellion of the first Tyrean colony at Utica, near the later site of Carthage.[8] The Bible says that he allied himself with King David of the United Kingdom of Israel as well and that the status of both Kings was equal and that the treaty between them was a parity treaty.[9] After the death of King David, Solomon, a son of David, succeeded to David's throne and Hiram continued the relation with Israel through King Solomon, the upcoming power of the region. They were also equal ("יהא," meaning "brothers").[10] Through the alliance with Solomon, Hiram ensured himself access to the major trade routes to Egypt, Arabia and Mesopotamia. The two kings also joined forces in starting a trade route over the Red Sea, connecting the Israelite harbor of Ezion-Geber with a land called Ophir.[11] Both kings grew rich through this trade and Hiram sent Solomon architects, workmen and cedar wood to build the first temple in Jerusalem. He also extended the Tyrean harbor, enlarged the city by joining the two islands on which it was built, and built a royal palace and a temple for Melqart.[12] Furthermore, we have this from the Bible:

> Now Hiram king of Tyre sent his servants to Solomon, because he heard that they had anointed him king in place of his father, for Hiram had always loved David .. So the Lord gave Solomon wisdom, as He had promised him; *and there was peace between Hiram and Solomon, and the two of them made a treaty together.*[13]

A thousand years later Josephus mentions this treaty and noted that copies of this alliance could be read in the public archives in Tyre:

> The copies of these epistles remain at this day, and are preserved not only in our books, but among the Tyrians also; insomuch that if any one would know the certainty about them, he may desire of the keepers of the public records of Tyre to shew him them, and he will find what is there set down to agree with what we have said.[14]

Therefore, the existence of King Solomon is now beyond question. Furthermore, we know he reigned sometime toward the beginning of the 10th century BC based on King Hiram's reign. Biblical scholars who believe in an historical Solomon argue that his regnal dates can be derived by independent methods: The division of the kingdom following Solomon's death occurred at some time in the year beginning in Nisan (in the spring) of 931 BC, as argued by Edwin Thiele,[15] so that his fourth year would have begun in Tishri (in the fall) of 968/967 BC. Solomon's fourth year, in which Temple construction allegedly began, is calculated by modern scholars from the Tyrian king list of Menander as the year 968 BC, without the use of biblical texts.[16] Therefore, we now have the beginning of the reign of Solomon in 971 BC, about 9 years after the start of King Hiram's reign.

The next important date is the beginning of the foundation for the Temple at Jerusalem. This will become important because from it we can go backwards to determine other important dates in the history of the Patriarchs. As just noted above, the beginning of the temple was started in 967 BC, determined from non-biblical sources, as noted above. However, the Bible confirms this as well:

> And it came to pass in the four hundred and eightieth year after the children of Israel were come out of the land of Egypt, in the fourth year of Solomon's reign over Israel, in the month Zif, which is the second month, that he began to build the house of the LORD.[17]

Then in verse 37 and following we see this:

> In the fourth year was the foundation of the house of the LORD laid, in the month Zif: And in the eleventh year, in the month Bul, which is the eighth month, was the house finished throughout all the parts thereof, and according to all the fashion of it. So was he seven years in building it.[18]

We are now in a position to move backward from our confirmed start date of 967 BC. From 1 Kings 6:1, we see that the Exodus (the coming out of the land of Egypt by the children of Israel) occurred exactly 480 years prior to the beginning of the Temple in Jerusalem. Therefore, from our start date of 967 BC, we will go backwards 480 years which will take us to the date that the Israelites left Egypt. This would bring us to 1447 BC. This is the date of the Exodus by Moses from Egypt.

The next important step is to determine the length of time that the children of Israel stayed in Egypt. Again, the Bible is quite specific on this:

> Now the sojourning of the children of Israel, who dwelt in Egypt, [was] four hundred and thirty years. And it came to pass at the end of the four hundred and thirty years, even the selfsame day it came to pass, that all the hosts of the LORD went out from the land of Egypt.[19]

Therefore, if we go backwards 430 years from the date of the Exodus, we get the date of the arrival of Jacob in Egypt to buy grain. That year is 1877 BC. We can move backward again to obtain the year of the birth of Jacob from the Bible. We know from the Bible how old Jacob was when he came into Egypt:[20]

> And Pharaoh said unto Jacob, How old art thou? And Jacob said unto Pharaoh, The days of the years of my pilgrimage are an hundred and thirty years: few and evil have the days of the years of my life been, and have not attained unto the days of the years of the life of my fathers in the days of their pilgrimage.[21]

Jacob was born in 2007 BC (by going backwards 130 years from 1877 BC).

The Bible also allows us to move backwards to determine the year of birth of the father of Jacob, who was Isaac:[22]

> And after that came his brother out, and his
> hand took hold on Esau's heel; and his name
> was called Jacob: and Isaac was threescore years
> old when she bare them.[23]

Issac was born in 2067 BC (going backwards 60 years from Jacob's birth).

Finally, we may also determine the year of the birth of Abraham in the same way:[24]

> And Abraham circumcised his son Isaac being
> eight days old, as God had commanded him.
> And Abraham was an hundred years old, when
> his son Isaac was born unto him.[25]

Abraham was therefore born in 2167 BC. In dealing with the Patriarchs, then, it is from this year, 2167 BC, that we must base our analysis. If we neglect this, then we are not being faithful to the clear references from the Bible. Also, we have no other references regarding the birth of Abraham from outside the Bible to dispute the Biblical record. However, we may find records that support this date from non-Biblical sources. We know from the Bible that Abraham lived 175 years in total. I will deal with this longevity issue in detail later. Assuming that this is true, and we have no reason to dispute it, unless we rely on pure prejudice, we can determine that Abraham died in 1992 BC. Non-biblical research for evidence of Abraham must then focus on the period between 2167 BC and 1992 BC, with the majority of it obviously starting at least 20 years after 2167 BC, since we are looking for evidence of him as an adult.

In confirmation of our dates, we may add the fact that in the Book of Jubilees Ur-Nammu, the King of Ur, assigned Abraham's father, Terah, to be the High Priest of the Temple of Nannar Sin in Ur. Ur-Nammu, as will be shown, was Terah's great-great-grandfather. From non-biblical archaeological sources, which I will show later when discussing Ur-Nammu, we know that Ur-Nammu died in 2095 BC.[26] Furthermore, Utu-Hegal was the king when Terah and his son Abraham lived in Ur as well. Utu-Hegal died in 2113 BC, meaning that Abraham had to have been born before that year as well. Therefore, we have non-biblical evidence that Abraham lived around the time that I have indicated (2167 BC to 1992 BC).[27]

Now that we have a firm starting and finishing date for the life of Abraham, we can determine from the biblical records the birth and death years of the other Patriarchs.

This can be done easily by using the clear dating in the Bible:

> These [are] the generations of Shem: Shem [was] an hundred years old, and begat Arphaxad two years after the Flood:
> And Shem lived after he begat Arphaxad five hundred years, and begat sons and daughters.
> And Arphaxad lived five and thirty years, and begat Salah:
> And Arphaxad lived after he begat Salah four hundred and three years, and begat sons and daughters.
> And Salah lived thirty years, and begat Eber:
> And Salah lived after he begat Eber four hundred and three years, and begat sons and daughters.
> And Eber lived four and thirty years, and begat Peleg: And Eber lived after he begat Peleg four hundred and thirty years, and begat sons and daughters.
> And Peleg lived thirty years, and begat Reu: And Peleg lived after he begat Reu two hundred and nine years, and begat sons and daughters.
> And Reu lived two and thirty years, and begat Serug: And Reu lived after he begat Serug two

hundred and seven years, and begat sons and
daughters.
And Serug lived thirty years, and begat Nahor:
And Serug lived after he begat Nahor two
hundred years, and begat sons and daughters.
And Nahor lived nine and twenty years, and
begat Terah:
And Nahor lived after he begat Terah an
hundred and nineteen years, and begat sons
and daughters.
And Terah lived seventy years, and begat
Abram, Nahor, and Haran.[28]

Based on this genealogical information we may arrive at the year
of birth and death of all of the Patriarchs after the Flood. Here is
the list:

Shem (3387 BC – 2787 BC)
Arphaxad (3285 BC – 2750 BC)
Cainan (3080 BC – 2620 BC)
Salah (3032 BC – 2572 BC)
Eber (2602 BC – 2198 BC)
Peleg (2568 BC – 2229 BC)
Ragau (2438 BC – 2099 BC)
Serug (2406 BC – 2176 BC)
Nahor (2276 BC – 2029 BC)
Terah (2242 BC – 2037 BC)
Abraham (2167 BC – 1992 BC)

I am aware that the lifetimes of these Patriarchs are larger than we
would expect and certainly longer than we live today. However,
this is what the biblical record gives as the lifetimes of these people. Before I address this, it is important to see how the longevity of these Patriarchs made it possible for communication across
multiple generations to occur. From the list above, one can see
that Abraham could have communicated with Ragau, his great

great grandfather. Simlarly, Shem could have communicated with Arphaxad, Cainan, and Salah. In short, and in theory, through only three persons all of the early Patriarchs could have passed along important information, even though there were 11 generations from the beginning (Shem) to the end (Abraham).

Is there any evidence outside the Bible that people lived longer lives at this time? In fact, there is. Flavius Josephus recognized that this might be a concern and he wrote the following in the First century AD:

> Now when Noah had lived three hundred and fifty years after the Flood, and that all that time happily, he died, having lived the number of nine hundred and fifty years. But let no one, upon comparing the lives of the ancients with our lives, and with the few years which we now live, think that what we have said of them is false; or make the shortness of our lives at present an argument, that neither did they attain to so long a duration of life, for those ancients were beloved of God, and [lately] made by God himself; and because their food was then fitter for the prolongation of life, might well live so great a number of years: and besides, God afforded them a longer time of life on account of their virtue, and the good use they made of it in astronomical and geometrical discoveries, which would not have afforded the time of foretelling [the periods of the stars] unless they had lived six hundred years; for the great year is completed in that interval. Now I have for witnesses to what I have said, all those that have written Antiquities, both among the Greeks and barbarians; for even Manetho, who wrote the Egyptian History, and Berosus,

> who collected the Chaldean Monuments, and
> Mochus, and Hestieus, and, besides these,
> Hieronymus the Egyptian, and those who
> composed the Phoenician History, agree to
> what I here say: Hesiod also, and Hecatseus,
> Hellanicus, and Acusilaus; and, besides these,
> Ephorus and Nicolaus relate that the ancients
> lived a thousand years. But as to these matters,
> let every one look upon them as he thinks fit. [29]

There is another clear non-biblical reference to long-lived persons. Gilgamesh is said to have lived in the 26th century BC.[30] I have estimated his birth in 2650 BC or thereabouts. Ur-Nammu, the king of Ur, who died in 2095 BC as just noted above, wrote a "praise poem" which was a record of his achievements in which he stated clearly that he was the "older brother" of Gilgamesh: "I am the older brother of Gilgamesh! I am the son borne by Ninsun."[31] If he was the "older brother of Gilgamesh as he says, and we have no reason to doubt it since it was in his own words, then he would have had to have been born around 2650 BC or before. Yet he died in 2095 BC. Therefore, he lived over 655 years. This record is from a NON-Biblical source and a first-person account!

We see, then, that many ancient historians state that the many post-Flood inhabitants had long life spans. Until shown otherwise, we might accept their witness. One must ask this question: other than from pure prejudice, on what basis could one deny this list of reputable historians? It runs against our intuition to believe that people actually did live longer lifetimes in the past. Yet, that is the witness of those closest to the events. There are books written as to how it might have been possible for people to live longer lives before and shortly after the Flood. These books also give possible explanations as to why the lifetimes fell from Noah (950 years) to Abraham (175 years) to Moses (120 years). I have no intention of dealing with these theories here, but I recommend for those who are concerned about this issue that they do their own research. I have done so myself and am comfortable that the lifetimes recorded in the biblical record reflect actual lifetimes and not mythological.

If I am able to show that the Patriarchs were real people, with other non-biblical names, and also am able to place them in their proper "*Sitz im leben,*" then I believe the argument over the longevity of the Patriarchs will be proven moot. I have included in the appendix a listing of biblical and non-biblical people and the lengths of their lives. Over the centuries their lives shortened until the time of Moses, who lived 120 years, according to the Bible. I will show that if we allow the record of the Bible to be the standard for dating that we will find that extra-biblical people will fit in quite well.

Identifying the Patriarchs

It is now time to identify the Patriarchs from non-biblical sources. If this is successful, then I will be able to show that the timeline discussed in the last chapter is accurate. If we accept the statement in the Bible that there was a Great Flood which wiped out almost all of mankind, then we must also accept that the world was repopulated by only a few people, including the family of Noah. Even if there were a few others who survived the Flood, which is a possibility that I do not discount out of hand, the earliest rulers of the post Flood world would almost certainly have had to have been descended from the sons of Noah. As we proceed I will identify many early rulers in Sumeria and nearby areas who were the descendants of Shem and Ham, two of the sons of Noah.

The Bible states that the Ark landed in "the mountains of Ararat."[32] Typically the mountain of Agri Dag in this range is sited as the best candidate since it is the highest peak in the area and would have been the first to appear. If, during the process of the water receding from the Flood the lands also were pushed upward, which is a current theory regarding getting rid of all the water, it would also explain that the water did not have to be this deep (over 28,000 feet, if Everest existed prior to the Flood!). Given that hypothesis, then, the mountain of Agri Dag may not be the landing site of the Ark.

Once again there are many books on this subject and it is not my intention to review the speculative theories on this matter. Suffice it to say that the "mountains of Ararat" is clear enough for us to know that the Ark settled in eastern Turkey near the Russian border. For our purposes going forward this is sufficient. Work by Simcha Lev-Yadun of Israel's Agricultural Research Organization and his colleagues suggest the first farms may have been farther north, between the Tigris and Euphrates rivers in what is today northeastern Turkey and northern Syria.[33]

Incidentally, Lake Van is in this area as well. Archaeologists have found evidence of extremely old villages along the shores of Lake Van.[34] Presumably the first settlements of the family of Noah took place there before the migration out of the mountains and into the valleys. As Noah sent his sons out into the world to repopulate it, it would have been natural to follow a stream or small river downhill until the plains below were reached. In doing so they would have naturally followed the courses of streams that eventually create the Tigris and Euphrates rivers.

We know very little about the family of Japheth. There are traditions that state that he headed into southern Russia and Europe, rather than heading south and west into the Middle East. We will not be following this line in this book. In the prologue, I offered some clues as to his identity, but in my opinion he disappears from "history" as we know it and must be relegated into the "pantheon of the gods." Instead, I will follow the families of Shem and Ham. The family of Shem initially settled at the base of the mountain range in what is now Syria, Lebanon, and northern Iraq. It was the family of Arphaxad who settled in the Syria/Lebanon area. His older brother, Elam, stayed to the east of the Tigris and Euphrates Rivers and traveled between them and the Zagros mountains in what is called Iran today, settling farther and farther down that val-

ley. His land was called after his name, Elam. Because these brothers were close, as I will show, they remained in contact with each
other and their children and grandchildren intermarried, as I will
also show. I will deal with Arphaxad and Elam, the sons of Shem,
together. Later I will address the sons of Ham.

Chapter Two

Arphaxad (3285 BC – 2750 BC), Aram, and Elam (3288 BC – 2900 BC)

A ccording to the biblical account, Arphaxad was born in 3285 BC and died in 2750 BC at the age of 535 years. These dates are calculated from the foundation of the Temple of Jerusalem in the same way that I determined the date of the birth of Abraham.

Arphaxad's brother, Elam, was older than Arphaxad, so he was born before 3285 BC. My research has led me to believe that Elam died before his brother Arphaxad, around 2900 BC. Elam was the founder of the Elamites, who inhabited what is now known as southwestern Iran, at the base of the Zagros mountains.[35] Elam is listed as the apparent firstborn of Shem. The country named after him to the east of southern Mesopotamia was for many years believed to have been settled by people who were not Shemites, and the biblical statement was challenged. Subsequent excavations, however, have shown that the earliest people to settle here were indeed Shemites. S. R. Driver was forced to admit that "inscriptions recently discovered" have shown that in very early times, Elam was peopled by Shemites. He could not help but add that the Biblical statement probably originated because Elam was dependent in much later times upon Semitic Babylonia: he assured his readers that "it is very unlikely" that the original author of Genesis 10 could possibly have known what we [only] now know.[36] This confirms the ancient authenticity of the book of Genesis in the Bible.

But since Driver's time, further excavation has provided very strong evidence of direct cultural links between some of the earliest cities in Sumer and the lowest strata at Susa, the capital of Elam.[37] The evidence indicates the presence in the earliest times of Greater Mesopotamia (before 3000 BC) three distinct groups of people, the Sumerian Hamites, Shemites, and a group of people whom both V. G. Childe and M. E. L. Mallowen properly refer to as Japhethites, or Indo-Europeans. Childe put it this way:

> From later written records, philologists deduce the presence of three linguistic groups – 'Japhethites' (known only inferentially from a few place-names); Semites (speaking a language akin to Hebrew and Arabic); and the dominant Sumerians.[38]

The picture as presented elsewhere by Childe reveals that the first people to enter Mesopotamia came from the East and were not Sumerians, but were Shemitic Elamites, descendants of Elam, who founded such early cities as Al-Ubaid and Jemdet Nasr.[39] These people established themselves first in the south at the Persian Gulf and gradually spread toward the north, but without losing the cultural links which take us back to Elam. In additon were Japhethites, who clearly moved on, and Sumerians, whom I will show were descendants of Ham, or Hamites.

The Book of Jubilees offers an even more specific plan by Shem for the dispersion of his sons:

And Shem also divided amongst his sons, and the first portion came forth for Ham and his sons, to the east of the river Tigris till it approaches the east, the whole land of India, and on the Red Sea on its coast, and the waters of Dedan, and all the mountains of Mebri and Ela, and all the land of Susan and all that is on the side of Pharnak to the Red Sea and the river Tina.

And for Asshur came forth the second Portion, all the land of Asshur and Nineveh and Shinar and to the border of India, and it ascends and skirts the river.

And for Arpachshad came forth the third portion, all the land of the region of the Chaldees to the east of the Euphrates, bordering on the Red Sea, and all the waters of the desert close to the tongue of the sea which looks towards Egypt, all the land of Lebanon and Sanir and 'Amana to the border of the Euphrates.

And for Aram there came forth the fourth portion, all the land of Mesopotamia between the Tigris and the Euphrates to the north of the Chaldees to the border of the mountains of Asshur and the land of 'Arara.

And there came forth for Lud the fifth portion, the mountains of Asshur and all appertaining to them till it reaches the Great Sea, and till it reaches the east of Asshur his brother.[40]

From this record, we see that Ham received lands to the east of the Tigris River all the way down to India. As will be shown, these lands eventually ended up largely in the hands of Elam. Asshur was given the lands at the north end of the Mesopotamian Valley, including Nineveh, which city he founded. Arphaxad was offered the lands of the "Chaldees", named after his son Kesed, east of the Euphrates River but but also down to the southwest toward Egypt. In addition, he was offered what is now known as Lebanon and Syria. His brother Aram was offered the main portion of the Mesopotamian Valley between the two rivers, the Euphrates and the Tigris, from the Gulf to the north all the way to the "mountains of Ararat."

As I will show shortly Aram was squeezed out of the Mesopotamian Valley and ended up having properties only at the north of that valley, close to the base of the "mountains of Ararat" in Syria, near to his brother Arphaxad. Similarly, Elam was forced out of the Mesopotamian Valley and moved to the east to the base of the Zagros mountains in what is now Iran. Arphaxad was also squeezed out of his portion and ended up at the far northwestern portion of the Mesopotamian Valley, although he also controlled the Elamite territory after the death of his brother Elam.

Childe, then, correctly proposed that a second wave of immigrants into Mesopotamia followed, who this time were not Shemites but Sumerians, or the sons of Ham. These people brought new civilizing influences with them which led to considerable cultural advance, until by the time of the Uruk period (down to about 2900 BC), though still a minority, had become the rulers. Meanwhile, further to the north, in Assyria, the Shemites continued their slow development with the sons of Arphaxad. To the east the sons of Elam also held lands along the Zagros mountains in Iran, lands that they controlled for another 1000 years or more, where they made excursions back into their original promised lands from their ancestor Shem, namely the Mesopotamian Valley.

Mallowen emphasizes the distinctions between these two dominant types, the Sumerians and the Akkadians, or in other words the Hamites and Shemites, in this early period of the country's development.[41] At the same time, he also underscores that there was another group, whose existence is only well attested on linguistic grounds. Speiser proposed the name Japhethite for these people, known very early in the hill country east of the Tigris.[42] This is the area that eventually became Elamite lands, including Aratta, about which I will have more shortly. The Japhetites were noted especially for their fairness of skin. That they did penetrate southern Mesopotamia, at least in some numbers in very early times, has been noted by Campbell Thompson as well as by Speiser.[43] The general picture supports the statements made in Genesis 10. Shem's offspring, Arphaxad, Aram, and Elam, came out of the "mountains of Ararat" and then split, with Arphaxad and Aram moving generally westward along the base of the "mountains of Ararat" to found the empire that eventually was known as Assyria (in Syria, Lebanon, and northern Iraq). Elam moved down the valley east of the Tigris River between that river and the Zagros mountains, founding cities far down the valley in what is now southern Iran. Although the historic record is not complete enough to show this, it is also likely that, at least originally, these three brothers also spread into the Mesopotamian Valley. However, Ham, while beginning at the base of the "mountains of Ararat" in northeastern Iraq, near the base of the top of the Zagros mountain range, shortly thereafter moved into the Mesopotamian Valley between the Tigris and Euphrates rivers, an area that came to be known as Sumer. In other words, he invaded the area orignally given to Elam by Shem.

Although we have no direct link to the descendants of Elam here is a brief history and some names of his descendants:

> Beginning with the semi-mythical period, we have the story of the fight of the Babylonian hero Gilgamesh with the Elamite tyrant Humbaba, who was defeated by the hero and his helper Enkidu, and beheaded.[44] The earliest really historical reference to the Elamites as the foes of Babylonia, however, is apparently that contained in a letter from the priest Lu-enna to the priest En-e-tarzi announcing that the Elamites had invaded Lagash in Sumer and

carried off considerable booty. The writer, however, had attacked the Elamites, and taken plunder from them in his turn.[45]

Around the time of Abraham (ca. 2050 BC) we find the following names of kings and princes of Elam, undoubtedly descended from Elam the son of Seth:

> Kudur-Lagamar (the biblical Chederlaomer)
> Kudur-Mabug (son or brother of Kuder-Lagamar; known as the father of the Amorites)
> Eri-Aku (son of Kudur-Mabug and the same as the biblical Arioch of Larsa and Ur).

At some early point the descendants of Elam lost control of their territory in the valley around the Tigris and Euphrates. The first kings of Elam are not known, although Elam, the son of Shem, must have headed the list. We do not have a non-biblical name for Elam. The first known King of Elam was called Peli and he was probably the great-grandson of Elam the son of Shem. Nothing much is known about Peli. After his death, or removal, the Elamite kingdom moved into the hands of Arphaxad, the brother of Elam, until Arphaxad's death. Arphaxad may have been an overlord to the sons of Elam who were the actual rulers.

Arphaxad was known then by the Akkadian name **Igrish-Halam (or Igrish-Haltam)**. He was the king of Ebla which is in Syria today. This area (Syria and Lebanon, once called Assyria) is the territory that Arphaxad and his sons initially settled after having departed from the area around the Ark after it landed. There is no evidence that they controlled the Mesopotamian Valley for any length of time, initially. However, over time they did regain control of this valuable land, as will be shown.

Arphaxad extended his rulership to include the lands formerly ruled by the descendants of Elam. He became the King of Awan near the center of the valley in Iran west of the Zagros mountains. This city-state is over 300 miles from Ebla, which is far to the northwest. This is convincing evidence that Igrish-Halam of Ebla and Awan, and Igrish-Halam of Ebla, was in fact Arphaxad of the Bible. The manner by which this happened, however, was not just the death of his older brother, even though that was obviously the trigger point. Instead, the ancient records show that Arphaxad had married Rasu'eja, the granddaughter of Elam:

> Arpachshad took to himself a wife and her name was Rasu'eja, the daughter of Susan,[46] the daughter of Elam, and she bare him a son in the third year in this week, and he called his name Kainam.[47]

From this marriage Arphaxad had a legal claim to the royal bloodline of the family of Elam because the Elamites recognized a *matrilinear* line of descent.

> In that turbulent period Elam's unique system of *matrilinear succession* emerged; sovereignty was hereditary through women, in that a new ruler was always "son of a sister" of some member of an older sovereign's family.[48] (Italics mine)

Fig. 1 Remains of Shusan in Elam

The marriage of Arphaxad to Elam's granddaughter Rasu'eja gave him the right as the "new ruler" to rule over the lands of "some member of an older sovereign's family." Elam was the "older sovereign" and Rasu'eja was the bloodline person who, through marriage to Arphaxad, gave him the right to rule Awan in Elam (and probably the other Elamite city states at that time, Susa, Anshan, etc.). The marriage of Arphaxad to Rasu'eja explains the fact that Igrish-Halam (Arphaxad) could be both the ruler of Ebla and then the ruler of Awan, even though these lands were separated by nearly 300 miles.

The meaning of Arphaxad is shown as follows:

> Shem's son 'Arphaxad' is better vowel-pointed as **Arpha-Khashd** where **Arpha** is the Hurrian word for "town" (and the name of their biggest town in particular, now Kirkuk, Iraq.[49]

Arphaxad's name means from the town of Khashd which is Kirkuk, Iraq, today. Arphaxad had a son whom he named after his town of birth. That son was Kesed (Khashd), and Kesed became one of the most famous Patriarchs of the Bible. While not mentioned in Genesis, his name is found elsewhere in the Bible, where he is the son of Nahor, an ancestor of Abraham.[50] However, in *The Book of Jubilees* he is specifically identified. I will devote an entire chapter to Kesed and many more to his descendants.

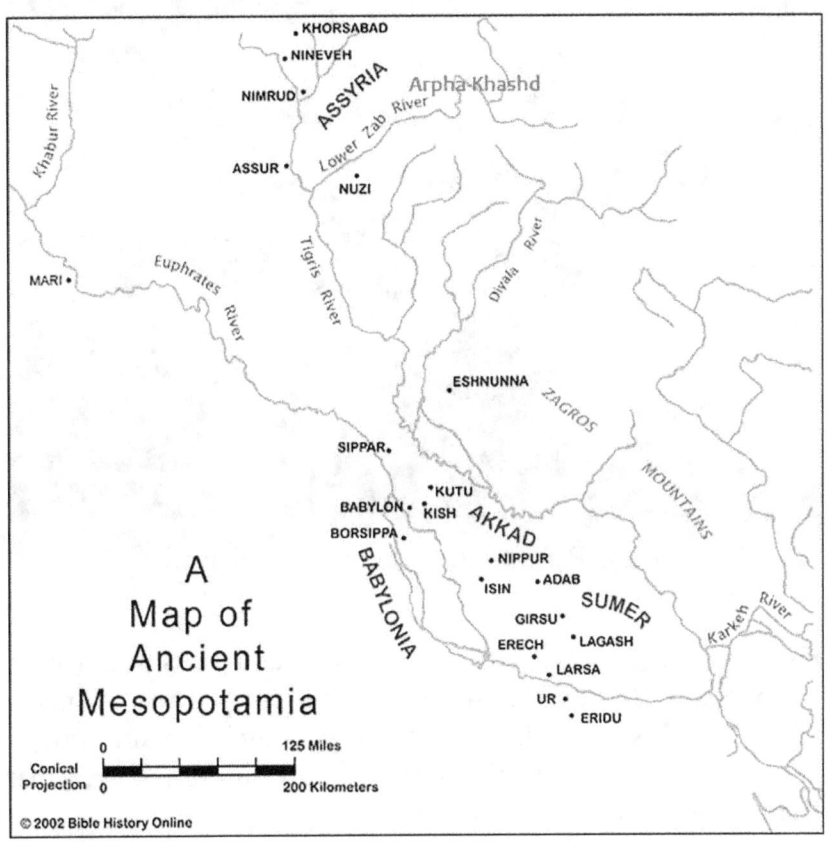

Fig. 2 Map showing home of Arphaxad, Arpha-Khashd

Since Arphaxad lived a long time, we should expect to see evidence of him as a ruler in one of the earliest areas to be settled after the Flood. We find the name of Igrish-Halam in the ancient Elamite city of Ebla, one of the oldest cities in the world. Igrish-Halam was the king of Ebla as well as the king of Awan.

Fig. 3 Palace of Ebla, home of Arphaxad

Ebla dominated northern Syria, Lebanon, and parts of northern Mesopotamia (modern Iraq) and enjoyed trade and diplomatic relations with states as far away as Egypt (Ham's domain through his son Cush), Iran (Elam's domain), and Sumer (an area that Ham's sons and descendants overran).

Giovanni Pettinato provides a list of the kings of Ebla: Igrish-Halam, Irkab-Damu, Ar-Ennum, Ebrium, Ibbi-Sipis, and Dubuhu-Ada.[51] Working backwards from Ebrium, the fourth king of Ebla, was the same as Eber, the Patriarch of the Bible. His father, Ar-Ennum, was the third king of Ebla, the Biblical Salah. Ar-Ennum's father, Irkab-Damu, was the second king of Ebla, the Biblical Cainan. Irkab-Damu's father was Igrish-Halam, the first king of Ebla the Patriarch Arphaxad of the Bible.

We have an even better clue that this is the correct identification of Arphaxad, Cainan, Salah, and Eber:

> There are sporadic references [in the Ebla Tablets] to other rulers, the most ancient king mentioned being Sa-mi-u.[52]

The amazing similarity of the word "Sa-im-u" to Sem or Shem of the Bible cannot be overlooked. I would suggest that the oldest king of Ebla was in fact Shem of the Bible. Given this information, then, we can tabulate what we have found as follows:

Biblical Name	Eblaite Name
Shem (Sem)	Sa-im-u (oldest King of Ebla)
Arphaxad	Igrish-Halam (Igrish of Haltamtu)
Cainan	Irkab-Damu
Salah	Ar-Ennum
Eber	Ebrium
Brother of Eber	Ibbi-Sippish

Dubuhu-Ada (son of Ibbi-Sippish)

Arphaxad married his brother Elam's granddaughter, whose name was Rasu'eja, the daughter of Sushan, according to the ancient *Book of Jubiliees*. Presumably, Elam predeceased his brother Arphaxad. Since Arphaxad had married Elam's granddaughter he had a legitimate claim to the throne of Awan, which was in Elamite territory 300 miles to the east and south. He then reigned over both Ebla and Awan, giving us the key clue that Igrish-Halam was Arphaxad of the Bible. Another interesting quote from the *Eblaitica* mentioned just above is referenced here:

> The king, together with his rather extensive family, dominated all major political, economic, and religious activites of the city-state by means of an elaborate hierarchy of officials. The consort of the ruler, particularly prominent in religious affairs, was the primary wife of the king, whose title was "ma-lik-tum," "queen." Other royal wives were designated simply "dam en," "woman of the king." These ladies were grouped into two ranks: dam-mah-en, "senior royal wife" and dam-en-tur, "junior royal wife." The mother of the king (ama-gal en) was also an important court figure, as were his siblings (ses-en, "brother of the king" and nin-ni-en, "sister of the king").[53]

The earliest traditions among the royals of Ebla are nearly identical to what we know about early Egyptian royals, as well as Sumerian royal traditions. One could speculate that they all have a common origin. That origin would be the head of the family, Noah. It seems reasonable that Noah would have instituted a method for the procreation of the planet as well as for control of the leadership of the families. Furthermore, from the *Eblaitica* we find this:

> It is apparent from the [Ebla] texts that the traditions of monarchy were already well established at Ebla long before these documents were composed. The various archives preserved in Royal Palace G, namely L.2586, L.2712, L.2752, L.2764, L.2769, and L.2875, contained administrative texts that spanned a period of at least three generations of rulers. But the ritual texts found among these documents provide

> evidence that the traditions of the monarchy were much older. Indeed, it seems that the kingship was already **centuries old** when the great royal residence of Ebla was destroyed by fire. The primary evidence for this conclusion are the references to **the worship of a long line of deceased former kings of Ebla** [emphasis mine].
>
> The evidence that the deceased kings of Ebla were deified and worshiped in rather elaborate rituals comes from a group of offerings lists and ritual texts, which refer by name to the deceased and deified former rulers…One of these texts… describes a series of rituals performed for the departed ruler. In this ceremony, the new king (en gibil) offered sacrifices at a mausoleum (e ma-dim), and the names of several deceased rulers were invoked.[54]

Within a few centuries after the landing of the Ark, and the separation of the sons from Noah, it did not take long before ancestor worship crept into the religious life of the people. The lifespans of persons who came after the Flood fell dramatically over the 11 generations from Noah, who lived 950 years, to the time of Abraham, who lived 175 years. This is a drop of an average of 65 years per generation. It is not difficult to see how, several generations away from the earliest survivors of the Flood, people could look back on their long-lived ancestors, who remained alive as they aged, and attribute divine qualities to them. As the newer generations lived shorter lives while the Patriarchs were still alive, it would seem that the Patriarchs themselves were divine. We could certainly see Shem, Arphaxad, Cainan, and Salah falling into this category. When they finally did die, people would naturally idolize them for their longevity, which led to their divinization. The worship of deceased ancestors was not limited to the survivors of the Flood. It almost certainly included, initially, the pre-Diluvian Patriarchs as well.

In Ebla, there was a religious tradition to worship these deceased kings/gods in pairs, or couples.

Stieglitz has listed three for us:

1. Ni-da-kul wa Be sal
2. Ra-sa-ap wa **A-dam-ma**
3. A-gu wa Gu-la-du

The first name is the wife/consort name. Then the "wa" means "and." The second name would be the name of the deified King.[55] The name of the second King who was being worshiped is the same name as Adam of the Bible. Is this a coincidence? Perhaps, but with the other evidence that the family of the Bible settled the Kingdom of Ebla, it is likely that this is an actual record of the worship of the progenitor of the family of Noah, namely Adam himself.

> Within the *Eblaitica* is an article written by Michael C. Astour dealing with dating of the Ebla texts. He states that they were contemporary to the three kings, namely Igrish-Halam (Arphaxad), Irkab-Damu (Cainan) and Ar-Ennum (Salah).[56] He then goes on to state:

The Ebla texts have yielded no datable synchronisms with Mesopotamian [Sumerian] rulers attested in other cuneiform sources. Of the seven pre-Sargonic kings of Mari whose names appear in local inscriptions, only two - Anusu (Hanusum) and, prominently, Iblul-Il - are mentioned at Ebla.[57]

However, we know that in about 2580 BC, King Ar-Ennum of Ebla (Salah of the Bible), or his son Ebrium, defeated and deposed Iblul Il, the King of Mari, a town situated southeast of the Ebla.[58] Iblul Il was the son of Anpu, the first king of Mari.[59] Anpu may have been a son of Arphaxad. Salah reigned over the two city states, Ebla and Mari, followed by his two sons and heirs, Ebrium and Ibbi-Sipish, until the start of the dynasty of Akkad, led by Sargon the Great. Therefore, we can date the Ebla texts to fall within the lives of these three Patriarchs.

The real surprise at Ebla was the language used in the tablets. Alongside the traditional Sumerian terminology borrowed from Mesopotamia, the scribes also wrote entries in their own language - Eblaite.[60] This was a North-West *Semitic* dialect, showing close links in its grammar and vocabulary with later Biblical Hebrew, Canaanite and Phoenician. Dated at around 2500 BC, Eblaite is the oldest known language of this group, up to 1000 years before the tablets of Ugarit, for example. In Biblical terms, it is over 1000 years before Moses.[61] Furthermore, it is a *Shemitic* dialect, having come from the family of Shem.

Part of Ebla's prosperity stemmed from its agricultural hinterland, in the rich plain of northern Syria, where barley, wheat, olives, figs, grapes, pomegranates, and flax were grown and cattle, sheep, goats, and pigs were raised. Linen and wool, including damask cloth, were the main products. Metalworking, including the smelting and alloying of gold, silver, copper, tin, and lead, was the second most important activity. Ebla also controlled a group of 17 city-states, probably in what is now Lebanon and southeastern Turkey, areas rich in silver and timber. The city proper was a manufacturing and distribution center. Woodworking and the production of olive oil, wine, and beer also were important. Trade was the third support of Ebla's economy. Cloth, manufactured goods, and olive oil were its main exports; imports included gold, silver, copper, tin, precious stones, and sheep. Because of its geographic location, Ebla grew wealthy on transit trade. Materials from Iran, Anatolia (Turkey), and Cyprus were transshipped to states as distant as Sumer and Egypt.[62] The Egyptian trade passed through Byblos. Byblos is in what was known as Phoenicia at that time and is located along the coast of the Mediterranean Sea. Egyptians would transport their wares by sea to Byblos and then across the Arphaxadian territory, through Ebla, just to the east of Byblos into Sumer and finally to Elam.

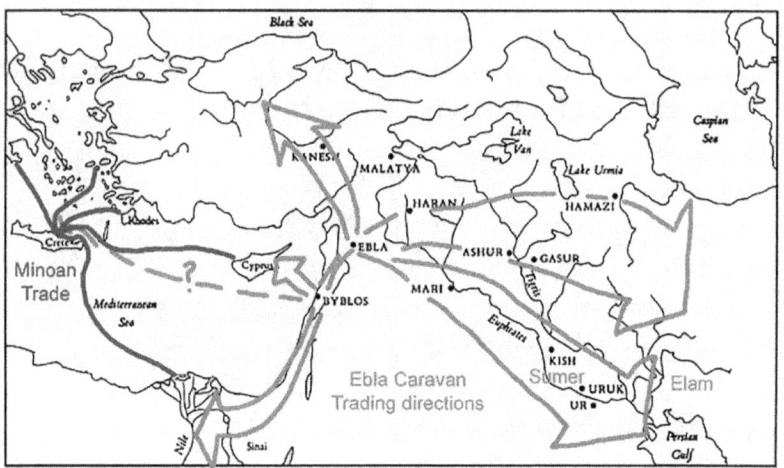

Fig. 4 Ebla, the center of early trading

Not coincidentally, Ebla is located at the base of the mountain range where it is believed that Noah's Ark had landed in the "mountains of Ararat." It is about midway between where the Ark landed and the Mediterranean Sea to the southwest. It was a natural location for a city to be founded as the earliest survivors of the Flood began their expansion. Archaeologists determined that Ebla was founded between about 3300 BC and 3100 BC.[63] Arphaxad was born in 3285 BC. Therefore, it is likely that Arphaxad (Igrish-Halam) was the founder and first king of Ebla. Another possibility is that Su-am-i (Shem of the Bible), the father of Arphaxad, was the founder of Ebla.

The Ebla texts also mention an area 34 miles northeast of Ebla known as A-ra-mu, or Aram. Arphaxad (Igrish-Halam) had a brother whose name was Aram. It was probably this brother

Aram who had founded A-ra-mu, a trading partner with Ebla.[64] The area of A-ra-mu is known as Aleppo in Syria today. The Ebla tablets refer to extensive trade between these two "brother" cities, although there are also descriptions of fighting between them.[65] That two sons of Shem, Arphaxad (Igrish-Halam) and Aram, ruled over city-states so close to each other is further confirmation that Arphaxad and Igrish-Halam were the same person.

Returning to Elam, the area of Elam is one of the oldest civilized areas in the world. Awan is one of the four oldest cities of the Elamites.[66] It would appear that Elam and Arphaxad were close to each other as the civilization around the base of the "mountains of Ararat" developed. Since they were born just shortly after the Flood and then lived another 500 years or more, there were more and more people living around them.

Using a standard of 2 children per decade, through the power of compounding (2,4, 8, 16, 32, etc.), by the middle of the lifetime of Arphaxad there would be at least 500,000 people of the descendants of Noah, if not many more. Ebla is said to have grown to about 250,000 persons at its height during the reign of Ebrium, the Biblical Eber.

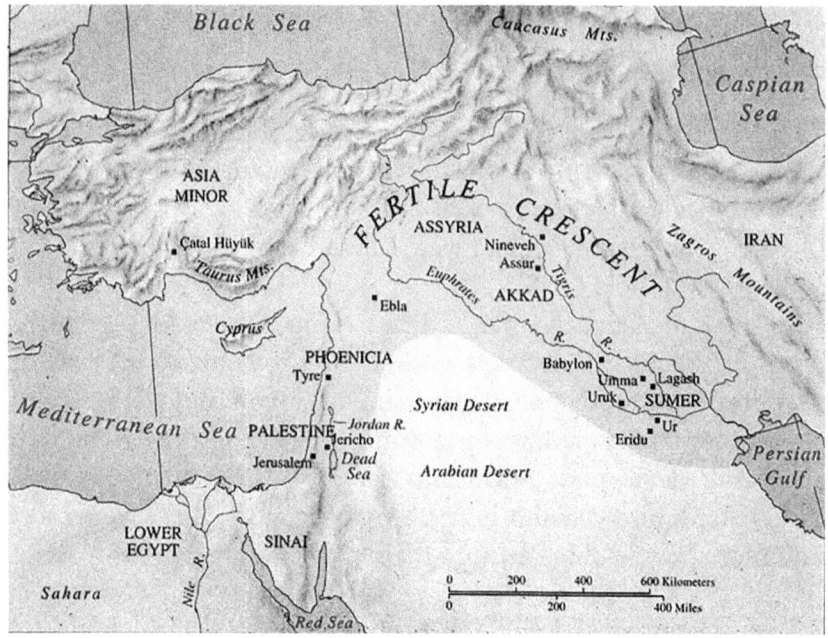

Fig. 5 Map of The Fertile Cresent,
showing Ebla in the center

The form of the kingdom's name, "Elam" ("highland"), is Akkadian, while in the original Elamite form it was Haltamtu or Haltamti.[67] Igrish-Halam can also be called Igrish-Haltam, meaning Igrish of the land of Haltam(tu). Haltamtu was also known in classical writings as Susiana, from the city state which usually formed its capital, Susa. The kingdom's four major cities were Awan, Anshan, Simash and Susa, the capital. The rulers practiced kingship by matrilineal descent, being referred to as "son of a sister." As shown earlier, this explains how Arphaxad (Igrish-Halam) became the king of Awan after he married to Rasu'eja, the granddaughter of Elam.

The inhabitants of Elam spoke an agglutinative language unrelated to the Sumerian, Semitic, or Indo-European languages. After 3000 BC, the Elamites, influenced by the system of writing developed by the neighboring Sumerians (Hamites), began to record their language in a native semi-pictographic script known today as Proto-Elamite.[68] At about the same time the original Eblaite language of Ebla was also being transformed. Eventually, the Sumerian cuneiform writing took over the area. Proto-Elamite is the oldest known writing system from Iran.[69] It was used during a brief period (ca. 3100 BC - 2900 BC); clay tablets with Proto-Elamite writing have been found at different sites across Iran.[70] The Proto-Elamite script is thought to have developed from early proto-cuneiform.[71] The fact that this language was used during a narrow period, 3100 BC to 2900 BC, coincides with the biblical dates for Arphaxad and Elam.

Susa, the capital of the burgeoning empire of Elam, was probably founded by Shem shortly after the Flood in 3287 BC. It is the oldest of the four cities in the ancient Elamite kingdom, and was founded before Elam and Arphaxad were born. It is located at the foothills of the Zagros Mountains in central western Iran. Archaeologists say that the city was founded as early as 4000 BC, but this is not likely since it would have been destroyed by the Flood. Of course, the dating of the Flood is based upon the biblical records as I have indicated. It is possible that the Flood occurred prior to this date, but we have no way of proving this.

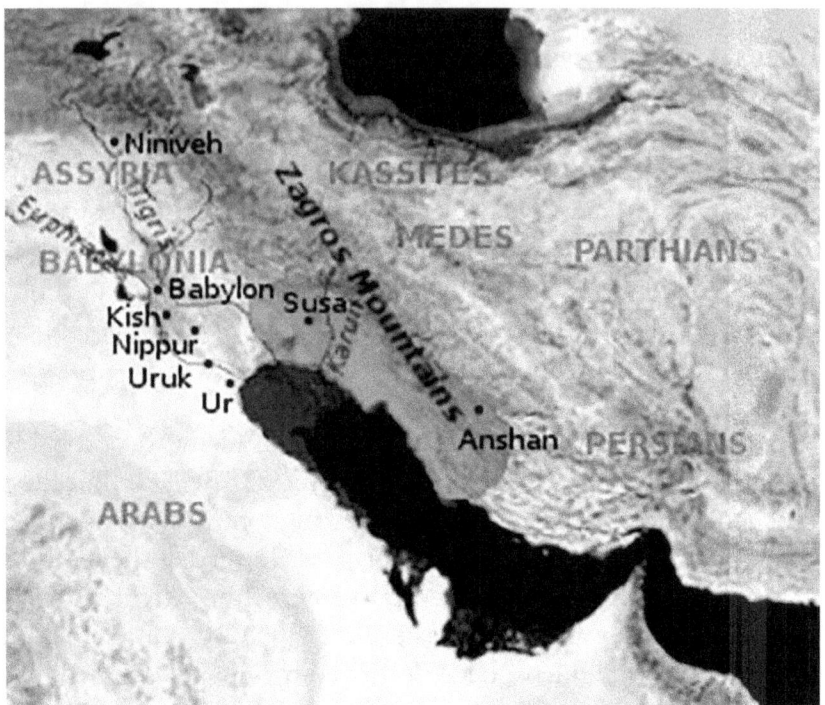

Fig. 6 Map showing the location of Susa

Susa began to be influenced by the cultures of the Iranian Plateau to the east, and dominated the lowlands to the west of the Zagros Mountains. Approximately 350 miles to the south, Anshan became prominent and expanded in size, dominating the highlands of the southern mountain range of Iran.[72]

The Old Elamite Period is the beginning of the historical era in relations between Elam and the Sumerian (Hamite) city states. Three dynasties of kings ruled, with the last of them forming a short-lived empire.[73] It seems that at various times, Anshan and Susa were ruled as separate kingdoms, and were perhaps only briefly united within one state. However, Sumerian writings start referring to them as the land of Elam, suggesting an element of unity, perhaps as a loose coalition of city states. The known sons of Elam were Sushan, Machul, and Harmon.[74] It seems that the Kingdom of

Susa would have been founded by Sushan, the names being nearly identical. The other two sons, Machul and Harmon, were possibly the progenitors of the other two founding Elamite dynasties. Those dynasties would have been the city-state of Anshan and the city-state of Awan.

The exact location of Awan is not known, but it was an old city or area of Elam and is often believed to be north of Susa. This would place it closer to the "mountains of Ararat" where the Ark landed. The lands of Arphaxad and his brother Elam comprised most of what is now Iran, to the east of Iraq, as well as the base of the mountain area below the "mountains of Ararat" (eastern Turkey), now known as Syria and Lebanon. The sons of Ham settled in what is now known as Iraq but was then called Sumer.

The Sumerian King List has a dynasty from Awan that exerted dominance in Sumer at one time. It mentions three successive kings, reigning in all 356 years, although their names are obliterated.[75] It shows that Awan had great political importance in the lifetime of Arphaxad, the end of the 4th millennium BC and the beginning of the 3rd millennium BC. These 3 successive kings could have been Igrish-Halam, Irkab-Damu, and Ar-Ennum (Arphaxad, Cainan, and Salah of the Bible).

A later royal list found in Elam gives 12 names of the kings in the Awan dynasty. These would also be the descendants of Arphaxad and/or Elam. As there are very few sources for this period, these names are not certain. Few facts of these kings' reigns are known, but Elam seems to have kept up a heavy trade with important Mesopotamian cities like Lagash in Sumer, importing foods and exporting cattle, wool, slaves and silver, among other things.[76] A text of the time refers to a shipment of tin to the governor of the Elamite city of Urua, which was committed to work the material and return it in the form of bronze, perhaps indicating a technological edge enjoyed by the Elamites over the Sumerians.[77]

It is also known that the Awan kings carried out incursions into Sumer, where they ran up against the most powerful city-states of this period, Kish and Lagash.[78] Kish was the oldest city in all of

Sumer, and was founded by Cush, the son of Ham. He was a first cousin of Arphaxad and Elam. Lagash, while ruled by Hamites, was eventually ruled by descendants of Arphaxad who recovered it, as I will show later. One cause of conflict between these relatives was apparently a Sumerian king's attempt to seize the "et at Warakshe," a kingdom further east of Elam on the Iranian plateau, rich in luxury products of all types, especially precious stones.[79] Toward the end of his life, Arphaxad engaged in efforts to recover lands in Sumer which were, at his death, ruled by the descendants of Ham, the brother of his father Shem. These efforts were continued by his son, Cainan (Irkab-Damu).

Chapter Three

Cainan (Irkab-Damu), the Son of Arphaxad (Igrish-Halam) (3000 BC - 2380 BC)

C ainan lived about 620 years. He was probably born in Ebla in what became part of the Assyrian Empire during his lifetime. Ebrium (or Ibrium) is named as the last ruler of Awan. He is the same as the Patriarch Eber in the Bible. His father was Ar-Ennum, Biblical Patriarch Salah. Ar-Ennum's father was Irkab-Damu, Biblical Patriarch Cainan, and his grandfather was Igrish-Halam, the Biblical Patriarch Arphaxad.

In Sumerian mythology, **Damu** was a god of vegetation and rebirth. He was a son of Enki and Nininsinna, and he kept the sap flowing and helped to regulate the death-rebirth cycle of nature.[80] Damu also seems to be a local offshoot of Tammuz. The name Irkab-Damu, then, might mean Irkab "son" of Damu, or "protected by" Damu. This would be an interesting change in the lineage of the family of Arphaxad if this theory is correct, because it would mean that as early as 3000 BC, only 285 years after Arphaxad had been born, the influence of the Sumerian gods had begun to infiltrate the family of Arphaxad. The family of Ham had become enamored with the Sumerian theocracy very early. Through trade among the sons of Shem (Arphaxad, Aram, and Elam), their new religion must have spread rapidly.

An ancient example of diplomatic language can be found in the treaty of peace and friendship concluded around 2500 BC, found in the Royal Library of Ebla, and now in the Archaeological Museum of Damascus.[81] The treaty was between the two kingdoms of Ebla and Hamazi. In its opening statement, engraved in clay it reads:

> Thus says Ibubu, the director of the king's palace, to the messenger: "You are my brother and I am your brother. As a brother I will grant whatever you desire, as you will grant whatever I desire. Give me good mercenaries (or, work-animals). Please send them. You are my brother; I am your brother. Ten beams of boxwood, two sledges of boxwood, I, Ibubu, have given the messenger (for you). **Irkab-Damu, king of Ebla, is brother of Zizi, king of Hamazi,** and Zizi, king of Hamazi, is brother of Irkab-Damu, king of Ebla." Thus Tira-Il, the scribe, has written. For the messenger of Zizi.[82]

From this we see that Zizi, the King of Hamazi, was a brother of Irkab-Damu. This would make Zizi another son of Arphaxad (Igrish-Halam). The exact location of Hamazi is not known, but historians believe that it is located midway between Elam and Assyria, possibly in northern Iran or in northern Iraq.[83] This would place it at the base of the "mountains of Ararat" where the Ark landed after the Flood and roughly midway between the lands of Arphaxad and those of Elam, which Arphaxad eventually ruled as well. Since this area was under the control of Araphaxad, it is likely that this was one of his sons, as the record shows. His name, Zizi, King of Hamazi (d. about 2430 BC), is attested only in extra-biblical sources, however. The Sumerian King List has him as the sole king of Hamazi who reigned 420 years. He defeated the Second Dynasty of Kish (a Hamite) to claim supremacy in Sumer, although his reign there did not last long.[84] He was defeated around 2430 BC, meaning he was born before 2850 BC, and rulership of Hamazi was transferred to Uruk.[85] Uruk at this time was ruled by Enshukeshdanna, the son of Enmerkar, who was the son of Meshkiaggasher, whom I will show later was Nimrod of the Bible. Nimrod's father was Cush, the son of Ham. Therefore, when Zizi was overrun by Enshukeshdanna, this was a case of the Hamites overruling the Shemites. The entire history of the Mesopotamian Valley will be shown to be an interfamilial fight between the Hamites, who invaded the areas that Shem had given to his sons, the Shemites, and their descendants.

Fig. 7 Treaty between Zizi of Hamazi and
Irkab-Damu (Cainan), sons of Arphaxad

Shortly before his death, Arphaxad, the father of Cainan, had made excursions into the Hamitic lands of Sumer, which were south and east of where Arphaxad had originally settled and ruled from Ebla. However, the Eblan king, Cainan (Irkab-Damu), overthrew the Ur

41

Dynasty sometime during his reign. Along with his brother, Zizi, he continued work that had been begun by his father.

In approximately 2600 BC, Gilgamesh became the king of the First Dynasty of Uruk. Gilgamesh was the son of Kesed, who was the son of Arphaxad. Kesed had been a commander in the army of Enmerkar, who was the son of Nimrod (Meshkiaggasher) of the Bible. Kesed became a High Priest in the city-state of Kullab, next to Uruk. He was probably instrumental in making his son, Gilgamesh, the king of Uruk, even though it had been earlier ruled by Enmerkar, a descendant of Ham through Cush and his son Nimrod. Uruk is a city at the southern end of today's Iraq near the Persian Gulf. It would have been substantially south and east of the empire of Arphaxad in Syria/Lebanon, but just southwest of Awan in the territory of Elam. Arphaxad had taken control of Elam after Elam's death (c. 2900 BC); however, he died in 2750 BC. We don't have a record that his son, Cainan (Irkab-Damu) ever controlled Uruk. Instead, the record shows that Gilgamesh, the son of Kesed, son of Arphaxad, and therefore a nephew of Cainan, who was born about 2750 BC, was given control over Uruk when he came of age. I will discuss Gilgamesh and his relationship to the family later. Uruk, one of the oldest post-deluvian city-states, was probably originally founded by Shemites but shortly thereafter overtaken by Hamites. Thus, placing Gilgamesh in control of Uruk around 2725 BC was probably handled by Irkab-Damu (Cainan) in an inter-familiar resolution with Cush, the son of Ham. Cush was the ruler of Kish, named after himself. The transfer back to the family of Shem at this early date was apparently handled peacefully, but would eventually lead to a dispute again over rulership of this key early Mesopotamian Valley city-state.

There is some question as to whether Cainan was the son of Arphaxad, since some ancient manuscripts of the Bible do not include him. Besides the evidence from Demetrius and Polyhistor, we also have the *Book of Jubilees*, written perhaps about 100 BC, based on much earlier tradition. In *Book of Jubilees* it says:

In the 29th Jubilee, in the first week, in the beginning thereof, took to himself a wife and her name was Rasueja, the daughter of Susan, the daughter of Elam, and she bare him a son in the third year in this week, and he called his name Kainam. And the son grew, and his father taught him writing, and he went to seek for himself a place where he might seize for himself a city. And he found a writing which former (generations) had carved on the rock, and he read what was thereon, and he transcribed it and sinned owing to it; for it contained the teaching of the Watchers in accordance with which they used to observe the omens of the sun and moon and stars in all the signs of heaven. And he wrote it down and said nothing regarding it; for he was afraid to speak to Noah about it lest he should be angry with him on account of it. And in the 30th Jubilee, in the second week, in the first year thereof, he took to himself a wife, and her name was Melka, the daughter of Madai, the son of Japheth, and in the fourth year he begat a son, and called his name Shelah . .[86]

The *Book of Jubilees*, sometimes called the Lesser Genesis (Leptogenesis), is an early Jewish religious work, considered one of the Pseudepigrapha by most Roman Catholic, Eastern Orthodox and Protestant Christians. It was well known to Early Christian writers in the East and the West. Later, it was so thoroughly suppressed that no complete Hebrew, Greek or Latin version had survived. It is considered canonical for the Ethiopian Orthodox Church, where it is known as the *Book of Division*. In the modern scholarly view, it reworks material found in the biblical books of Genesis and Exodus in the light of concerns of some Second century BC Jews. However, it contains tidbits of information that "fit in" with the historical record and therefore cannot be thrown out summarily.

Until the discovery of the Dead Sea Scrolls, the only surviving manuscripts of the *Book of Jubilees* were four complete texts dating to the 15th and 16th centuries, and several fragmentary quotations in Greek, mainly found in a work by Epiphanius, with a few others.

Between 1947 and 1956, approximately 15 of the *Book of Jubilees* scrolls were found in five caves at Qumran, all written in Hebrew. The large quantity of manuscripts (more than any biblical books except for Psalms, Deuteronomy, Isaiah, Exodus, and Genesis, in descending order) indicates that the *Book of Jubilees* was widely used at Qumran. A comparison of the Qumran texts with the Ethiopic version, performed by James VanderKam, found that the Ethiopic was in most respects an accurate and literalistic translation.[87]

As we see, Cainan's name must have been in the copy of Genesis used by the author of the *Book of Jubilees*. (Note that while the Septuagint says Cainan was 130 years old when he begot Salah, the *Book of Jubilees* says Cainan was only 57 years old.) It will be shown as I proceed that the Septuagint is probably the accurate number since the other would only place the life of Cainan another 73 years backward in history into a period that is already shady, at best.

Cainan was known to Jewish writers as early as the 200's BC, while it is only with Philo Judaeus in the early first century AD that we have evidence of the absence of this name from Abraham's genealogy. What is likely to have happened is that at some point between 200 BC and the birth of Christ, a scribe must have accidentally skipped over Cainan in Genesis 11, thus creating a family or tradition of manuscript copies that left him out. In time, scribes who were confused by Cainan's absence from Genesis 11 but presence in Genesis 10 and I Chronicles 1 would have begun to "correct'" their copies by deleting him from Genesis 10 and I Chronicles 1. This would explain why the Septuagint, Demetrius, Polyhistor, and Jubilees include Cainan, while Philo, Josephus, Africanus, the Vulgate, and the Masoretic omit him. Because Luke followed the Septuagint, his genealogy includes Cainan.

However, others claim that the second Cainan did not originally appear in the Old Testament, but was interpolated at some point.[88] While not impossible, no one has ever been able to come up with a satisfactory reason for the addition of a generation to Abraham's genealogy, while an accidental omission of part of Genesis 11, followed by later harmonizing deletions, is quite plausible and understandable. Some who argue that Cainan is spurious have pointed out that his presence in Abraham's genealogy supposedly destroys the numerical symmetry of the genealogical lists in Genesis 5, Genesis 11, and Exodus 6. Without Cainan, there are ten generations inclusive from Adam to Noah, ten generations inclusive from Shem to Abraham, and seven generations inclusive from Abraham to Moses. The Jews have long viewed the numbers 10 and 7 as particularly significant. With Cainan, there would be eleven generations inclusive from Shem to Abraham.

The argument from numerical symmetry is a two-edged sword. Besides the numbers 10 and 7, the Jews also regard 3 and 22 as significant. What we find in Genesis 5 are indeed ten generations, but the tenth generation (Noah) had three notable sons (Shem, Ham, Japheth). With Cainan included, what we find in Genesis 11 are ten generations just as before, with the tenth generation (Terah) again having three notable sons (Abraham, Haran, Nahor). That gives us a total of 22 generations inclusive from Adam to Abraham, the same number of letters in the Hebrew alphabet and number of scrolls in the Hebrew canon of scripture. Also, from Adam to Moses would be 28 generations inclusive, and 28 is a multiple of 7. Without Cainan added, this numerical symmetry is lost. Furthermore, the genealogy of Luke has exactly 77 names inclusive from Jesus Christ to God. Without Cainan, there would be only 76 names. Jews would naturally see 77 as symbolic or significant, especially when associated with the genealogy of the Messiah, but wouldn't necessarily see the number 76 in the same way.

Attempts to "infuse" numerology into the biblical narrative are a perfect example of eisigesis. Cainan was in the original biblical record and was dropped as a scribal error. Therefore, I include Cainan in the genealogy of the Patriarchs, as did Luke in the New Testament. The weight of the evidence points to the conclusion that Cainan was an original and authentic part of Genesis and I Chronicles. Though the name dropped out of the Hebrew text before the birth of Christ, the Greek Septuagint fortunately preserved this generation of Abraham's pedigree.[89]

Finally, as stated above, there were 3 kings of Ebla and Awan, namely Igrish-Halam, Irkab-Damu, and Ar-Ennum. I have identified them as Arphaxad, Cainan, and Salah, respectively. If Cainan is left out, then who would Irkab-Damu have been? Ar-Ennum's son was Ebrium, who is obviously the Eber of the Bible. Therefore, the argument for the inclusion of Cainan is also supported from outside the Bible as well.

The Ebla texts differ from the Sumerian texts in that they called their leaders either *en* or *malikum*, which could roughly be translated as "king." The Sumerians, on the other hand, used the word *lugal* for king. The Eblaites used lugal as "governor," a position slightly lower than "king." In addition, however, the Eblaites had a term that meant "vizier." This all becomes important because the three rulers of Ebla and Awan, Igrish-Halam (Arphaxad), Irkab-Damu (Cainan), and Ar-Ennum (Salah) were called by various titles at different times. In particular, they were all called *en*, or king, and they were also called *malikum*, the Hebrew word that came to mean king. But by the time of Ar-Ennum, whom I will show was also called Arrukum, his title was also "vizier." The rule of Ebla was followed by the "vizier" Ebrium, whom I have identified as Eber the Patriarch of the Bible. Based on the lineage that has been presented, and the fact the Ebrium became the most famous of the rulers of Ebla, it seems evident to me that Ebrium was the son of Ar-Ennum. Furthermore, it also seems evident that the title, while it changed over time, did not change the power of the position. Therefore, while there are no records yet that show Ebrium to be the *en* of Ebla, the simple fact that as "vizier" he ruled an area that competed with Sargon the Great would imply that he was, in fact, the king of Ebla.

Cainan (Irkab-Damu), as *en*, or king, of Ebla, sent the commander of his army, Enna-Dagan, to overthrow the powerful coalition formed by Iblul-Il, the king of Mari. This was successful and Enna-Dagan took the title of Lugal, or governor of that city-state. As I just noted, lugal is a Sumerian term and meant "great man," and meant "king" in other parts of Sumer. In Ebla, it was used as the title of a governor. After Cainan overthrew him, Iblul-Il returned to Mari as a governor,[90] with Enna-Dagan as the overseer, or possibly vizier. This may be an indication the Iblul-Il was related to Cainan (Irkab-Damu), since he was not removed totally from his position as a ruler in Mari. Mari was not one of the oldest cities in the post-diluvial world. It was created during the reign of Igrish-Halam, Arphaxad, as a "go between" from Ebla to "the Chaldees," which is located at the southern end of the Mesopotamian Valley at the Gulf. Mari is located in Syria on the west side of the Euphrates River. Therefore, it was Arphaxadian territory. It is not clear just how Iblul-Il was related to Arphaxad or to his son Cainan, but it is likely that they were directly related, since his name is Akkadian. Perhaps Iblul-Il was a younger brother of Cainan.

Mari is not considered a small settlement that later grew,[91] but rather a new city that was purposely founded during the Mesopotamian Early Dynastic period I about 2900 BC, to control the waterways of the Euphrates trade routes that connect the Levant with the Sumerian south. The city was built about 1 to 2 kilometers away from the Euphrates river to protect it from floods,[92] and was connected to the river by an artificial canal that was between 7 and 10 kilometers long depending on which old meander it used to be attached with, which is hard to identify today.

The city-state of Mari had for many years had difficult relations with Ebla. The problems began with Igrish-Halam (Arphaxad), the father of Irkab-Damu (Cainan).

As the second of the Ebla kings who ruled over the powerful kingdom in the middle of the third millennium, Irkab-Damu is mentioned in the administrative texts of the city. He married his daughter, whose name is not mentioned, to the ruler of Emar.[93] Emar was an ancient Amorite city on the great bend in the mid-Euphrates in northeastern Syria. Emar was strategically sited as a trans-shipping point where trade on the Euphrates was reloaded for shipping by overland route. In the middle of the third millennium BC, Emar came under the influence of the rulers of Ebla; the city is mentioned in archives at Ebla.[94] It has been the source of many cuneiform tablets, making it rank with Ugarit, Mari, and Ebla among the most important archaeological sites of Syria.[95]

We begin to see that as we move from Arphaxad to his son Cainan there is greater commerce, and with that greater commerce there is the necessity for alliances and negotiations to allow for these new city-states to cooperate commercially. We also see that there is more activity that is directed toward power struggles. Since these earliest city-states were ruled by members of the descendants of Noah, largely through Shem's son Arphaxad and Ham's son Cush, as I will show later, these power struggles were, ultimately, sibling rivalries.

The earliest settlement appears to have been at Ebla, in the north. Cainan, following in his father Arphaxad's footsteps, made excursions into the Hamite (Sumerian) territories and overtook, among others, the city-states of Ur and Kish, well into the Mesopotamian Valley. At the same time, however, we begin to see the influence of cultural differences intermingling between the family of Shem and the family of Ham. In the process of incursion back into the Hamite territories that were originally promised to Arphaxad and Elam, the influence of the religion of Ham largely overtook the original Noahic monotheism, eventually snuffing it out almost entirely from the Shemitic lie.

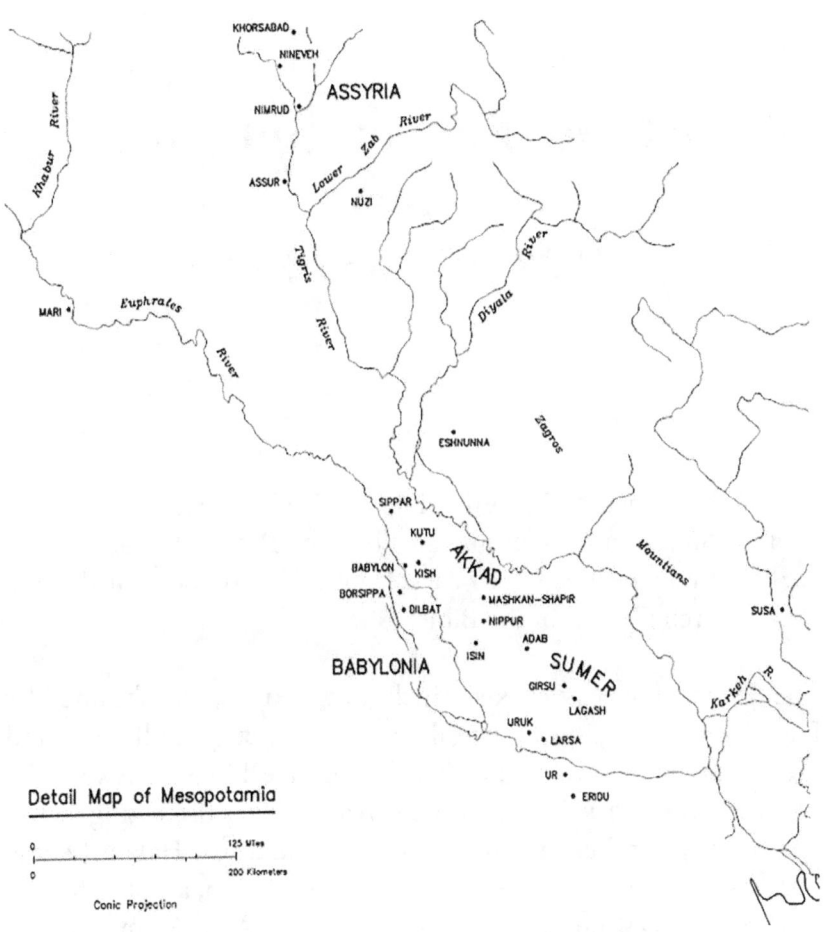

Fig. 8

Chapter Four

Salah (Ar-Ennum), the Son of Cainan
(3032 BC - 2572 BC)

The father of Ebrium of Ebla, the Patriarch Eber of the Bible, was Ar-Ennum of Ebla, the Patriarch Salah of the Bible. He lived 460 years. He was the son of Irkab-Damu, the Patriarch Cainan of the Bible.

The Second Dynasty of Kish, including 8 kings, was founded by Lugal-shumgal (King Shumgal), whose father, grandfather, and great-grandfather, were the three successive kings of Awan, the Elamite city-state as I have shown already. These three kings were, respectively, Ar-Ennum, Irkab-Damu, and Irgish-Halam. These persons were the Biblical Patriarchs Salah, Cainan, and Arphaxad. Therefore, Lugalshumgal was a son of Salah (Ar-Ennum of Ebla). This means that by the end of the reign of Salah (2572 BC) the Shemite family had once again taken over one of the oldest cities in the post-deluvian world, Kish, which may have originally been founded by a Shemite but, by the time history recorded its name, was named after Cush (Kish), the son of Ham.

King Iblul-Il of Mari is credited with having conquered Ebla (and its subject city of Haran), temporarily, in about 2700 BC. While Ebla may have been able to hold him off in this skirmish, it appears that it was more expedient to agree to the terms of surrender, which included making payments to the Mari king. The annual payments, or war indemnity, were made at Mane. Mane lies at the farthest southern border of territory claimed by Ebla and the farthest north by Mari. Therefore, it was the "line of demarcation" between the two city-states. It is highly likely that Iblul-Il was a relative of Salah (Ar-Ennum). His father was Anpu, who was the first king of Mari and was, therefore, probably a son of Arphaxad or Cainan. In about 2580 BC, just a few years before his death, Salah, as King Ar-Ennum of Ebla, defeated and deposed Iblul II, the King of Mari.[96] Salah then reigned over the two city-states, followed by his two sons and heirs, Ebrium and Ibbi-Sipish, until the start of the dynasty of Akkad.

However, Salah, the ruler of Ebla, was driven out of Sumer by Enshakushanna of Uruk. Enshakushanna was a king of Uruk around 2700 BC. He is named on the Sumerian King List, which states his reign to have been 60 years. He conquered Hamazi (whose king Zizi was a brother of Cainan), Akkad, Kish, and Nippur claiming control over all of Sumer.[97] He adopted the Sumerian title *en ki-en-gi lugal kalam-ma*, which may be translated as "Lord of Sumer and King of the land" (or possibly as "*en* of the region of Uruk and *lugal* of the region of Ur"), and could correspond to the later title *lugal ki-en-gi ki-uri*, "lord of Sumer and Akkad" that eventually came to signify kingship over Babylonia as a whole. He was the brother of Enmerkar and both were sons of Nimrod, the son of Cush, who was the son of Ham, the son of Noah. Enshakushanna was the "Lord of Aratta" when Enmerkar, his brother, was the king of Uruk but also later became a ruler of Uruk after his brother left for Egypt. These persons (Cush, Nimrod, Enmerkar, and Enshakushanna) were the Hamites who for many decades fought with the Shemites (Arphaxad, Cainan, Salan, and Eber) for control of the Mesopotamian Valley that they had usurped when Shem originally allocated the lands to his sons.

Ancient Sumer was overtaken by the sons of Ham. Several important city-states were formed very early after the Flood, including Kish, Lagash, Nippur, Uruk, Ur, and others, by his family, even though Shem had promised this land to his own sons. The history of Sumer is largely the history of the descendants of Ham trying to either wrest control of city-states from the sons of Shem, or to retake it from them, or to wrest it from their own siblings. The family of Arphaxad, including Cainan and Salah, participated in these "sibling rivalries" as they fought for control over larger and larger territories in Sumer that they felt were theirs by right from their ancestor Shem. The Shemite Patriarch ruler Serug, who was the same person as Sargon the Great, finally managed to conquer all of Sumer and Akkad (Assyria) under his own singular control.

After a promising start, Ar-Ennum (Salah) was less fortunate than his father Cainan (Ikab-Damu) in Ebla. He was pestered by Hadanish, the king of Hamazi, his cousin (being the son of Zizi, the brother of Cainan), as well as Iblul II, the King of Mari, who was also his cousin (being the son of Anpu, the brother of Cainan). To his east, on the middle Euphrates, King Iblul-II of Mari had gained control over southern Assyria. But then Salah (Ar-Ennum) of Ebla sent his general Enna-Dagan, who had served under his father Cainan (Irkab-Damu) eastwards, where he conquered the young "empire'" of Mari, compelling Iblul II to pay a massive tribute to Ebla of 11,000 pounds of silver and 880 pounds of gold. The vast city of Ebla with an area about ten times that of Solomon's Jerusalem, enjoyed a comparably larger administration. Where Solomon in Jerusalem and its surrounds, had 12 officers in Israel to provide the royal supplies (1 Kings 4:7), the kings of Ebla had 103 "leaders" (nase) and 210 "aides" to look after services for the four palaces of their acropolis, not to mention the staff of 4,700 people employed there.[98] (I might note here, as an aside, that the term "nase" eventually became "nasi" and was used to denote the "leader" of the Sanhedrin during the time of King David of Israel down to the fall of Judea in 73 AD). The general Enna-Dagan was then put in charge of Mari as a vizier, as a subject of the king (en) Salah (Ar-Ennum) of Ebla, with Iblul II as "governor" (lugal).[99]

Ebla was populated by gods (about 500 of them) as well as by over 250,000 people. In such a large city-state, it is the leading figures who mattered.

Through trade with Canaan, Sumer and Anatolia (Turkey), Ebla drew its chief gods from at least these three regions. Most at home were the West-Semitic deities. These included: Il or El, the "senior god;" Dagan (Dagon of the Bible); Rasap (Resheph of the Bible); the sun-god Sipish (Babylonian Shamash; Shemesh in the Bible); Adad; Ashtar, a male equivalent of Astarte (Ashtoreth in the Bible); the goddess Ashera (Asherah in the Bible); Kashalu, perhaps the same as Koshar, the artificer-god of later Ugarit; Malik; and Kemish, possibly familiar centuries later as Kemosh, god of the Moabites.[100] Distinguished foreign members of Ebla's pantheon included such venerable Sumerian deities as Enlil, lord of the world order, and Enki (or Ea), the god of magic and wisdom.
The Sumerian-Eblaite vocabulary tablets show us how the theologians of Ebla equated Syrian deities with their Sumerian cousins. Thus, Resheph equaled the Sumerian Nergal,[101] and Sipish was the same as Utu, for example.[102] This influx of foreign religion into the formerly pure monotheism of Noah was becoming rampant in the days of Salah.

The ancient gods of Ebla had to be housed, fed and honored as befitted their station in life. On its surface, this would tend to indicate that these "gods" had a human form. The administrative tablets of Ebla mention the temples of Dagan, Ashtar, Resheph and Kemish. The regular cult of the gods required bread and drink offerings, plus animal sacrifices, especially on festival days such as on the feasts of Ashtabi and Adammu, for example. [103]

The royal family became the patrons of the state gods. In one month, the king (*en*) of Ebla gave as offerings "11 sheep to Adad," "12 sheep for Dagan," "10 sheep for Resheph." The literary texts preserve brief hymns sung to the gods, probably on such occasions. The actual temples of the golden age of Ebla (around 2300 BC) lie buried for the most part under later remains. However, the excavations have unearthed several temples of the later periods, around 2200 BC to 2000 BC, and especially around 2000 BC to 1650 BC. The lower city boasted three in the south quarters and one in the northern districts. These sometimes had a large sanctuary within massive walls that once towered up to some height, with service-rooms around the outside. Most impressive of all was the great temple on the acropolis, with portico, vestibule and ample sanctuary, a distant forerunner in its layout of Late Bronze and Iron Age temples in Hazor and north Syria. The furnishings of such a temple are illustrated by the fine stone libation-basin sculptured with scenes of the gods, doubtless used in the long, complex rituals of offerings customary in all other temples in the greater area. From the tablets of around 2300 BC, we learn also about the servants of the gods in such temples: priests, priestesses, and "prophets." For this latter group, two terms are used: mahhu (already known from later Akkadian), and nabi'utum, a word related to the Hebrew nabi, "prophet."[104] This innovation of priests, priestesses, and prophets proved important in the expansion of the family of the sons of Shem. In some ways, Salah was fortunate. While he had to deal with the Kings of Mari and of Hamazi, he did not have to vie with Akkad. That would be left for his son, Ebrium, the Biblical Patriarch Eber.

Chapter Five

Eber (Ebrium), Ruler of Ebla, the Son of Salah (Ar-Ennum) (2602 BC-2198 BC)

Eber (Ebrium of Ebla) was born in Ebla, Syria, and lived 404 years. As such it would have been possible for him to have known Terah, the father of Abraham. Flavius Josephus wrote that his name was the source of the name "Hebrews," as his descendants came to be known later on.[105] We know that Salah was Ar-Ennum, King of Ebla. His son was Ebrium, and he assumed the role of King of Ebla on the death of his father in 2572 BC. He would have been only 30 years old at that time. His long reign allowed him to become known as the greatest king of Ebla.

Zechariah Sitchin, the eminent Sumerian linguist has this to say about Eber:

> The term *Ibri* ('Hebrew') by which Abraham and his family identified themselves clearly stemmed from *Eber*, the father of Peleg, and from the [Sumerian] root 'to cross.' Instead of seeking the meaning of the epithet-name in

the Hapiru notions or in Western Asia, it is our conviction that the answer is to be found in the Sumerian origins and the Sumerian language of Abraham and his ancestors. Then a new solution emerges with startling simplicity: The biblical suffix 'I,' when applied to a person, meant 'a native of;' Gileadi meant a native of Gilead and so on. Likewise, *Ibri* meant a native of the place called 'Crossing'; and that, precisely, was the Sumerian name for Nippur: NI.IB.RU – the Crossing Place.... The dropping of the "n" in transporting from Sumerian to Addadian/ Hebrew was a frequent occurrence. In stating that Abraham was an Ibri, the Bible simply meant that Abraham was a *Ni-ib-ri, a man of Nippurian origin!*" [106]

While some of Sichins' theories are not widely accepted, the fact that he recognized in the name Ebrium that this was an ancestor of Abraham is significant. Based on his view, then, Abraham was apparently born in Nippur. Nippur was one of the earliest of all the Sumerian cities. It was the special seat of the worship of the Sumerian god Enlil, the "Lord Wind," ruler of the cosmos, subject to the supreme god An alone. Nippur never enjoyed political hegemony in its own right, but its control was crucial, as it was considered capable of conferring the overall "kingship" on monarchs from other city-states. It was distinctively a sacred city, important from the possession of the famous shrine of Enlil.[107]

The *Tummal Chronicle* states that Enmebaragesi, an early ruler of Kish, was the first to build up this temple at Nippur.[108] His influence over Nippur has also been detected archaeologically. The *Tummal Chronicle* lists successive early Sumerian rulers who kept up intermittent ceremonies at the temple: Aga of Kish, son of Enmebaragesi; Mesannepada of Ur; his son Meskiang-nunna; Gilgamesh of Uruk (the brother of Ur-Nammu, King of Ur); his son Ur-Nungal; Nanni of Ur and his son Meskiang-nanna. It also indicates that the practice was revived in Neo-Sumerian times by Ur-Engur, and then later by his brother Ur-Nammu of Ur (older brother of Gilgamesh and son of Kesed of the Bible).[109] I will identify all of these persons as part of the extended family descendants of Noah as I proceed.

King Ur-Nammu of Ur, the nephew of Eber, being the son of Kesed (brother of Cainan and therefore great uncle of Eber as well as grandfather of Eber through Muak his daughter, who married Salah, the father of Eber), gave to the temple, many years later (about 2110 BC) its final characteristic form. Partly razing the constructions of his predecessors, he erected a terrace of bricks, some 12 meters high, covering a space of about 32,000 square meters. Near the northwestern edge, towards the western corner, he built a ziggurat of three stages of dry brick, faced with kiln-fired bricks laid in bitumen. On the summit stood, as at Ur and Eridu, a small chamber, the special shrine or abode of the god. Access to the stages of the ziggurat, from the court beneath, was by an inclined plane on the south-east side. To the north-east of the ziggurat stood, apparently, the House of Bel [Enlil], and in the courts below the ziggurat stood various other buildings, shrines, treasure chambers, and the like. The whole structure was oriented with the corners toward the cardinal points of the compass.[110]

The Biblical Patriarch Eber married Azura,[111] the daughter of Nimrod and the Sumerian goddess Inanna. In the *Book of Jubilees,* she is called the daughter of Nebrod, which is the Septuagint name for Nimrod.[112] The marriage of Eber and Azura was very important because it was a *dynastic marriage.* Eber, the great grandson of Arphaxad, married Azura, the granddaughter of Cush. Therefore, this *dynastic marriage* eventually proved effective in the future control of parts of Sumer in Hamite territory. The marriage occurred about 2580 BC.

Between this date and around 2250 BC the city-state of Ebla reached its peak of achievement and development. The Eblaites elected a local "merchant ruler" as their king (although the use of this is disputed by scholars, with some preferring to use the term "minister"), with each term of office lasting for seven years. The names of the three known merchant kings match those which are sometimes ascribed to the Awan kings of Elam, so if they are one and the same, perhaps the "elections" were nothing of the kind, and this was a simple way of allowing the people to think that their rulers were "democratically" elected, however anachronistic that may seem.[113] We now know that for at least 4 generations these "ministers" or "merchant rulers" were in fact the Kings of Ebla, Igrish-Halam (Arphaxad), Irkab-Damu (Cainan), and Ar-Ennum (Salah). The last ruler was Ebrium, the Biblical Patriarch Eber.

Sargon of Akkad, later known as Sargon the Great, was born in 2406 BC, the son of Ragau of the Bible, the grandson of Peleg of the Bible, and the great-grandson of Eber of Ebla. Eber was almost 200 years old when Sargon was born. Sargon, as I will show, was the Biblical Patriarch Serug. He grew into a great leader and had won control of southern Mesopotamia by the time he was in his 30's. He then looked northwestwards to Syria and Anatolia (Turkey), sources of valuable timber and metal. He conquered Mari and then much of Assyria, and hammered at the gates of Ebla itself, whose submission and tribute he exacted, perhaps before claiming sovereignty up to the Taurus Mountains and returning in triumph to Akkad. However, we have no record that he ever conquered Ebla.[114] Instead, the powerful dignitary (the term given to him then was "vizier" even though he was truly a king), Ebrium (Eber), had taken over the rule of Ebla from his father Salah (the vizier Ar-Ennum) and had diligently restored the widespread rule of Ebla throughout north Syria and beyond. Since Eber was a relative of Sargon the Great, being his great grandfather, there was no need or desire, I suspect, of Sargon the Great (Serug the Patriarch of the Bible) to conquer him. However, in due time, in Sargon's old age (he died in 2176 BC, only 22 years after Eber had died), Eber had once more begun to extend the influence of Ebla south and eastwards. He had again subdued Mari as his father Ar-Ennum (Salah) had done, even having installed his own son Shura-Damu as the vassal-king there.[115] After both Sargon (Serug) and Eber were dead, however, the empire of Akkad under Sargon's son Rimush was powerless to fight back. The new ruler of Akkad was too beset by revolts nearer home to worry about lands in the distant northwest.

Going one step farther, the ambitious Eber succeeded in imposing an international commercial treaty upon a new king of Assyria, Tudiya, in 2350 BC.[116] Tudiya was the lesser partner in the treaty based on the wording of the document. Until recently, Tudiya has been known to us only as the first name in the Assyrian King List, first of 'seventeen kings who lived in tents,' so remote did he and they seem in later tradition. This treaty is but one of several international treaties found in the Ebla archives, heralds of seventeen centuries of ancient Near Eastern treaties. This one contains an introduction, listing the leading dignitaries of Ebla, then proceeds in twenty paragraphs of main text with the founding and regulation of a commercial center (karum) and its merchants, and ends with a splendid curse-formula as sanction upon the Assyrian king Tudiya, should he break the treaty, clearly making him virtually Ebla's vassal.[117] What is unknown but fascinating, however, is that Tudiya (c. 2600 BC– c. 2000 BC) was the son of Asshur, who was the son of Shem of the Bible. Since Asshur and Arphaxad were brothers, Tudiya and Eber were cousins, although two generations removed.[118] Such, now, was the triumph of Ebla that even Akkad itself paid tribute, perhaps not from the capital but from some northern province only, to buy off Ebla's encroachments. In other words, during the troubled reigns of Sargon's sons, Rimush and Manishtushu, the eyes of Akkad looked south and east, leaving the northwest to Ebla's supremacy.[119]

In the relatively long reigns of Eber and his son and successor Ibbi-Sipish, we see the golden age of the empire of Ebla. From almost all quarters of the ancient Near East, messengers, merchants and tributaries formed the sinews of the influence and power of Ebla.

Among the hundreds of place names in the commercial and diplomatic texts, of special interest to biblical scholars are references to places and vassal cities in Palestine like Hazor, Gaza, Lachish, Megiddo, Akko, Sinai, and even Jerusalem itself (Urusalima).
But perhaps the most intriguing names are those personal names which also appear in the Bible; names from the "Patriarchal Age" like Ab-ra-mu (Abraham), E-sa-um (Esau), Ish-ma-ilu (Ishmael), even Is-ra-ilu (Israel), and from later periods, names like Da-'u'dum (David) and Sa-'u-lum (Saul). All of these names are found in the Ebla Tablets.

The commercial city of Ebla dominated the Western Lands during this period and much is known about it due to the archives found at Tell Mardikh. In the 26th century BC, it dominated all commerce in the west if not in the entire Middle East. At its height, the city-state of Ebla had 250,000 persons. At this early time, weaker dynasties ruled in Sumer, making it possible for cities like Ebla to obtain and retain a strong sense of independence. Because of its strategic location astride the trade routes from Sumer to the Mediterranean, Ebla became a commercial power with influence over most of the city-states of the Middle East. It was a big plum that was not to be ignored by the rulers of Sumer who, by tradition, tried to lay claim to this whole area.

The archives of Ebla reveal many commercial and trading relationships as, for example, a special affinity to the city of Mari on the Euphrates, the midway point for goods going from Sumer up to the northwest and then to the coast of the Mediterranean, from which point it could go to Egypt, Phoenicia, and other countries along the coast of this sea. Besides trade treaties, the two cities cooperated in various academic matters such as in the training of scribes, a very important profession at the time. Another text recovered was found to be a geographical list of cities trading with Ebla. They included Byblos, Sidon, Ashdod, Megiddo, Jaffa, Carchemis, and many others not yet located. These lists also provide a catalog of viable cities of the era and provide a means to date these activities more accurately. As noted above, the language used in Ebla was Eblaite which, by the time of Eber was a very old language already. It undoubtedly was the language of Shem.

Ebla's importance in the absorption of Sumerian culture is attested to by the use of *en* to denote the king. It reveals a special status as well as close relations with Sumerian Uruk in that only the kings of Uruk, the sacred city of An, were allowed to use this prestigious title. Earlier I had noted that Uruk was ruled by Gilgamesh, a son of Kesed and grandson of Shem. Thus these two city-states shared the original family view of authority, namely that it was to Shem's descendants, and not to those of Ham, that the Mesopotamian Valley (Sumer) ultimately belonged. Other sovereigns of Sumer were called *lugal*.[120] As noted above, the Eblaite royalty also used the word *lugal*, but for them it meant "governor." The oldest reference to Ebla in cuneiform literature in Sumer dates to the period of the Akkad dynasty, 2334 BC- 2176 BC. Sargon the Great, the founder of the dynasty, boasts of having conquered Ebla. He did not despoil the city since it survived his reign.[121] As I have shown, just the opposite occurred, and Sargon was forced to leave Ebla alone. Sargon the Great is the same person as Serug the Patriarch of the Bible. As noted above, he did not despoil Ebla because his own great grandfather ruled that city-state, namely Eber, the Patriarch.

One of the Ebla tablets names the five cities of Genesis 14:2 in the same order as they existed in the Old Testament: Sodom, Gomorrah, Admah, Zeboiim and Zoar.[122] It is likely that the book of Genesis was compiled from ancient literature that existed in Ebla (the home of Eber, Salah, Arphaxad, Cainan, and possibly Shem) shortly after the Flood. Another intriguing possibility is that the first part of Genesis was brought to Ebla by Shem himself, and then added to by the Patriarchs as time passed. In any case, it seems clear that the origin of the book of Genesis was not in 600 BC, as some Biblical scholars and critics have thought, but that it was, in fact, written by the Patriarchs themselves and is contemporary with the times about which it speaks, at least for purposes of this book which deals with the period from the Flood until Abraham.

While it is not my intention in this work to do an extensive investigation into the dating of the book of Genesis, it is important that the idea that people wrote this book around 600 BC should be dispelled. There are several factors that lead to the conclusion that the book of Genesis was written and then complied in ancient times.

The first error to dispel is that Moses wrote the book of Genesis. The Bible does not say that Moses wrote the book of Genesis. Instead, it is implied that he "compiled" the book. The implication here is that the book was brought together by Moses but was originally written by several different persons. This fact can actually be shown to be true from the book's writing itself.

Assume for a moment that the book of Genesis was originally written by the Patriarchs themselves at the times about which it speaks. If that is the case then the book would have been written on clay tablets just as ancient Sumerian documents were written at that time. Is there evidence within the book of Genesis that it was not only written on clay tablets but also that it was originally written by several different persons? The answer to this question is an unqualified "yes."

Ancient Sumerian tablets often had writings on them that forced the writing to go from one tablet to the next tablet. The Sumerians did not have page numbering systems such as we use today to go from one page to the next. Instead, they would repeat the last line on the first tablet at the beginning of the first line of the next tablet. Within the book of Genesis we find evidence of this method of moving from one table to the next.

The vocabularies at Ebla were distinctively Semitic: the word "to write" is k-t-b (as in Hebrew), while that for "king" is "mali-kum,"and, that for "man" is "adamu." The closeness to Hebrew is surprising.[123] At Ebla, the king had the Sumerian title "en," and according to the vocabulary lists already referred to, the Paleo-Canaanite equivalent is "Malek." This is virtually the same as the Hebrew word for "king" in the Old Testament "melek." The elders of the kingdom were the "abbu," reasonably close to abba" (father) of the Old Testament. At many points the similarity to Old Testament Hebrew is very close.[124]

There is a creation record reasonably similar to the Genesis account. There are dealings with Hittites long before Abraham purchased the Cave of Machpelah from the Hittites. There are treaties and covenants similar to those in Exodus, and for the protection of society there are laws that point towards the concept of justice so prominent in Exodus. There are ritualistic sacrifices long before those of Leviticus, and before the Canaanites from whom some critics claimed that the Hebrews had borrowed them. There are prophets proclaiming their message long before the nevi'im (prophets) of the Old Testament, though the Old Testament's superiority in the realms of ethics, morality, and spiritual values stands unchallenged.[125]

During the reign of Eber, Dr. Pettinato noted, a change occurred "in the theophoric element, from -el to -ya(w), so that Mi-ka-ilu became Mi-ka-ya(w) and so on. It is quite clear that both of the endings are divine names, either names of gods or words simply meaning "god;" so it looks as if Eber made some major alteration in the religion of Ebla at this time. Whether ya(w) is related to the Biblical Yahweh, the one God of Israel whose name replaced the earlier form of El, is a matter for debate.[126]

Diplomacy and limited warfare supported Ebla's commercial activities. Emar, a city strategically located at the confluence of the Euphrates and Galikh rivers, was tied to Ebla by a dynastic marriage. Khammazi (Hamazi) was Ebla's commercial and diplomatic ally in Iran and probably ruled by a close family relative, Zizi, a brother of Cainan. Commercial treaties were drawn up with other cities. Mari, on the Euphrates River to the southeast, was Ebla's great commercial rival. Twice, an Eblaite army marched against it, and, for a time, Ebla ruled Mari through a military governor, Enna-Dagan.[127]

As noted above, the religion of Ebla was polytheistic and primarily Canaanite. The language of Ebla was a hitherto unknown Canaanite dialect, most closely akin to the Northwest Semitic languages. The script of the tablets, however, is Sumerian cuneiform. Texts reveal that Sumerian teachers came to Ebla, and the presence of a "Canal of Ebla" near Adab attests that Eblaites went to Sumer as well. Vocabularies, syllabaries, gazetteers, and student exercises that have been recovered show that Ebla was a major educational center. Ebla's texts are so complete in comparison to the fragments found in Sumer that the Sumerian texts are augmented by the texts from Ebla.[128]

Most of Syria west to the Mediterranean, south to Hamath, north well beyond Aleppo (Aram), and east to Mari and Assyria and into Elam, was ruled by the kings of Ebla, often through vassals who were family members. But commercial and trading relations reached even farther.[129] Northwards, Ebla's envoys climbed through the Taurus Mountains into the Anatolian (Turkish) plateau to trade with the famous center at Kanesh and even to Hattu, a future Hittite capital. Eastwards there were cities such as Carchemish, Urshu, Mari, Tuttul, and Nahur (possibly founded by Nahor, son of Serug of the Bible). Southwards through Syria, via Hamath, and ports like Ugarit or Byblos or Tyre on the coast, Ebla's commercial tentacles reached on into Palestine, already termed "Canaan" at the time of Eber.[130]

The fifth and last king of Ebla during this period was Ebrium's son, Ibbi-Sipish.[131] Often thought to be the first to succeed in a dynastic line I have shown that the dynasty began with Irgish-Halam (Arphaxad), followed by his son Irkab-Damu (Cainan), then Ar-Ennum (Salah) and then Ebrium (Eber), all Patriarchs of the Bible. This absolutism over inherited succession may have contributed to the unrest that was ultimately instrumental in the city's decline. Meantime, however, the reign of Ibbi-Sipish, Ebers's son, was considered a time of inordinate prosperity, in part because the king traveled abroad frequently. It was recorded both in Ebla and Armi, named after Aram, a brother of Arphaxad, he concluded specific treaties.[132] Monarchy had already openly hereditary by the time of Eber, including the extensions to his sons ruling over nearby towns. By the Ebla there is no way that his "reign" as an elected official could have been for only 7 years as the Ebla Tablets indicate is the term for elected officials. This administrative rule did not apply to the king, or his family, although it may have applied to lower level dignitaries. However, even with those second-level dignitaries, such as Enna-Dagan, who became governor of Mari under the King of Ebla (Salah), he must have served more than one "term" based on the amount of trade that occurred between the two city-states.

After the reign of Ibbi-Sipish, Ebla disappears from the history records. It was destroyed by the grandson of Sargon the Great (Serug the Patriarch of the Bible), namely Naram-Sin.

Chapter Six

Peleg, the Son of Eber
(2568 BC-2229 BC)

The son of Eber in the Bible was Peleg. Peleg lived 339 years. His father, Eber, outlived him by 31 years. This period included the rise of Sargon the Great, one of the most powerful rulers in the Mesopotamian Valley. Therefore, it would be unusual if evidence of Peleg was not found. Here is what we know about Peleg.

In the Bible, it is stated that Peleg was given his name because, "in his days the land was divided."[133] According to Flavius Josephus in his work *Antiquities of the Jews,* the reason for the division is because the languages of the people were divided, forcing them to move apart into other lands.[134] The ancient book *The Cave of Treasures,* written in about 373 AD offers this:

> And in the days of Peleg all the tribes and families of the children of Noah gathered together, and went up from the East. And they found a plain in the land of Sên`ar (Shinar, Sumer), and they all sat down there; and from Adam until this time they were all of one

speech and one language. They all spake this language, that is to say, SORYÂYÂ (Syrian), which is ÂRÂMÂYÂ (Aramean), and this language is the king of all languages. And after the division of tongues [in 2229 BC] Peleg died in great sorrow, and with tears in his eyes and grief in his heart, because in his days the earth was divided. And his son Reu, and Serug, and Nâhôr buried him in Peleghîn, the city which he had built after his own name. And there were seventy-two tongues in the earth, and seventy-two heads of tribes (or families), and each tribe and tongue made unto themselves a chief like a king.[135]

It appears, then, that around 373 AD, when *The Cave of Treasures* was written (although based on older traditions and writings), the phrase "earth was divided" referred to the separation of languages. This coincides with what Josephus had said in his *Antiquities* as well. Since we know the dates for the life of Peleg (2568 BC - 2229 BC) from the Bible, we should expect to see the lifetime of Nimrod to coincide, at least in part, within this range since it was Nimrod's building of the Tower of Babel that led to the confusion of languages among the people. As I will show, Nimrod lived a much longer lifetime than Peleg and was born over 400 years before Peleg.

From the *Book of Jubiliees* comes this amazing story:

And in the three and thirtieth jubilee, in the first year in the second week, Peleg took to himself a wife, whose name was Lomna the daughter of Sina'ar, and she bare him a son in the fourth year of this week [2438 BC], and he called his name Reu; for he said: "Behold the children of men have become evil through the wicked purpose of building for themselves a city and a tower in the land of Shinar [Sumer]."

For they departed from the land of Ararat eastward to Shinar [Sumer]; for in his days they built the city and the tower, saying, "Go to, let us ascend thereby into heaven."

And they began to build, and in the fourth week they made brick with fire, and the bricks served them for stone, and the clay with which they cemented them together was asphalt which comes out of the sea, and out of the fountains of water in the land of Shinar.

And they built it: forty and three years were they building it; its breadth was 203 bricks, and the height (of a brick) was the third of one; its height amounted to 5433 cubits and 2 palms, and (the extent of one wall was) thirteen stades (and of the other thirty stades).

And the Lord our God said unto us: Behold, they are one people, and (this) they begin to do, and now nothing will be withholden from them. Go to, let us go down and confound their language, that they may not understand one another's speech, and they may be dispersed into cities and nations, and one purpose will no longer abide with them till the day of judgment."

And the Lord descended, and we descended with him to see the city and the tower which the children of men had built.

And he confounded their language, and they no longer understood one another's speech, and they ceased then to build the city and the tower. For this reason the whole land of Shinar [Sumer] is called Babel, because the Lord did there confound all the language of the children of men, and from thence they were dispersed

into their cities, each according to his language
and his nation.[136]

Peleg was the father of Ragau (Reu), the Biblical Patriarch, and
the grandfather of Serug (Sargon the Great), another Bibilical
Patriarch. It will be shown that Serug was the great king Sargon the
Great. Therefore, it is almost impossible that we would not find out
the identity in the Mesopotamian Valley of his grandfather, Peleg.

There are three persons who could be the same person as Peleg.
The first two are known as sons of Eber from the Ebla documents.
These are Shura-Damu and Ibbi-Sipish.

Shura-Damu, son of Eber

Shura-Damu was briefly theking of Ebla after his father Eber
(Ebrium). King Eber had diligently restored the widespread rule of
Ebla throughout north Syria and beyond. In due time, in Sargon's
(Serug) old age, Ebrium once more extended the sway of Ebla
eastwards. He again subdued Mari as his predecessor had done,
installing his son Shura-Damu as vassal-king there. This time,
the empire of Akkad under Sargon's son Rimush was powerless
to reply. The new ruler of Akkad was too beset by revolts nearer
home to worry about lands in the distant northwest.

Ibbi-Sipish, son of Eber

The fifth and last king of Ebla during this period was another of
Ebrium's sons, Ibbi-Sipish, the first to succeed in a dynastic line,
thus breaking with the established Eblaite custom of electing its
ruler for a fixed term of office, lasting seven years. This absolutism may have contributed to the unrest that was ultimately instrumental in the city's decline. The reign of Ibbi-Sipish was considered a time of inordinate prosperity, in part because the king was
given to frequent travel abroad. It was recorded both in Ebla and

Aleppo that he concluded specific treaties with neighboring Armi, as Aleppo was called at the time.

Lugalshumgal, brother of Eber

Shura-Damu and Ibbi-Sipish stayed relatively close to home while still extending the range of city-states under the control of their father, Eber.

The Second Dynasty of Kish, including 8 kings, was founded by Lugalshumgal (King Shumgal), whose father, grandfather, and great-grandfather were the three successive kings of Awan, a city-state in Elam as has been shown. These three kings were, respectively, Salah, Cainan, and Arphaxad. Their names in the historical records are Ar-Ennum, Irkab-Damu, and Irgish-Halam. Since the father of Lugalshumgal was Salah of the Bible, then Lugalushumgal was either the same person as Eber of the Bible or his brother. We have no records to indicate that Eber was Lugalshamgal, but instead have shown that he was Ebrium (Ibrium) of Ebla, so therefore Lugalshumgal was Eber's brother. Lugalshumgal was a king of Kish, which had been founded by Cush in the First Dynasty. Cush was a Hamite, the son of Ham of the Bible.

We know that Salah was Ar-Ennum, king of Ebla. His son was Ebrium, the fourth and greatest king of Ebla. Ebrium's son was Peleg. And Peleg's son was Ragau, or Reu. Ragau, who lived 339 years, became a king of Lagash in Sumer. This easily could have happened when his grandfather, Eber, made excursions into Sumer and conquered several of the city-states there, including Kish and Lagash. Eber apparently made his brother, LugalShumgal, the first king of Kish's second dynasty.

Kish had been founded, as I will show later, by Cush, the son of Ham, the son of Noah of the Bible. The name Kish is taken from the name Cush. The city-state therefore was named after himself. The next 21 rulers of Kish, from about 3100 BC to 2550 BC, were probably all descendants of Cush. However, in about 2550 BC Lugalshumgal became the first king of the second dynasty of Kish. It is not clear how he obtained this position other than the fact that his brother, Eber, was still living and had become more and more influential in Sumerian political affairs. The change of rulership from the descendants of Ham to a descendant of Shem may have been accomplished through military conquest, although there is no direct record of a coup having taken place. In any case, the arrival of Lugalshumgal into the rulership of Kish was a significant intrusion of Shemites into land that had originally been Hamite territory. It should be noted that when Noah divided the lands among his sons the area of Kish was supposed to have gone to Shem's line but was instead taken by Ham's family. Therefore, the placement of Lugalshumgal as a King of Kish was a "recovery" of lands originally promised to the descendants of Shem.

Lugalshumgal was also, however, the first king of the second dynasty of Lagash. The first dynasty of Lagash had begun with Enhengal, a son of Gilgamesh. Gilgamesh, as I will show later, was the son of Kesed, who was a brother of Cainan. He was thus a son of the Biblical Patriarch Arphaxad (Igrish-Halam), the son of Shem. Therefore, the last king of the first dynasty of Lagash, namely Enhengal, was a Shemite. When Lugalshumgal became king of Lagash, this was not a second dynasty after all but was an extension of the Shemite first dynasty through a cousin of Enhengal, namely Lugalshumgal. In any case, Lugalshumgal, the brother of Eber, brought the rulership of Lagash into this side of the family. This is important, because the son of Peleg, Reu or Ragau, was also a king of Lagash. The means by which the rulership moved from a descendant of Lugalshumgal to a descendant of his brother, Eber, gives us a clue to the identity of Peleg, the son of Eber.

At some point the rulership of Lagash moved from Lugalshumgal to Peleg after whom it was passed to Ragau. The second king of the second dynasty of Lagash is named Puzer-Mama in the Sumerian records. Therefore, Puzer-Mama is the same person as Peleg, the Biblical Patriarch.

Eber's son Peleg must have also been granted land at some point, since we see that this royal family had all of its members as kings of city-states (Shura-Damu over Mari, Ibbi-Sipish over Ebla, Eber himself over Ebla, and Lugalshumgal over Kish). Therefore we should look to Peleg as having become a king of a city-state as well.

Determining which city-state Peleg ruled can be done by looking to his son, Reu, or Ragau. The Biblical Patriarch Ragau became a ruler of the city-state of Lagash. Therefore, in finding the name of Peleg in Sumer we should look to the King of Lagash prior to Ragau.

As noted just above, Lugalshumgal became the first king of the second dynasty of Kish. He was the brother of Eber.

Chapter Seven

Ragau (Reu), the Son of Peleg (2438 BC-2099 BC)

Fig. 9 Artists rendering of the City of Lagash

W hat we know is that during Eber's reign he was moving south into the areas of the Hamite cities. He was having a good deal of success. In fact, he had fended off Sargon the Great, his own great-grandson, in his own city of

Ebla. Yet, even Eber had no idea just what was about to happen. Only time would reveal it, and it did. Eber's grandson Ragau, who was probably not the eldest son, was able to make inroads into another family with "connections" as well. This is very early in the history of these two individuals, so there was no dynastic marriage taking place here. However, Ragau married into this "connected" family. These people met, fell in love, and married, around 2415 BC. No one at the time was even aware of who they were, beyond their family and friends. However, as time passed, and as their lives were longer than they are today, this particular marriage turned out to be a turning point in the history of the people of Israel many centuries later. The young maiden that Ragau married was named Ora, the daughter of Ur-Nammu, who was a son of Kesed, both descendants of Shem.

Now Kesed, and Eber, Ragau's grandfather, were also related, Kesed being Eber's grandfather, through his mother, Muak; therefore, given the inter-marrying traditions of the day, it was natural that these two cousins once removed, Ragau and Ora, should marry. They were all descendants of Shem as well, Shemites. It is only later that events unfolded that showed us that this particular marriage, along with one other, was a determining point that would lead to the problem that Abraham would have to face centuries later in obedience to his single God, Yahweh. We are now dealing with a very fluid time in the early recorded history of the post-diluvian world, and the number of players tends to increase exponentially. From here on the players are all related, and I will show this clearly. The relationships will determine the events, rather than the other way around. The relationships will be shown to be seminal in the unfolding of the events that lead to our key Patriarch, Abraham. We must follow Ragau first, now, because his involvement with his father-in-law, Ur-Nammu, won't occur for another hundred years or so. It is the longevity of lives that makes this so complex. Yet he, his father-in-law, his grandfather-in-law, and his own descendants, became embroiled in the events that determined how Abraham appeared, became what he was, and led to what he became.

Ragau, then, was married to Ora the daughter of Ur-Nammu, the future King of Ur. We must consider this an "accident" at best. None of the parties were powerful at the time. Ragau's father, Peleg, if he held a position of power in any part of Mesopotamia, which is not likely, disappeared from the scene later; so, from his perspective no case can be made that this was a "dynastic marriage." On the other side, Ur-Nammu, the son of Kesed, was the older brother of Utu-Hegal, who himself would eventually rule Ur as would Ur-Nammu, but at this time he himself was a "pretender" to the throne, at best. Their common older brother happened to be Ur-Engur, who would become the founder of the Second Dynasty of Ur, but not yet. In addition they had another brother, Gilgamesh, about whom I will write shortly. So, what led this couple together? The answer, surprisingly, was that it was Eber and Kesed. As I have shown above, Eber had married Azura, the daughter of Nimrod and the granddaughter of Cush.[137] She was, therefore, of the line of Ham, not Shem. Eber and Cush must have known each other. It was Eber who overtook the First Dynasty of Kish, which had been formed by Cush. Nimrod was the ruler of nearby Babylon. As Eber moved into this Hamite territory a true "dynastic marriage" was arranged. Eber was espoused to Nimrod's daughter Azura, thereby stopping the wholesale routing of these Hamite city-states by Eber. Through the marriage of Azura, daughter of Nimrod, the intermingling of these two Noahite families had finally begun. Therefore, the relationship between Nimrod and Eber had to have been close, even if somewhat edgy. Each wanted to "rule the world."

Here is how this must have worked. Eber, as the greatest king of Ebla during its most impressive period from 2572 BC (the year of the death of his father Salah), had built his city-state into a power-house of the north. Notice that he had married Azura only about 8 years prior to taking over Ebla, in 2580 BC, so the marriage may have been arranged by Nimrod out of a realization that Nimrod would have to eventually deal with the kingdom of Ebla. The city-state of Ebla had fought off many foes to become the ruler that he was, including the King of Mari and the King of Hamazi. He was an "up and coming" "lugal." As he had aged, however, Eber had become more and more power hungry and, finally, had laid designs on the northern parts of the Sumerian, or Hamite, city-states. Eventually, he achieved his "entry point," as it were, through his "dynastic marriage" with Azura. Remember that power in all of these early Noahic families followed a matrilineal descent. Having married Azura, therefore, Eber became the "pretender" to the throne of Nimrod himself. As I will show, Eber's grandfather, Kesed, was the High Priest of the temple of Ninsun at Kullab. He was therefore familiar with all of the "players" in the city-state of Uruk, including the current reigning King Nimrod. He obviously played a role in the later overtaking of the Hamite rule in all of Sumer in favor of the Shemites.

I had stated that Eber, the king of the northern Arphaxad lands (Syria, Lebanon, and Elam to the east) and Kesed, the aging ancestor who was the High Priest at the Temple of Kullab, in what was then Hamite territory, came to an agreement. They found a solution. They would arrange the marriage of their own grandchildren, Ragau of the family of Eber, and Ora of the family of Kesed. Through this they would, eventually, have an inroad into the rulership of Uruk, and then all of Sumer. Eber was the last of the family of Shem to stem the tide of his own descendant, Serug (Sargon), from overtaking all of Sumer into the Arphaxadian northern kingdom of Ebla. He made an agreement through this marriage that would procure Sumer, for all time, as Shemite territory.

The entire Sumerian valley had been in the control of Sargon at one time. As Sargon aged, and as Eber aged, it would only have been natural that Eber would arrange a dynastic marriage to resolve a political problem. However we need not even expect that this might have happened. As then emperor, Sargon more likely determined that it was important that he place a person into a position that would both protect his own position but at the same time empower him with the divine knowledge he needed to continue that empire that he had built. In Kesed, the grandfather of Eber, he found the right person. He installed Kesed as the High Priest of the Temple of Kullab. This would have happened somewhere around 2350 BC, during Sargon's middle age when he was obtaining more and more control. Kesed would have been older by far, about 350 years old in fact at that time. I will show shortly just how important this position was, and relate it to the gods of Sumer who allowed this to occur.

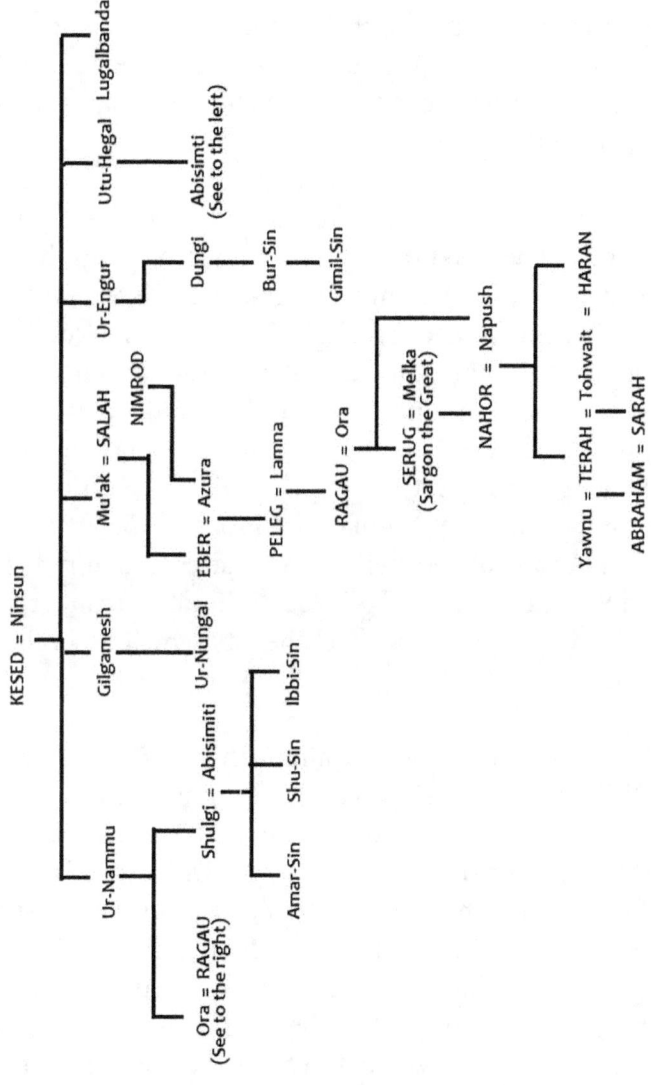

Fig. 10 Kesed's Line

The position for Kesed proved to be important because it allowed him not only to have access to the royal family in Uruk, which was changing every decade or so during this period, but also to have influence with his descendant, Sargon (Serug), at the same time. Kesed became an insider, a role that he had held to a great extent before, but to which he needed to be in that position during the reign of Sargon. As I will show, however, Kesed was not thrust into this position; in fact, he was the key player in the control of Sumer throughout his lifetime. While never a king, he remained the High Priest. That position proved to be much more powerful than even the role of the king.

According to the *Book of Jubilees*, Ragau (Reu) was an idol worshipper, having learned the secrets of divining from the family of his father-in-law, Ur-Nammu, whose father, Kesed, was the High Priest of Ninsun at her temple in Kullab, near Uruk.[138] Ninsun was a goddess of Sumer, the daughter of Nannar-Sin. She was also the mother of Ur-Nammu, who had built a temple at Ur for her father, Nannar-Sin. It is perhaps for this reason that Ur-Nammu placed young great-great-grandson Terah in a position of authority within the temple of Nannar-Sin. From the *Book of the Cave of Treasures*: "And Reu died, being two hundred and thirty-nine years old, and Serug his son, and Nâhôr and Tarah (Terah, grandson of Reu) buried him in Aor`în [Ur] the city which he built after his own name."[139]

Leading up to the reign of Ur-Nammu, historians cite three dynasties rather than two. However, Ur-Nammu, king of the Third Dynasty, was actually related to Utu-Hegal, last king of the Second Dynasty. Therefore the Third Dynasty of Ur is actually a continuation of the Second and not a new dynasty at all. The First Dynasty of Ur was established by the king Mesannepada, who is on the Sumerian King List and is named as a son of Meskalamdug on one artifact.[140] Based on the outline that I have laid out, Meskalamdug and his son Mesannepada had to have been descendants of Ham of the Bible. In fact Meskalamdug was almost certainly the son of

Cush, who was the son of Ham. However, Cush, having been the first ruler in Sumer, as King of Kish, was in control of all of Sumer and, through his son Nimrod, future "Emperor" of Sumer and Akkad, all of the other later city-states were set up with rulers of the Hamite line.

Meskalamdug, whose name means "hero of the good land" was an early ruler of Ur although his name does not appear in the Sumerian King List. His tomb was discovered by English archaeologist Sir Leonard Wooley in the Royal Cemetery of Ur in 1924.[141] It contained numerous gold artifacts including a golden helmet with an inscription of the king's name, indicating that he was the King of Ur at that time. His wife's name was Queen Ninbanda. Meskalamdug was also mentioned on a seal in another tomb in which he held the title lugal, which we have shown meant "king" in Sumer at that time. His own tomb lacked attendants, so Woolley assumed that he did not rule over Ur. The controversy remains though, because he is named on a bead inscription discovered in Mari by French archaeologist Andre Parrot ten years later, as the father of King Mesannepada of Ur, who appears in the King List and in many other inscriptions. It is my supposition, and only that, that Meskalamdug was a younger son of Cush. His rule over the young city of Ur was not as significant as his son's, and was, therefore, not mentioned. As Ur became a more important city-state around 2700 BC, it was more appropriate to allow the son of Meskalamdug, namely Mesannapada, to take the realm. It is also possible that Meskalamdug predeceased his son.

Therefore, we have the beginnings of the First Dynasty of kings at Ur. Meskalamdug, the first king (or his son, as I have just noted), was followed by his own son, Mesannepada. Mesannepada's son, Nanni, followed, and then his other son, Meskiang-nanna, followed by Elulu, and finally, Balulu. The time period for this dynasty lasted about 200 years, from 2750 BC to 2550 BC Recall that people lived longer lives during this period, as I will prove later. Therefore, Meskalamdug, the first king or proto-king of the

First Dynasty of Ur, was almost certainly a son of Cush, the son of Ham, if not indeed a son of Ham himself.

Meskiang-nanna's reign was ended by an incursion from Elam, which could not have occurred before about 2400 BC, after which Elam lost control. Therefore, we see a glimpse of another line of the family of Cush, through Meskalamdug, Mesannepada, and Meskiang-nanna, that was Hamite. While we know the names of the son and grandson of Meskiang-nanna, we do not know that they ruled Ur.

The First Dynasty, according to the list, ended when Ur was defeated and the kingship was taken to Awan, a city-state in Elam. I have noted above that Arphaxad, after the death of his brother Elam, had taken control of the Elamite territories through his marriage to Elam's grandaughter Rasueja. I also suggested that Arphaxad had made excursions into lower Sumer (Hamite territory), which his son, Cainan, had continued. Therefore, the First Dynasty of Ur, under Meskalamdug and his son Mesannepada, both Hamites, ended when Cainan extended his control from Awan into southern Sumer, conquering the city-state of Ur for the Shemites. This would have occurred roughly around 2325 BC It is for this reason that the descendants of Mesannapada (Nanni, Meskiang-nanna, Elulu, and Balulu), while shown as having "reigned" over Ur, were actually "patesis" or governors of the city-state. It also explains why we have no information of their contributions and are only lucky to have their names. An estimate of the "reigns" of these rulers of the First Dynasty of Ur is as follows:

Name	Estimated Reign
Meskalamdug	2582 BC to 2502 BC
Mesannapada	2502 BC to 2422 BC
Nanni	2422 BC to 2422 BC
Meskiang-nanna	2422 BC to 2386 BC

Elulu	2386 BC to 2361 BC
Balulu	2361 BC to 2325 BC

In about 2325 BC Cainan then installed Lugalzagezi as ruler over this area, which included Ur, Umma, Larsa, Lagash, and Uruk. Lugalzagezi is shown as the first king of the First Dynasty of Uruk, but he also controlled Ur during his lifetime. He reigned about 2325 BC to 2300 BC, consistent with the transfer from Balulu of Ur as noted above. Lugalzagezi was descended from Kesed, the brother of Arphaxad. Here is the family tree:

Kesed had Gilgamesh. Gilgamesh had Ur-Lugal, or Urnugal, who became a king of Uruk. He is named as a son of the "divine" Gilgamesh and reigned for 30 years:

Name	Estimated Reign
Urnugal	2602 BC to 2572 BC
Utul-Kalamma	2572 BC to 2557 BC
Labasher	2557 BC to 2548 BC
Ennundaranna	2548 BC to 2441 BC
Meshede	2441 BC to 2405 BC
Melamanna	2405 BC to 2399 BC
Lugalkidul	2399 BC to 2363 BC
Lugal-Kinishe-Dudu	2363 BC to 2355 BC
Lugalzagezi	about 2355 BC

We can see, then, that my chronology now is well aligned with the Sumerian King List, even though the dating is long. At the very end of the reign of Balulu, descended from Cush, in the same time frame, we see Lugalzagezi, a descendant of Shem, through his son Kesed, taking over the rule of Ur as an addition to the long reign of the dynasty of Uruk. This, then, is also the dynasty started by Gilgamesh, son of Kesed, who ruled over Uruk.

Lugalzagezi is mistakenly called an "ensi" of Umma, rather than a King of Uruk in the dynasty of Gilgamesh.

Before we continue with the normal biblical line of the Patriarchs, we need to deal with the most important figure involved in the mixing of the family of Shem with the family of Ham. His name is Kesed.

Chapter Eight

Kesed, Brother of Cainan and Son of Arphaxad (c. 2900 BC-c. 2200 BC)

Kesed was the son of Arphaxad and he therefore may have lived as much as 700 years. Kesed was the grandson of Shem. Although his father remained faithful to the warnings of Noah, Methusaleh, and Enoch that they should have no contact with the Nephilim, Kesed, who described as a "lillu", or spirit, a demonic sort, was enticed to have intercourse with Ninsun, a Sumerian goddess, by whom he had Gilamesh, Utu-Hegal, and Ur-Nammu.[142]

The origin of the term "lillu" follows:

> Lilith (Belit-ili) was the screech owl goddess, a sort of winged demon associated with the night. She made her nest in the huluppa tree that grew along the bank of the Euphrates. It was uprooted by wind and Flood, and found and planted by Inanna in her holy garden. It was cut down by Gilgamesh to make a throne

for Inanna, causing Lilith to fly away to the wild lands. Her children are the Lillu or Lilim.... Huwawa (Humbaba) as well as some Sumerian Kings lists indicate that Gilgamesh was the son of a Lillu.[143]

In the Sumerian King List the actual statement is this, regarding Gilamesh: "*whose father was a phantom (lillu), the lord of Kulaba.*"

Kulaba was the city-state honoring Ninsun. There was no other "lord of Kulaba" other than the High Priest of her temple there, namely Kesed. Furthermore, Kesed was not a "lillu", or phantom. In the "Letter of Gilgamesh", in the Akkadian language of the neo-Assyrian period, Gilgamesh refers to himself as "Sar Urim, mar Kullab", "King of Ur, native of Kullab."[144] Kesed was that High Priest of the temple at Kullab, which honored Ninsun, the goddess and daughter of Nannar-Sin, the Moon god. Therefore, Kesed was the father of Gilgamesh through a relationship between himself and the goddess Ninsun, in whose temple he was the High Priest.

Another story says that Ninsun had Gilgamesh by Lugalbanda.[145] However, the 3rd Dynasty of Ur kings often claimed Gilgamesh's divine parents, Ninsun and a High Priest of Kullab, as their own, probably to evoke a comparison to the epic hero. In fact Gilgamesh called himself "semi-divine", which indeed he was! His divine nature came from his mother, Ninsun. However Kesed is more likely the father of Gilgamesh, rather than Lugalbanda, since Kesed was the High Priest within the Temple of Ninsun at Kullab and he had the position that made this liason possible through the "Sacred Marriage" rite. The Sumerian King List indicates that Gilgamesh was born of Ninsun and a "Lord of Kullab," who had to be Kesed. I will deal more extensively with the issue of the "Sacred Marriage." The result was that the bloodline of the family of Shem was polluted with the commingling of human and "godly" genes.

Ninsun had apparently become enamored of Kesed as her High Priest. He became her High Priest at Kullab, and through that was inducted into a hierarchy of power that included her father Nannar-Sin, the Moon god. In time, as I will show, Kesed had great influence over the secular power of Sumer. The *Book of Jubiliees* names Ur-Nammu, King of Ur, as the son of Kesed:

> "And in the thirty-fifth jubilee, in the third week, in the first year thereof, Reu took to himself a wife, and her name was 'Ora, the daughter of 'Ur, the son of Kesed, and she bare him a son, and he called his name Seroh [Serug], in the seventh year of this week in this jubilee." [146]

Abraham is named as having been born in Ur of the Chaldees, which is a corruption of Ur of the Kasidim. The Kasidim were the ancestors of Kesed, who was the father of Ur-Nammu, King of Ur. The daughter of Ur-Nammu, Ora, was the wife of Reu (Ragau). Reu was the father of Serug (Sargon the Great), whose son Nahor was the father of Terah, the father of Abraham. Therefore, Abraham was the great-great-grandson of Kesed of Ur and also of Ninsun, the goddess.

Cainan, the brother of Kesed, came under the special tutelage of his father Arphaxad and learned the art of writing. One day on the foothills, he uncovered a stone stele with writings which he soon identified as the writings of the Watchers, the fallen angels, who had wreaked such genetic havoc in the antediluvian world.[147] These writings included the "astrology of the sun and the moon and the stars and in all the signs of heaven."[148] Cainan hid the writings from the knowledge of Noah but passed the secret mysteries to his brother, Kesed and then to Kesed's son, Ur-Nammu, the builder of the city of Ur of the Kasidim (i.e. of Kesed). It was, then, Ur-Nammu who transported this information of the new mystery religion of the Kasidim and was the first to sculpt molten images for worship. The formation of idol worship was started by Ur-Nammu, the son of the High Priest Kesed of Kullab. As the older brother of Gilgamesh and Utu-Hegal, also kings of Uruk and Ur, the influence of Ur-Nammu cannot be understated. I will develop this in more detail when we talk about Terah and his son Abraham.

Four of the sons of Kesed became Kings of Ur. They are Gilgamesh, Ur-Engur, Utu-Hegal, and Ur-Nammu. The kingship of Ur remained in the family from 2481 BC until the destruction of Ur in 2023 BC, a period of nearly 460 years, except for the period during which Sargon the Great controlled it. Of course Sargon was also a descendant of Shem as is shown elsewhere. I will now discuss the sons of Kesed.

Chapter Nine

Gilgamesh, the Son of Kesed (c. 2650 BC-c. 2475 BC)

Gilgamesh was the son of Ninsun, a comparatively obscure goddess who had a palace-temple in Uruk.[149] I have already shown that Gilgamesh is, in fact, the son of Kesed of the Bible, High Priest of Ninsun's Temple at Kullab, which was a part of Uruk,. Gilgamesh is the fifth king on the Sumerian King List and reigned in Uruk from around 2600 BC for 126 years to about 2475 BC He was the ruler of Uruk (biblial Erech). He was also known as the ruler of Kullab, the city where his mother's temple was located and where his father, Kesed, held the position of High Priest.

Fig. 11 Gilgamesh

After the Flood the first city that had "kingship" was Kish. This is also confimed in the Bible, but my statement comes from the Sumerian texts. At some point in time kingship over the land was transferred to Uruk (Erech in the Bible), due to the ambitions of the Sumerian goddess Inanna, again according to the Sumerian texts. I will develop this scenario completely later. Gilgamesh built the walls of the city Uruk, and the Eanna (house of An) Temple complex there, dedicated to Ishtar, who is the same as Inanna. After this episode, he apparently took Nippur from the son of the founder of the First Dynasty of Ur, who was Mesh-ki-ang-nanna, the son of Mesannapeda. Mesannapeda was the son of Meskalamdug, whom I have shown was the son of Nimrod. Thus began the transfer of power from the sons of Ham to the sons of Shem.

Ur was one of the first village settlements founded by the so-called Ubaidian inhabitants of Sumer. Before 2800 BC, Ur became one of the most prosperous Sumerian city-states.[150] According to ancient records, Ur had three dynasties of rulers who, at various times, extended their control over all of Sumer. The founder of the First Dynasty of Ur was the conqueror and temple builder Mesannepada (he reigned about 2670 BC), the earliest Mesopotamian ruler described in extant contemporary documents. His father was Akalamdug, whose father was Meskalamdug, the son of Cush, the son of Ham. He was therefore a Hamite. His son Aanepadda (he reigned about 2650 BC) built the temple of the goddess Ninhursag, which was excavated in modern times at Tell al-Obeid, about 5 miles northeast of the site of Ur. Therefore, the ruler whom Gilgamesh overthrew was apparently Mesannepada.

One of the most famous tales of the era of Gilgamesh is the *Epic of Gilgamesh*, a summary of which I have included in an Appendix. Within this tale is a similar tale to that of the story of Noah and the Great Flood. In addition, Gilgamesh states clearly that his mother is the goddess Ninsun. Archaeologists in Iraq believe they may have found the lost tomb of King Gilgamesh - the subject of the oldest "book" in history. I am reproducing the article here:

> A German-led expedition has discovered what is thought to be the entire city of Uruk - including, where the Euphrates once flowed, the last resting place of its famous King. "I don't want to say definitely it was the grave of King Gilgamesh, but it looks very similar to that described in the epic," Jorg Fassbinder, of the Bavarian department of Historical Monuments in Munich, told the BBC World Service's Science in Action programme.

Magnetic

In the epic written on a set of inscribed clay tablets, Gilgamesh was described as having been buried under the Euphrates, in a tomb apparently constructed when the waters of the ancient river parted following his death.

"We found just outside the city an area in the middle of the former Euphrates river the remains of such a building which could be interpreted as a burial," Mr Fassbinder said. He said the amazing discovery of the ancient city under the Iraqi desert had been made possible by modern technology. "By differences in magnetisation in the soil, you can look into the ground," Mr Fassbinder added. ""The difference between mudbricks and sediments in the Euphrates river gives a very detailed structure." This creates a magnetogram, which is then digitally mapped, effectively giving a town plan of Uruk.

'Venice in the desert'

"The most surprising thing was that we found structures already described by Gilgamesh," Mr Fassbinder stated. Iraq has long been the site of some of the most important historical finds.

"We covered more than 100 hectares. We have found garden structures and field structures as described in the epic, and we found Babylonian houses." But he said the most astonishing find was an incredibly sophisticated system of canals. "Very clearly, we can see in the canals some structures showing that Flooding destroyed some houses, which means it was a highly developed system. "[It was] like Venice in the desert." [151]

I will now deal with two of the sons of Kesed: Ur-Engur and Utu-Hegal.

Chapter Ten

Ur-Engur (c. 2700 BC-2390 BC) and Utu-Hegal (c. 2550 BC-2113 BC), the Sons of Kesed

I have aready discussed Gilgamesh, one of Kesed's four sons. In this chapter I will talk about 2 more brothers of Gilgamesh. Then in the next chapter discussion will cover Lugalzagesi, a descendant of Gilgamesh who was an active player just prior to the last brother's reign, Ur-Nammu, who is a very important person at the time of Terah and Abraham.

Ur-Engur, Son of Kesed

Historians call Ur-Engur, who lived about 210 years, the first King of the Second Dynasty of Ur. In fact he actually took over from Lugalzagesi, who was also of the family of Kesed, although many generations removed due to the shorter lives of this particular branch of the family. At the beginning of his reign Ur-Engur held only the city of Uruk (the biblical Erech) which Lugalzagesi had held. He decreed that here the first measure undertaken must be the rebuilding of the city wall as a measure of protection. His first conquest made him "Lord" of Uruk. About the same time came the capture of Lagash, for the year following the installation of Ur Abba, as patesi, is ed in the date formulas by that of Ur-Engur's son as High Priest of Inanna in Uruk. That Larsa belonged to his kingdom is proved by a building inscription, and others show his lordship over Nippur, Adab, and Umma. At Lagash he dug a boundary canal which reminds us of the one dug long centuries before between that city and its rival Umma.[152] Therefore, it is clear that due to the overlordship of Sargon (Serug), his relative, he obtained the same control that Lugalzagesi had held prior to his removal by Sargon. In short, the removal of Lugalzagesi was not a matter of "conquest" but was instead an issue of "family matters." Sargon didn't get along with Lugalzagesi, apparently, but he wasn't about to throw the entire southern portion of Sumer away. Instead, he took his grandfather Kesed's advice and installed a son of Kesed, Ur-Engur, in the position that had been held by Lugalzagesi (who himself was a descendant of Kesed through his son Gilgamesh). This act of placing Ur-Engur into a significant position of power in southern Sumer is a clear indication of the influence of Kesed. This influence outlived the power of Sargon. Through this action the dynasty of Gilgamesh was transferred to Ur-Engur, his brother, both being the sons of Kesed.

After the conquest of Nippur, Ur-Engur assumed the title "King of Sumer and Akkad," though the only portion of northern Babylonia that we may conjecture belonged to him was Ishkun Sin, whose patesi, Hashhamer, made a dedication in his honor. That Ur-Engur actually did make at least one expedition into this part of Babylonia is proved by a date formula which tells how he "took his way from the Lower to the Upper Country."[153]

We are now able to piece together the formal statements in the royal records. Further hints we find in a hymn. We hear of the city wall of Ur, fallen through age, of the palace burned by fire, of the plundered home of the shepherd, his wife lost, his son not permitted to grow upon his knees. But Ur-Engur, the brother of Gilgamesh, became the shepherd of the people.[154] The deities had compassion on him. Those whom he plundered followed him in tears; his ships were seen in places hitherto unknown. The faithful wood of the oars brought its wealth to Gu-edin and at the same time came the gifts of Kish. There was a rebellion, but the foe who was hostile to the land was thrown down, the chariot overthrown, and the expedition annihilated, though the leader was not captured. The seven foreign lands brought gifts. At the name of Ur-Engur terror was felt in the foreign lands and then the lands were at peace. The reign of Ur Engur, which ended in 2390 BC, had resulted in a reable increase of power for the Ur dynasty, and he well deserved all the praises of the scribes. Unlike his successors, he was not deified, either in his lifetime or in the lifetime of his deified descendants. His son Dungi, in his long rule of fifty-eight years (2390-2332 BC), secured deification, possibly because of his expansion of his domains. There are inscriptions which prove that all of southern Sumer was under the control of Ur-Engur, including Nippur, Adab, Umma, Lagash, the nearby Dungi Babbar, whose name identified the king with the sun-god, but only his inscriptions from the Elamite capital of Awan point to actual conquests.

King Ur-Engur proclaimed his code of laws in the name of the great god Utu in Sumer. Government had, at the very start of human civilization, recognized the political expediency of gaining heaven's blessing for its actions.[155] Ur-Engur and Dungi, his son, had indeed become the founders of a new empire. In this were united the entire south of Sumer, which had belonged by right of long occupation to the Hamites, but in it he also listed Akkad, the land which would subsequently be won by the Shemites under Sargon. Therefore, almost all of Sumer, as well as the original Assyrian (Akkadian, or Arphaxadian) lands were now Shemite lands. There were pockets of Sumer that were still controlled for a time by Hamites.

All over his kingdom Ur-Engur built great structures for protections, for civil use, or for the worship of the gods. In his own chief city of Ur he built the great temple to the moon god, Nannar-Sin.

In the city of Uruk he erected a temple to the goddess Nina. At Larsa, also, there are found unmistakable evidences that it was he who built there the shrine of the sun god Utu (Shamash). In Lagash he erected a temple to Enlil, and dug a canal, intended not only to supply water but also to serve as a boundary.[156] In Nippur he built a great ziggurat, whose base was a "right-angled parallelogram nearly fifty-nine meters long and thirty-nine meters wide. Its two longest sides faced northwest and southeast respectively, and the four corners pointed approximately to the four cardinal points. Three of these states have been traced and exposed. It is scarcely possible that formerly other stages existed above. The lowest story was about six and a third meters high, while the second (receding a little over four meters from the edge of the former) and the third are so utterly ruined that the original dimensions can no more be given. The whole ziggurat appears like an immense altar. [157] The defensive walls of Ur were also built by Ur-Engur, who seemed to be building for all time.

Utu-Hegal, Son of Kesed and Brother of Gilgamesh, Ur-Engur, and Ur-Nammu

Utu-Hegal was the younger brother of Ur-Engur, both being the sons of Kesed, the High Priest of Kullab, whose consort was Ninsun, who was the daughter of Nannar-Sin, the god over Ur. He lived about 437 years. Utu-Hegal took over the realm of his brother as King of Ur, which included the city-states of Umma, Uruk, Larsa, and Lagash as had been controlled by his brother. The meaning of his name is "The Sun God is Exuberance" or "The Exuberance of the Sun God."[158] He worshiped Nannar-Sin, the sun god who was his grandfather, the father of his mother Ninsun!

He reigned over Uruk from the death of his brother in 2390 BC until his own death in 2113 BC Utu-Hegal of Uruk is given credit for having overthrown Gutian rule by vanquishing their king Tirigan (the Biblical Terah) along with two generals. Tirigan had been on the throne for only forty days. They fought at a place called Ennigi. Tirigan was defeated and fled but was captured and returned to Utu-Hegal.[159] Tirigan is the same person as Terah, the father of Abraham. Utu-Hegal called himself "Lord of the four quarters of the earth" in an inscription, but this title, adopted from Akkad, is more likely to signify political aspiration than actual rule.[160] Utu-Hegal was a brother of Ur-Nammu,[161] who founded the 3rd Dynasty of Ur ("3rd" because it is the third time that Ur is listed in the Sumerian King List, when in fact it was a continuation of the Second Dynasty, started by Ur-Engur as shown above). Under Ur-Nammu and his successors Shulgi, Amar-Sin, Shu-Sin, and Ibbi-Sin, this dynasty lasted for 385 years (2408 BC to 2023 BC). Ur-Nammu was at first "governor" of the city of Ur under Utu-Hegal. What is amazing is that this dynasty continued to exist during the reign of Sargon the Great. We must ask ourselves how this is possible, since Sargon the Great (Serug of the Bible) conquered all of Sumer and Akkad. Sargon was directly related to all of the kings in this dynasty of Ur. He, therefore, did not need to conquer them and destroy their city-states. Instead, all he needed to do was obtain their allegiance, which he clearly did. Therefore, while he was the "Emperor of Sumer and Akkad", his cousins Ur-Engur and Utu-Hegal were at the same time rulers over the city-states listed above.

Utu-Hegal, following in his brother Ur-Engur's footsteps, managed to maintain Sumer under his control in his reign and continued the peace that his brother had established.[162] After having captured Tirigan (Terah), Utu-Hegal made the young ex-king a High Priest in the temple of Nannar-Sin in Ur. He did this because Terah was a relative. We know that Terah was in fact a High Priest in Nannar-Sin's temple during the reign of Ur-Nammu, the brother of Utu-Hegal.[163] Since the father of Utu-Hegal was Kesed, the High Priest of Ur, it would have been easy to have Terah placed into a position within the priesthood. Terah was also the great-great-grandnephew of Utu-Hegal, being in the line descended from Kesed. Utu-Hegal may have died accidentally as a text states that "his body was carried off by the river."[164] On the other hand, there is some indication that he was overthrown by his ambitious brother, Ur-Nammu, and some texts do allude to his being assassinated. Ur-Nammu was a general whom his brother, Utu-Hegal, had promoted to that position in the city of Uruk before he became the ruler of Ur.[165] It is also possible that Utu-Hegal sent his brother to Ur to become the "patesi" or underlord and that then Ur-Nammu became the King on the death of his brother in 2113 BC.

The following is from *The Babylonian Empire* by A. T. Olmstead:

> The long agony of Babylonia under the sway of the barbarian Guti was brought to an end by the Shumerian Utu-Hegal. In an inscription unique for freshness of expression among the royal records of early Babylonia he tells us of his operations. Gutium is the "dragon of the mountains, the enemy of the gods, which had ravished the wife from her husband, their infants from the parents, and caused woe and evil in the land." Utu-Hegal, the king of Uruk, the king of the Four World Regions, prayed to Inanna for aid, since Enlil had granted to him that the kingdom of Sumer should be independent. Meanwhile the Guti king, Tirigan, had thought, "No one will come against me, the Tigris has Flooded the country, below in Shumer it has covered the fields, it has covered the roads, the roads of the land are covered with torn-off plants." From Uruk, Utu-Hegal sallied forth and moored his boat at the temple of Ishkurra, whence issued his proclamation to the people, informing them that Enlil had given him Gutium, that the lady Inanna was his aid, that the old hero of Uruk, Gilgamesh [the brother of Utu-Hegal, long since deceased], had given him protection. To the people of

Uruk and Kullab he brought joy of heart; his city like one man marched behind him; to the same purpose they turned their face. From the temple of Ishkurra he weighed anchor. In five days he came to the dam of Ilitabbeka, where the lieutenants of Tirigan arrived with a message and were captured. On the sixth day Utu-Hegal anchored at Muru; the wall of Gutium he broke through; soldiers he brought within. Tirigan, alone and on foot, fled to his fortress of Dubrum. The people of that town, knowing that Utu-Hegal was the king to whom Enlil had given the might, gave not the hand to Tirigan. Through the messenger of Utu-Hegal they made Tirigan, his wife, and his children prisoners in Dubrum; on his hands they placed fetters. Utu-Hegal took him. Prostrate before his conqueror the Guti king threw himself, and Utu-Hegal placed his feet on his neck. So Utu-Hegal established Sumer in its independence and began the fifth and last dynasty of Uruk. Yet it wasTirigan and not Utu-Hegal who was remembered a thousand years hence as the founder of a city.[166]

Here is another analysis of the situation between the Gutians and the Sumerians:

Semitic-Sumerian Conflict

Indeed, the Gutians appear to have been initially hailed by the Sumerians as deliverers from the Semitic Akkadian oppressors. The reason given for the Gutian attack on the Akkadians by the Sumerians is the destruction of the main Sumerian religious shrines by the fanatical

Akkadian ruler Naram-Sin [the son of Sargon]. The work 'The Curse of Agade,' composed by a Sumerian, indicates the revulsion which the Sumerians felt at this senseless act of Akkadian destructiveness:

"In searching for the causes behind the humiliating and disastrous Gutian invasion, the author comes upon what he thinks is undoubtedly the true answer and informs us of an outrage committed by Naram-Sin, unknown as yet from any other source. According to our author [of *The Curse of Agade*], Naram-Sin had sacked Nippur and committed all sorts of desecrating and defiling acts against Enlil's sanctuary, and Enlil had therefore turned to the Gutians and brought them down from their mountain abode to destroy Agade and avenge his beloved temple. Moreover eight of the more important deities of the Sumerian pantheon, in order to soothe the spirit of their ruler Enlil, laid a curse upon Agade that it should remain forever desolate and uninhabited. And this, added the author at the end of his work, was indeed the case: Agade had remained desolate and uninhabited."[167]

What we see, then, is that Naram-Sin, who was the son of Serug (Sargon), a biblical Patriarch, had stepped over the line. Enlil was outraged and spoke through Nahor who was the High Priest in the Temple of Enlil at Nippur, and as such was the "voice" of the god Enlil. As that "voice", he called upon his own son, Terah, who lived among the Gutians, to avenge Enlil. Now at this time Terah was most likely not the king of Gutia, but he was in line to become the king shortly. The king of Gutia at the time was Siu or Sium, although in Gutia the kingship was not handed down through families. Therefore Terah was not related to Sium.

According to the Sumerian King List, "In the army of Gutium, at first no king was famous; they were their own kings and ruled thus for 3 years."[168] Naram-Sin was also of the family of Terah, however, being the son of Serug (Sargon). Sargon (Serug) was also related to Utu-Hegal, although somewhat distantly. Their common ancestor was Arphaxad, who had Cainan and Kesed. Naram-Sin was descended from Cainan, while Utu-Hegal was descended from Kesed, being, in fact his son. Naram-Sin, on the other hand, was not the son of Cainan but was in fact the 5th great-grandson of Cainan and the 4th great-grandson of Mu'ak, a daughter of Kesed. Due to the longevity of lives at this time, still, these mult-generational relationships existed. Naram-Sin had stepped over the line in attacking Nippur, the home of Enlil the god. Enlil had turned to Utu-Hegal for support, and Utu-Hegal sought out the Gutians for support. They in turn routed Naram-Sin. In giving Utu-Hegal the authority to route Naram-Sin and the Akkadians, Enlil also said that Akkad, their capital, would never be inhabited again. When it was finally destroyed in the next generation, the devastation was total. To this day Akkad, the home of Sargon the Great, has not been found. Later, when Utu-Hegal had to also undo the Gutian empire, since Terah was related to Utu-Hegal, he elected to give him the position of High Priest of the temple in Ur, rather than kill him. Utu-Hegal was followed by his brother Ur-Nammu as king of Ur.

Chapter Eleven

The Issue of Dating
and Longevity

D ue to the longevity of lives during this ancient period I have to develop the next segment through a chart. The chart will show that the family of Kesed, through Gilgamesh, will have to have had intercourse with the descendants of Ham, through his son Cush. The following is a list of descendants of Cush, known as Jusher (also transliterated **Jucur, Gushur, Gishur**) in the King List. I have included in this list an average age between father and son of 25 years. It could have varied much more than that, but the oldest son is often born around the 25th year of the parents. Given that, I present this possible scenario.

Name	Estimated Birth	Name	Estimate Birth
Jusher (Gusher, Cush)	3100 BC	Mashda	2850 BC
Kullassina-Bel	3075 BC	Arwium	2825 BC
Nangishlishma	3050 BC	Balih	2800 BC
En-Tarah-ama	3025 BC	Enmennuna	2775 BC

Balima (Babum)	3000 BC	Melam-Kish	2750 BC
Buanum (Paunnum)	2975 BC	Barsal-Nuna	2725 BC
Kalibum	2950 BC	Zamug	2700 BC
Galimum	2925 BC	Tizkar	2675 BC
Zukakin ("Scorpion")	2900 BC	Ilku	2650 BC
Atab	2875 BC	Iltasadum	2625 BC

The next four kings on the list are as follows:

Enmenbaragesi	**2600 BC**
Agga of Kish	**2575 BC**
Uhub	**2550 BC**
Mesilim	**2525 BC**

I want to deal with three of these kings of Kish. Enmenbaragesi, who was a king of Kish, according to the Sumerian King List reigned around 2600 BC according to the general consensus of the scholars.[169] [170] The list states that he subdued Elam, but was captured single-handedly by Dumuzid "the fisherman" of Kuara, who was the predecessor of Gilgamesh. I will show that the scholars have rightly placed Gilgamesh as having flourished around 2600 BC Therefore, Dumuzid would have been before him, say 2650 BC Finally, we can see that Dumizid and Enmenbaragesi are contemporaries of one another by using this simple dating system. In other words, Enmenbaragesi falls where we would expect him to by just placing 25 years between each of the kings of Kish on the Sumerian King List.

Enmenbaragesi is also mentioned in a section of the original Sumerian *Epic of Gilgamesh,* called *Bilgamesh and Aga,* as the father of the Agga who laid siege to Unug. The Sumerian King List and the *Tummal Chronicle* concur with the *Epic of Gilgamesh* in making him the father of Agga, who was also a king of Kish. Thus the fragments verifying Enmenbaragesi's historicity enhance the notion that Gilgamesh is also historical.[171] Furthermore, this evidence of his historicity is also evidence that verifies the dating scheme throughout this book, using the sources themselves rather than trying to impose an artificial "sitz im leben" on the characters.

The later 3rd Dynasty of Ur, King Shulgi, addressed one of his praise poems to Gilgamesh which credits Gilgamesh with capturing and defeating Enmebaragesi. We can see, again, that Enmenbaragesi was also a contemporary of Gilgamesh.[172] The next king of Kish on the list above is Agga. The following story comes from Sumerian tablets called "Gilgamesh and Agga:"

> King Agga of Kish sent an ultimatum to Uruk. Gilgamesh tried to convince the elders that Uruk should sack Kish in response, but the elders wanted to submit. He responded by taking the matter to the men of the city, who agreed to take up arms. Agga laid seige to Uruk and Gilgamesh resisted with the help of his servant, Enkidu. He sent a soldier through the gate to Agga. The soldier is captured and tortured with a brief respite while another of Gilgamesh's soldiers climbs over the wall. Gilgamesh himself then climbs the wall and Agga's forces are so taken aback by the sight of them that Agga capitulates. Gilgamesh graciously accepts Agga's surrender, praising him for returning his city. [173]

Again, by using only 25 years per generation between the long list of the kings of Kish, from Cush to Agga, I have arrived within the lifetime of Gilgamesh, the son of Kesed. I have shown that Gilgamesh was born about 2650 BC Agga of Kish was born about 2620 BC, right in the lifetime of Gilgamesh. They were probably about the same age. Therefore it is highly likely that this dating system is roughly accurate. The next king of Kish that I have highlighted is Mesilim, who lived around 2480 BC, according to my estimates. We need to study Mesilim more carefully.

Mesilim, Descendant of Cush

Mesilim, who called himself the king of Kish, was, as I have shown, directly descended from Cush, the son of Ham and founder of the city-state of Kish. He erected a temple to Ningirsu in Lagash, for which he arbitrated a territorial dispute with Umma and set up a stela ing the border.[174] Therefore, in addition to being king of Kish, he was suzereign over Lagash as well. However, he was overthrown, as was the last king of Uruk, by the founder of the Ur dynasty, Mesannepadda. He and his successor rebuilt the Tummal Temple at Nippur which had fallen into ruin. The reader might want to look back where I made the following statement: "Mesannepada was followed by his son, Meskiang-nanna. His reign was ended by an incursion from Elam, which I have already shown **could not have occurred after about 2400 BC, after which it lost control.**" We see, then, that the life of Mesilim falls within a period when in fact he could have been overthrown by Mesannepada. This is a powerful argument in favor of a proper procedure for dating these rulers. It also supports the theory of longer lifetimes which I will prove conclusively from non-biblical sources. Mesilim of Kish does not appear on the king list, but his existence is confirmed from predynastic Lagash and from Adab. He is famous for drawing the border between Umma and Lagash, a contentious point between these two cities. His decision, accepted by both parties, appears to have favored Lagash over Umma.[175]

Kish, a powerful city to the north of Sumer, appears to have exercised political and religious control over several of the Sumerian city-states in the period 2700-2500 BC We, therefore, have further confirmation that our dating of the Patriarchs and their cousins, including Nimrod and Cush, is correct. According to The New Cambridge Ancient History:

It is in the city of Lagash that our knowledge of Sumerian history may be said to begin, to arrange her rulers for long periods in chronological order, and to reconstruct the part they played in conflicts between the early city states. It is true that some of her earlier kings and patesis remain little more than names to us, but with the accession of Ur-Nina we enter a period in which our knowledge of events is continuous, so far at least as the fortunes of the city were concerned.

With the growth of her power it is also possible to trace in some detail the relations she maintained with other great cities in the land.

At the earliest period of which we have any historical records it would appear that the city of Kish exercised a suzerainty over Sumer.[176]

Here ruled Mesilim (c. 2500 BC), to whom Lagash, and probably other great cities in the south, owed allegiance. During his reign a certain Lugal-shag-engur was patesi of Lagash, and we have definite record that he acknowledged Mesilim's supremacy. A votive mace-head of colossal size has been found at Tello, which bears an inscription stating that it was dedicated to Ningirsu by Mesilim, who had restored his great temple at Lagash during the time that Lugal-shag-engur was patesi of that city. The text, the brevity of which is characteristic of these early votive inscriptions, consists of but a few words, and reads :

Mesilim, King of Kish, the builder of the temple of Ningirsu, deposited this mace-head (for) Ningirsu (at the time when) Lugal-shag-engur (was) patesi of Lagash.[177]

In spite of its brevity the importance of the inscription is considerable, since it links these two early rulers of Sumer, one in the north and one in the south. Of Lugal-shag-engur we know nothing beyond his name, and the fact that he was patesi of Lagash at the time of Mesilim, but Mesilim has left a more enduring upon history. A later patesi of Lagash, Entemena, when giving a historical summary of the relations which existed between his own city and the neighboring city of Umma, begins his account with the period of Mesilim, and furnishes additional testimony to the part which this early king of Kish played in the local affairs of southern Babylonia.[178]

The Treaty Of Mesalim (c. 2500 BC)

> By the immutable word of Enlil, king of the lands, father of the gods, Ningirsu and Shara set a boundary to their lands. Mesilim, King of Kish, at the command of his deity Kadi, set up a stele [a boundary er] in the plantation of that field. Ush, ruler of Umma, formed a plan to seize it. That stele he broke in pieces, into the plain of Lagash he advanced. Ningirsu, the hero of Enlil, by his just command, made war upon Umma. At the command of Enlil, his great net ensnared them. He erected their burial mound on the plain in that place.

> Eannatum, ruler of Lagash, brother of the father of Entemena [who put up this inscription] . . . for Enakalli, ruler of Umma, set the border to the land. He carried a canal from the great river to Guedin. He opened the field of Ningirsu on its border for 210 spans to the power of Umma. He ordered the royal field not to be seized. At the canal he inscribed a stele. He returned the stele of Mesilim to its place. He

did not encroach on the plain of Mesilim. At the boundary-line of Ningirsu, as a protecting structure, he built the sanctuary of Enlil, the sanctuary of Ninkhursag . . . By harvesting, the men of Umma had eaten one storehouse-full of the grain of Nina [goddess of Oracles], the grain of Ningirsu; he caused them to bear a penalty. They brought 144,000 gur, a great storehouse full, [as repayment]. The taking of this grain was not to be repeated in the future.

Urlumma, ruler of Umma, drained the boundary canal of Ningirsu, the boundary canal of Nina; those steles he threw into the fire, he broke [them] in pieces; he destroyed the sanctuaries, the dwellings of the gods, the protecting shrines, the buildings that had been made. He was as puffed up as the mountains; he crossed over the boundary canal of Ningirsu. Enannatum, ruler of Lagash, went into battle in the field of Ugigga, the irrigated field of Ningirsu. Entemena, the beloved son of Enannatum, completely overthrew him. Urlumma fled. In the midst of Umma he killed him. He left behind 60 soldiers of his force [dead] on the bank of the canal [named]"Meadow-recognized-as-holy-from-the-great-dagger." He left these men--their bones on the plain. He heaped up mounds for them in 5 places. Then Ili, Priest of Ininni of Esh in Girsu, he established as a vassal ruler over Umma.

Ili took the ruler of Umma into his hand. He drained the boundary canal of Ningirsu, a great protecting structure of Ningirsu, unto the bank of the Tigris above from the banks of Girsu. He took the grain of Lagash, a storehouse of 3600 gur. Entemena, ruler of Lagash declared hostilities on Ili, whom for a vassal he had set up. Ili, ruler of Umma, wickedly Flooded the dyked and irrigated field; he commanded that the boundary canal of Ningirsu; the boundary canal of Nina, be ruined. . . Enlil and Ninkhursag did not permit [this to happen]. Entemena, ruler of Lagash, whose name was spoken by Ningirsu, restored their canal to its place according to the righteous word of Enlil, according to the righteous word of Nina, their canal which he had constructed from the river Tigris to the great river, the protecting structure, its foundation he had made of stone . . . "[179]

Chapter Twelve

Lugalzagesi, King of Uruk, Ur, and Umma in Southern Sumer

Lugalzagesi was a descendant of Gilgamesh. It is possible that some of these persons were brothers to one another, although most are father to son movements and are as follows:

> Gilgamesh (c. 2650 BC), died age 421
> Ur-Nungal (c. 2625 BC), died age 153
> Utul-Kalamma (c. 2600 BC), died age 143
> Labasher (c. 2575 BC), died age 127
> Ennundaranna (c. 2550 BC), died age 109
> Meshede (c. 2525 BC); died age 120
> Melamanna (c. 2500 BC), died age 101
> Lugalkidul (c. 2475 BC), died age 112
> Lugal-Kinishe-Dudu (c. 2450 BC)
> Lugalzagesi (c. 2425 BC)

Will our dating scheme work this time? Let's see. Lugalzagesi, the "priest-king" of Uruk and Umma (reigned from about 2355 BC (in Uruk) to 2330 BC (in Ur) was the last king before the conquest of Sumer by Sargon of Akkad and the rise of the Akkadian Empire, and was considered as the only king of the 3rd Dynasty of Uruk. He was arguably the first king to unite Sumer as a single kingdom.[180] He would therefore have been about 75 when he took the reign and died at about 95 to 104 years of age, based on his length of reign from the Sumerian King List. This, therefore, fits nicely for the dating scheme I have identified. It might be noticed that we know the dates of death of several of the ancestors of Lugalzagesi. I have put their "estimated" lifetimes to the right in the column above. The dates are estimated because the year of birth is estimated. The year of death is known when the reign changed. These falling ages confirm that Lugalzagesi had a shorter expected lifetime due to his ancestry. While he may not have been born exactly in 2425 BC it is likely that he did not live much beyond 100 years, which was unusual in the 25th century BC

Lugalzagesi pursued an expansive policy. He conquered several of the Sumerian city-states - including Kish, where he overthrew Ur-Zababa; Lagash, where he overthrew Urukagina; Ur, Nippur, and Larsa, as well as Uruk, where he established his new capital. He ruled for 25 (or 34) years according to the Sumerian king list.[181] He was the priest-king of Umma and overthrew Urukagina, the King of Lagash.[182] He also took Ur and Uruk, making Uruk his capital, and claimed an empire extending from the Persian Gulf to the Mediterranean. In a long inscription that he caused to be engraved on hundreds of stone vases dedicated to Enlil of Nippur, he boasted that his kingdom extended "from the Lower Sea (Persian Gulf), along the Tigris and Euphrates, to the Upper Sea" or Mediterranean.[183]

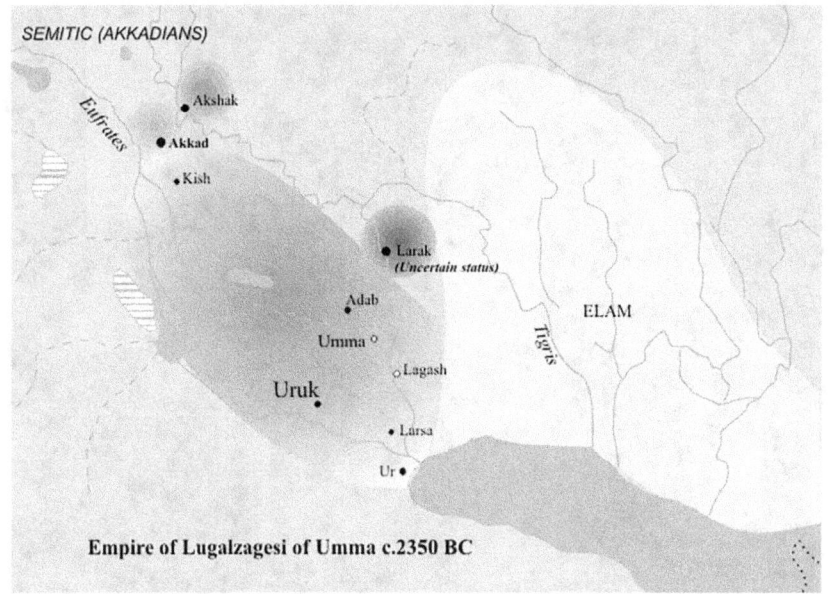

Fig. 12

According to later Babylonian versions of Sargon's inscriptions, Sargon of Akkad captured Lugalzagesi after destroying the walls of Uruk, and led him in a neck-stock to Enlil's temple in Nippur.[184] Lugalzagesi was a Shemite of the line of Gilgamesh. Even though Lugalzagesi was led away by Sargon the Great, Sargon himself (Serug of the Bible) was also a Shemite. Since Sargon was a Shemite, he recognized that the kings of Uruk were descendants of Kesed and his son Gilgamesh, also Shemites, and therefore enabled some form of peace between him and them. This is perhaps the reason why there is so little information about this period in the area of Uruk (and of Ur at this time, having also been ruled by Lugalzagesi). These city-states were being run by Shemites, not Hamites, so the situation did not require fighting for control. See the secton on the family of Kesed, the brother of Arphaxad in Chapter 8. Suffice it to say that Ur-Engur, Utu-Hegal, and Ur-Nammu were all Shemite kings.

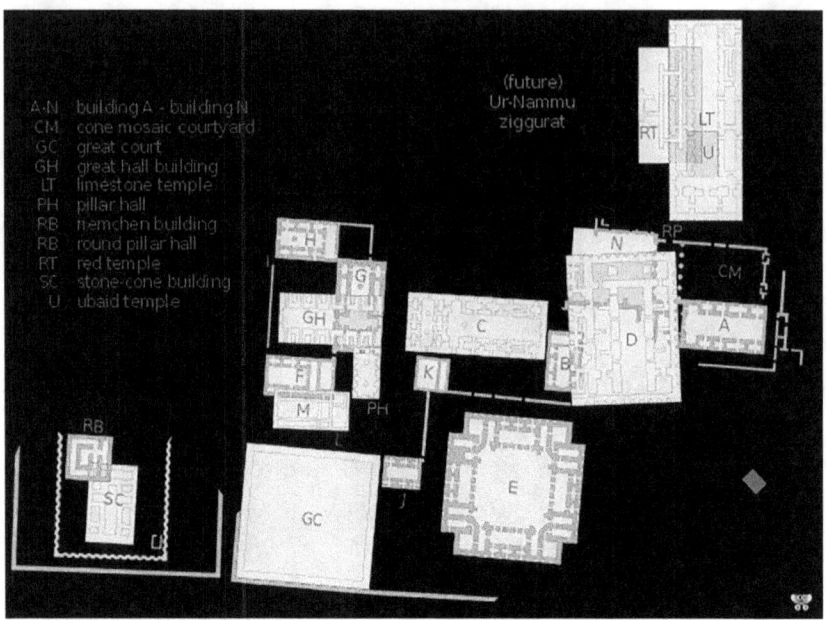

Fig. 13 Uruk, taken from Lugalzagesi
by Serug (Sargon the Great)

As kinsmen, Eber and Kesed must have designed a plan that would eventually lead to greater control of Sumer, a normally Hamite territory. But what was the solution? As High Priest of the temple of Kullab, Kesed was the "mouthpiece" for Ninsun, the goddess of the temple at that early time. Nannar-Sin was Ninsun's father. Ninsun was the consort of Kesed, High Priest of her temple. The result was the birth of Ur-Engur, then Ur-Nammu, then Gilgamesh, and then Utu-Hegal, as well as Mu'ak, a daughter, who married Salah, the father of Eber! All of the sons of Kesed listed above became kings of Ur, starting as early as 2600 BC This began almost 200 years **before Sargon the Great was born**. By the time that Sargon came to power around 2360 BC Kesed was about 500 years old. His children, Gilgamesh, Ur-Engur, Utu-Hegal, and Ur-Nammu, were all over 200 years old, at least.

Kesed worked his position to enable his sons to form a dynasty. Gilgamesh became a king of Uruk and ruled 126 years.[185] Ur-Engur, his oldest son, became the first king of the Second Dnasty of Ur. He reigned 18 years.[186] He was actually an extension of the First Dynasty, because the progenitor of Lugalzagesi was Gilgamesh, the son of Kesed. However, many generations of the sons of Gilgamesh reigned for shorter terms, from 8 to 40 years each, until it literally ran out of males to take the kingship of Ur. Utu-Hegal followed his brother Ur-Engur and reigned 22 years. He died in 2113 BC and his older brother Ur-Nammu took over and reigned 18 more years, until his death in 2095 BC.

Here is where the women come in, again. Sargon's mother, Ora, was the daughter of Ur-Nammu, the son of Kesed. Therefore, when Sargon (Serug) took Lugalzagesi out of control of Uruk and its sur-roundings, including Ur, he (Sargon) permitted the High Priest or Ur, Kesed, who was his great-grandfather, to appoint one of Kesed's own sons to be the new king of Ur, which had been a part of the greater Uruk over which Lugalzagesi had ruled. That son of Kesed was Ur-Engur, who was over 200 years old at the time. Then 18 years later, Kesed used his influence again with Sargon to have another of his sons, Utu-hegal, appointed to rule most of southern Sumer. Finally, assuming that Kesed was still alive, which is possible, after Utu-hegal died in 2113 BC (he drowned), his last surviving son, Ur-Nammu, who happened to be his second oldest son, took over as ruler of Ur and most of Sumer.

Since we are now approaching the times of Terah and Abraham, I will now deal with this great King of Ur.

Chapter Thirteen

Ur-Nammu, the Son of Kesed
(c. 2675 BC-2095 BC)

Fig. 14 Artist Rendering of Ur-Nammu

U r-Nammu was the brother of Gilgamesh, Ur-Engur, and Utu-Hegal. They were all the sons of Kesed of the Bible. Their mother was Ninsun, the Sumerian goddess. Kesed was the brother of Cainan, and both were the sons of Arphaxad, who was the son of Shem. Ur-Nammu became the first ruler of the 3rd Dynasty of Ur, which is misnamed because his brother, Utu-Hegal, and his older brother, Ur-Engur, had preceded him in the rulership of Ur. Therefore, his was a continuation of a Second dynasty of Ur, the first being held by the descendants of Gilgamesh, son of Kesed, whose descendant, Lugalzagasi, was the last king of the Gilgamesh line. According to his own extensive records, as soon as "Anu and Enlil turned over kingship to his city of Ur he was instructed to institute a new moral revival."[187]

Ur-Nammu was originally a general appointed by his brother Utu-Hegal, who was the ruler of southern Sumer. Either his brother, Utu-Hegal, was drowned or Ur-Nammu revolted and subsequently defeated him. He also defeated king Nammhani of Lagash (his great-granddaughter's husband) as well. However, some scholars dispute that Ur-Nammu revolted against his brother Utu-Hegal, since Ur and Uruk continued to have good relations after Ur-Nammu became king. It is more likely that Utu-Hegal drowned as written.[188]

Ur-Nammu, continuing the actions started by his brothers Ur-Engur and Utu-Hegal, was successful in maintaining a well organized empire, in which Sumer and Akkad were united. Recall that Akkad was the empire of Arphaxad, while Sumer had beenkesed the empire of the sons of Ham. But through a dynastic marriage of Eber (from Shem's line) and Azura (from Ham's line), the rulership of Sumer moved from the Hamites to the Shemites. In Ur-Nammu, finally, all vestiges of Hamitic control of Sumer were removed.

Fig. 15 Ur-Nammu

Upon the death of the king of Utu-Hegal, his brother, Ur-Nammu, became King of Ur, seized Uruk, and attacked and killed Nammhani, the traitor of Lagash. He ruled all of Sumer and much of Assyria and Elam, the latter two lands that had been held by his ancestors Arphaxad and Elam. Syria, including Ebla, paid tribute and may well have been part of the empire. Even Phoenician Byblos was forced to pay. Thus, we can divide the empire into two sections. The first was the empire proper: He ruled Sumer (the former Hamite lands) outright and imposed the State's will over all the cities. The second section could be called the dependencies or tributaries: The foreign lands which were forced, either by military conquest or threat, to send tribute to the Ur state. He called himself the "King of Ur, King of Sumer and Akkad". [189]

Ur-Nammu strived after the law and order of the past times when Arphaxad had controlled a great deal of the land. While he never knew Arphaxad his father Kesed certainly did, since Arphaxad was Kesed's father. Additionally, Kesed lived until 2200 BC, or thereabouts, and would have had several hundred years of contact with his son Ur-Nammu. Therefore they would have had many conversations about the religious beliefs of Arphaxad, as opposed to Kesed's beliefs. Arphaxad's moral tenets would have been well known to Ur-Nammu. Although he wanted a central authority, Ur-Nammu emphasized the local interests of cities and city deities by starting early in his reign the construction of temples in other cities. Usually, new rulers in their first years of reign were occupied with further military expansion and were only devoted to construction activities in the last part of their reign. Bur Ur-Nammu was different.

Fig. 16 Artistic Rendition of the City-State of Ur

Ur-Nammu built ziggurats with a three stage system and probably with a temple on the highest level. Different types of 'high terraces' were parts of many temples in Sumerian cities since the Ubaid period of very ancient times. Use was made of mud bricks each stamped with the name of the city, city deity and the name of the temple. His development in temple construction was an innovation which would be used for many centuries. The legendary Tower of Babel was possibly of this type and Ur-Nammu was living when it was constructed around 2500 BC He may well have used it as an example. Ur-Nammu rebuilt and enlarged one of the most famous temples in ancient time, the Ekur Temple in the city of Nippur devoted to Enlil, the chief god in the pantheon.

Ur-Nammu wrote of himself as follows:

> City of the finest divine powers, lofty royal throne-dais! Shrine Urim, pre-eminent in Sumer, built in a pure place! City, your well-founded great wall has grown out of the abzu! City, beautiful as the sky, endowed with beauty, colorfully decorated in a great place! Shrine Urim, well-founded jipar [Nippur], dwelling of An and Enlil! Your lofty palace is the E-kic-nujal, in which the fates are determined! Your pilasters heavy with radiance tower over all the countries! Its terrace like a white cloud is a spectacle in the midst of heaven. Its.. like flashing lightning shines (?) inside a shrine. Like a single bull under the yoke, ... Suen's [Nannar Sin] beloved pure table; E-kic-nujal, Suen's beloved pure table. The king, ornament of the royal offering place, occupies the august courtyard; Ur-Namma the exalted, whom no one dares to oppose, .. Urim, the wide city....

> 1 line unclear

...., the authoritative, praised himself exultantly: Under Ur-Nammu, king of Urim, for whom a favorable destiny was determined, the roads have been made passable. An opens his holy mouth, and because of me rain is produced. He directs it downward into the earth, and abundance is brought for me. Enlil treats me kindly, .. Enki treats me kindly, bestowing early Floods, grain and dappled barley. Nintud formed me; I am peerless. .. brought me up well; I am the king of the Land. I am...; under my rule the cattle-pens and sheepfolds are extended wide. Utu endowed me with eloquence (?); my judgments create concord in Sumer and Akkad. Ningubalag has given me strength. In the whole extent of heaven and earth, no one can escape from a battle with me.

I am Ur-Namma, king of Urim, the protecting genius of my city. I strike against those guilty of capital offences, and make them tremble. The fear I cause ... My judgments make Sumer and Akkad follow a single path. I place my foot on the necks of thieves and criminals. I clamp down on evildoers, who will be caught like snakes. I [stifle] fugitives, and their intentions will be set right. I make justice apparent; I defeat wickedness. As if I were fire, even my frowning is enough to create concord. My word .... .. the lands, the foreign countries .. Urim ... Their food offerings make Nanna rejoice in E-kic-nujal.

After my seed had been poured into the holy womb, Suen [Nannar Sin], loving its appearance (?), made it partake of Nanna's attractiveness.

119

Coming forth over the Land like Utu, Enlil called me by an auspicious name, and Nintud assisted at my birth. **As I came forth from the womb of my mother Ninsun**, a favorable destiny was determined for me.

Fig. 17 The Ziggurat of Ur-Nammu, at Ur

In me, Ur-Nammu, the lands of Sumer and Akkad have their protecting genius. I am a source of joy for the Land; my life indeed creates!...., the fields are resplendent (?) under my rule. In the fields growing with ..., .. did not multiply under my rule. In the desert, the roads are made up as for a festival, and are passable because of me. The owner of the fields ....; it rises (?) up to his chest. I have freed the sons of the poor from their duty of going to fetch firewood.

After the storm ..., and the month had been completed (?) for me, Enlil chose me by extispicy on a day very auspicious for him. He spoke fairly to Sumer, and caused me to arise (?) from my family (?). Because of my broad understanding and wisdom, An the king entrusted... into my hands. I am the foremost one of Sumer. I am ... good... I am ... I am .. of the Land.

3 lines fragmentary

I, the lord, ...

I, Ur-Nammu, born on high, ... shining. The people line up in front of me. Enlil has given me the task of keeping the Land secure, with unscathed (?) troops. I am clad in linen in the jipar [temple at Nippur]. I lie down on the splendid bed in its delightful bed chamber. I cause the people to eat splendid food; I am their Enkimdu [i.e. the god of irrigation and cultivation]. I am the good shepherd whose sheep multiply greatly. I open the ..... of the cattle-pens and sheepfolds. I am peerless...... the pastures and watering-places of shepherds (?).

Since I have been adorned (?) with their rulership, no one imposes taxes on my abundant crops which grow tall. My commands bring about (?) joy in the great fortresses of the mountains. The joy of my city and the territory (?) of Sumer delights me. I release water into the canals of Sumer, making the trees grow tall on their banks. I have lifted the yoke of its male prostitutes.

1 line unclear

I returned ..... to Urim. I made ..... return (?) to his country..... like ...... I loaded its grain on barges, I delivered it to its store-houses. I returned its ..... citizens to their (?) homes. I..... their earth-baskets. I ..... the savage hands of the Gutians, the ...... After I had made the evil-doers return (?) to their......, I restored (?) the walls that had been torn down; my outstanding mind .... the shrine of Urim ...... I am the foremost workman (?) of Enlil; I am the one who ..... food offerings.

Fig. 18 Ur-Nammu Foundation Statue

7 lines fragmentary or missing

..... at a banquet with me in the city. ..... joyful dance ...... I have brought abundance to Enlil's temple on the king's canal: I have directed ships both to the wine quay of Enlil and to the lapis-lazuli quay of Nanna. Alcohol and syrup have been poured out before Enlil. To me, the shepherd Ur-Nammu, let life be given as a reward! For Nanna, my master, I have built his temple; as if it were a verdant hillside, I have set up the E-kic-nujal in a great place. I have surrounded (?) its terrace with a gold and lapis-lazuli fence.

I am the creature of Nanna! I am the older brother of Gilgamesh! I am the son borne by Ninsun, a princely seed! For me, kingship came down from heaven! Sweet is the praise of me, the shepherd Ur-Nammu!"

Fig. 19 Ur-Nammu

A text known as "The Death of Urnammu," contains an under-world scene in which Ur-Nammu showers "his brother Gilgamesh" with gifts.[190] From his own words we see that he was the son of Ninsun and the older brother of Gilgamesh. I have shown earlier that his father was Kesed, High Priest of the temple of Nannar-Sin, whose daughter, Ninsun, became Kesed's wife/consort. Had Ur-Nammu written that Gilgamesh was his brother then we might take that to mean that he identified with Gilgamesh as a role model. But that is not what he said. He said that he was the "**older brother**" of Gilgamesh. **This is truly fascinating because it allows us for the first time to confirm from outside biblical sources that people did in fact live long lives.** Gilgamesh lived sometime around 2650 BC, according to most accepted histori-ans.[191] Ur-Nammu, however, is known to have died in 2095 BC Therefore, since he was the older brother of Gilgamesh, he had to have been at least 555 years old when he died!

King Ur-Nammu of Ur, the uncle of Eber, being the brother of Eber's mother Muak, daughter of Kesed, gave to the temple at Nippur its final characteristic form. Partly razing the construc-tions of his predecessors, he erected a terrace of bricks, some 12 meters high, covering a space of about 32,000 square meters. Near the northwestern edge, towards the western corner, he built a zig-gurat of three stages of dry brick, faced with kiln-fired bricks laid in bitumen. On the summit stood, as at Ur and Eridu, a small chamber, the special shrine or abode of the god. Access to the stages of the ziggurat, from the court beneath, was by an inclined plane on the south-east side. To the north-east of the ziggurat stood, apparently, the House of Bel, and in the courts below the ziggurat stood various other buildings, shrines, treasure cham-bers, and the like. The whole structure was oriented with the corners toward the cardinal points of the compass. The two most famous monuments of Ur-Nammu's reign are the great ziggurat (temple) at Ur and his stele, of which fragments remain.

Fig. 20 Another photo of the Ziggurat at Ur

Ur-Nammu was the promulgator of the oldest code of law yet known, older by about three centuries than the code of Hammurabi. It consists of a prologue and seven laws; the prologue describes Ur-Nammu as a divinely appointed king who established justice throughout the land. This code is of great importance to the study of biblical law, which it predates by about five centuries.[192]

Fig. 21 Ur-Nammu receiving a dignitary

From the *Book of Jubilees* we see the destructive influence of the pagan religion of Ur-Nammu:

> And 'Ur, the son of Kesed, built the city of 'Ara of the Chaldees [Ur], and called its name after his own name and the name of his father [Ur of the Kasidim, or Ur of the Kesed]. And they made for themselves molten images, and they worshipped each the idol, the molten image which they had made for themselves, and they began to make graven images and unclean simulacra, and malignant spirits assisted and seduced (them) into committing transgression and uncleanness. And the prince Mastema [Satan] exerted himself to do all this, and he sent forth other spirits, those which were put under his hand, to do all manner of wrong and sin, and all manner of transgression, to corrupt and destroy, and to shed blood upon the earth. For this reason he called the name of Seroh, [Serug, Sargon], for everyone turned to do all manner of sin and transgression.[193]

Serug was the son of Ora, daughter of Ur-Nammu, and her husband Ragau, the son of Peleg. He was also Sargon I (the Great), king of Akkad.

Assyriologists have given the name of "Code of Ur-Nammu" to a literary monument that is the oldest known example of a genre extending through the Code of Lipit-Ishtar in Sumerian to the Code of Hammurabi, written in Akkadian. (Some scholars have attributed it to Ur-Nammu's son Shulgi).[194] It is a collection of sentences or verdicts mostly following the pattern of "If A [assumption], it follows that B [legal consequence]." The collection is framed by a prologue and an epilogue. The original was most likely a stela, but all that is known of the "Code of Ur-Nammu", so far, are Old Babylonian copies. The term "code" as used here, is conventional terminology and should not give the impression of any kind of "codified" law; furthermore, the content of the "Code of Ur-Nammu" is not yet completely known. It deals, among other things, with adultery by a married woman, the defloration of someone else's female slave, divorce, false accusation, the escape of slaves, bodily injury, and the granting of security, as well as with legal cases arising from agriculture and irrigation. He initiated many building programs and promoted the Sumerian "way of life". Ur-Nammu "freed the land from thieves, robbers, and rebels," restoring order and peace. He re-fortified the towns of Sumer against any future unrest.

Fig. 22 Ur-Nammu

The first invasion of Palestine by Ur-Nammu was in 2108 BC soon after he consolidated his position among the cities of the valley of Sumer. The invasion is only implied in the book of Genesis, but it is described in the "*Antiquities*" of Josephus. At this time, Ur-Nammu forced a treaty and an assurance of fealty on the cities of the Valley of Siddim: Sodom, Gomorrah, Admah, Seboyim, and Zoar. These cities were at that time located in the valley now covered by the northern part of the Dead Sea. For twelve years, as reported in Genesis, the pact held firm; in the thirteenth year the cities rebelled and refused to pay tribute. In the fourteenth year, the eastern kings led by Ur-Nammu, who is called Amraphel King of Shinar in Genesis, invaded the lands.[195]

The rebellion was apparently fomented by the god Adad [named Prince Ishkur, Imperial Consort of Queen Ninkhursag], in 2096 BC, a few years before they rebelled, Abraham was sent to Canaan and then to Egypt, apparently to set up defenses against what was sure to be an invasion from the east.

The year before the invasion, Abraham returned from Egypt with a detachment of troops. Abraham went to Bethel near Ai where he divided his forces: Lot took his troops east to defend the city of Sodom in the Valley of Siddim. Abraham deployed his forces south to the Anakim fortress city of Hebron where he gained valuable allies of the Anakim.

Close-up - Foundation Figure of King Ur-Nammu
*The Inscription reads: Ur-Nammu, king of Ur,
king of Sumer and Akkad, the one who built the
temple of Enlil.*

The object on his head represents a basket of Earth:
symbolic of his carrying material to build the temple.
Sumerians "kept" the ancient African custom of
carrying heavy loads on their heads.

Fig. 23

Thus, the grand plan of Adad was to defend the land with a three-fold strategy:

> 1. A string of fortresses of the Rephaim in the
> Trans-Jordan defended the approach known as
> the King's Highway. They were believed to be
> impregnable.

2. The approach through the Jordan Valley was protected by the armies of the five cities of the Plain, reinforced by the army of Lot. Several major citadels like Beth-Shean and Jericho also blocked this approach.

3. The third possible invasion route was through the lands west of the Valley, through Jerusalem. It was protected by the forces of Abraham, supplemented with an Egyptian contingent and the Anakim, or Rephaim, allies at the fortress of Hebron.

The following year, the eastern kings under the leadership of Ur-Nammu invaded the Western Lands. This must have been a formidable army revealed in the Haggadah as numbering 800,000; they easily penetrated the Trans-Jordan and destroyed the fortifications of the Rephaim.

Fig. 24 Ur-Nammu (seated) bestows governorship on Hashamer, patesi (high priest) of Iskyn-Sin, from a cylinder seal impression, ca. 2100 BC Inanna was a consort of Ur-Nammu.

The rapidity with which they passed through this heavily defended area strongly indicates the use of special mass destructive weapons supplied by their deity Nannar-Sin, grandfather of Ur-Nammu and a Sumerian god. Abraham and his Anakim cavalry caught up with the rear guard of the army of Ur-Nammu at Dan. A second skirmish was fought near the city of Damascus and they managed to recover most of the booty and prisoners. In the melee' Ur-Nammu's chariot got stuck in the mud and he was thrown from it. The chariot, without his weight in it, was set free of the mud and rushed along without Ur-Nammu. Other chariots came from behind and apparently killed him.[196] The translation of a cuneiform tablet provided by J. V. Kinnier Wilson in his book *The Rebel Lands* provides the story of the expedition of Ur-Nammu and his death in a foreign land. The tablet describes how he fell ill [actually died] in "the mountain land" and was swiftly taken back to Ur where he was laid on a funeral bier at his palace in Ur.

The people of Sumer were in shock, for this was not supposed to happen in the cosmic scheme of things. The tablet complains how the king had been "abandoned on the battlefield like a crushed vessel."[197] Although he had served the gods well, so went the complaint, they failed to stand by him in his time of need. Ur-Nammu may have been the victim of his own ambition. In a tablet commemorating the death of Ur-Nammu it is implied that he used mass destructive weapons whose use may have backfired and caused his death. He boasts of using "the mighty udug weapon" which is said to have "reduced the enemy land to dust," and to have "overlaid it with poison." There are references to a "fiery gas" which blew into the "house of the rebel lands." These are all symptoms and consequences of weapons apparently having been granted to him from the gods, possibly even including nuclear and chemical warfare weapons.

Fig. 25 Artist Rendering of the Ziggurat at Ur

If this is true, then Ur-Nammu may have been deathly ill from the chemicals when he fell from his chariot. In that case, he not only would have caused his own sickness and death but he also would have devastated the lands of Trans-Jordan and the northern Sinai which caused them to remain unoccupied for hundreds of years. The cities of Sodom and Gomorrah were quite possibly destroyed by a similar nuclear holocaust.[198]

The cities of the Valley of Siddim had a short respite. The death of Ur-Nammu and the change of kingship, with the resultant disorganization, probably allowed them to continue their independent ways. But their doom was sealed. Eighteen years later the cities were destroyed in a cataclysmic explosion that also ruptured the geological fault that underlies the Jordan Valley, causing the ground to sink and seal off the effluence of the Jordan River. Thus, the Dead Sea was formed. Zechariah Sitchin has detailed all of this in his *Twelfth Planet* series, which explains the source of the weapon of mass destruction.[199] Shulgi then became king and a quiet period seems to have come over the land of Canaan. During this interim period, Abraham apparently broke relations with Egypt, as shown in the treatment of Hagar, his Egyptian wife, and their son and heir

Ishmael. The cities returned to the aegis of the eastern kings and reaffirmed their loyalty to the Dynasty of Ur.

Ur-Nammu's death is bemoaned in a lamentation hymn which is an example of a type of court poetry that became in use since this period in time.[200] In it is this sentiment:

> The mother, miserable because of her son, the mother of the king, holy Ninsun, was crying: "Oh my heart!" Because of the fate decreed for Ur-Namma, because it made the trustworthy shepherd pass away, she was weeping bitterly in the broad square, which is otherwise a place of entertainment. Sweet sleep did not come to the people whose happiness ......; they passed their time in lamentation over the trustworthy shepherd who had been snatched away.[201]

Fig. 26 The Ziggurat at Ur, as it might have looked

Fig. 27 Ziggurat at Ur, built by Ur-Nammu

Fig. 28 Ziggurat at Ur, built by Ur-Nammu

Fig. 29 Ziggurat at Ur, built by Ur-Nammu

Fig. 30 Ziggurat at Ur, built by Ur-Nammu

Fig. 31 Ziggurat at Ur, built by Ur-Nammu

Fig. 32 Artist Rendering of the Ziggurat at Ur

Fig. 33 Restored section of the Ziggurat at Ur

Fig. 343 Restored section of the Ziggurat at Ur

Chapter Fourteen

Ur-Bau, Son of Ragau
(c. 2250 BC-2080 BC)

U r-Bau succeeded his father Ragau as the King of Lagash.
The Sumerian King List incorrectly calls him the founder
of the Second Dynasty of Lagash, when in fact he was
continuing the dynasty of his father Ragau, King of Lagash. He
founded a "pro- Gutian" dynasty and he also controlled Ur.[202] He
was followed by three sons-in-law, according to one record.

Ur-Bau is somewhat less of a shadow, for we have his statue, with
mention of a building operation, a series of bricks, and other brief
inscriptions, as well as a date formula which tells us of his irrigation work. Nammhani, his successor, is likewise a little less of a
shadow, for we have, in addition to a date formula, various brief
inscriptions, a statue dedicated to his father, Nin-kagina, and a
mace head dedicated by his wife, Ningandu, which shows that he
was the son-in-law of Ur-Bau. Another daughter of Ur-Bau dedi-
cates a statue for Ur-Gar, who also belongs to this period. [203] [204]

A statue-inscription of Ur-Bau (ca. 2155-2142 BC) states:

He dug a foundation-pit(?) (to a depth) of x cubits; he heaped up the earth from it like stone and purified it with fire(?) like precious metal. As with a measuring-vessel he brought it to the broad place. He put the earth back and filled in the foundation with it. On it he built a kisu of ten cubits, and on the kisu he built "The House of Fifty Gleaming Anzu Birds," thirty cubits high. [205]

Ur-Bau, one of the most enlightened patesis of Lagash, may be placed shortly after Sharkalisharri, who was the son of Naram-Sin,[206] for he still employed the same huge brick-moulds of the size adopted by Naram-Sin. He built or rebuilt a great temple of Ningirsu on the terrace north of Girsu at Lagash. It was adorned with most readable statues of the two great patesis, Ur-Bau and Gudea. A diorite statue of Ur-Bau has been recovered. The figure is now decapitated, the body is abnormally squat and heavy, and in execution distinctly inferior to those of Gudea. The patesi is represented standing with hands clasped in liturgical pose, wearing the long shawl draped gracefully from the left shoulder. An inscription on it commemorates his construction of the temple E-ninni.[207]

Fig. 35 Ur-Bau

In Girsu he built a temple to the mother-goddess Ninkharsag of Kesh, one to the water-god, Enki of Eridu; one to Geshtin-anna, a title of the old virgin mother-goddess Innini of Erech; and one to Tammuz, her son and consort. In the neighboring city, Uru-kug, 'Holy City,' he built a temple to Bau, goddess of healing and consort of Ningirsu [Sumerian god Ninurta]. In the temple-mound the excavator, De Sarzec, recovered a bronze figurine of a god attached to a pillar in kneeling position with hands firmly placed at the top of the post as though in the act of planting the pointed end firmly in the ground. It is a new type of the old copper figurines of pre-Sargonic times, a post with the body of a female deity with a stone tablet on her head. It was enclosed in a clay vessel with the customary stone tablet on which was inscribed the record of Ur-Bau's pious works for the gods. This curious talisman represents the god of the city himself protecting the boundaries of his land, and reminds us of the Roman deity Terminus.[208]

Ur-Bau had more than local and contemporary fame, for in the times of Sainsu-iluna (21st century) a street at Erech was named after him. His are the first inscriptions which mention Ninagal, a variant of Ninegal, a form of Ereshkigal, goddess of the lower world; and he claims to have been her son. His two sons-in-law became patesis after him; they lived in a period when there was no strong central government, for they use their own year-dates, which would not have been permitted under the great kings of Agade, led by Serug (Sargon). Nammhani, who had married his daughter, Ningandu, seems to have been an important ruler. He was the grandson of Ka-Azag, the patesi who probably preceded Ur-Bau. His father, Ninkagina, dedicated a statuette of himself to the goddess Bau for the life of his son and patesi. The wife of Ur-gar, a patesi, and another son-in-law of Ur-Bau, likewise dedicated a statuette of herself for the life of her husband. Nammhani's monuments are many; they include a fine large circular dish of veined onyx dedicated to Ningirsu by his wife; a marble mace dedicated to a god, Dunshaggana, and another dedicated to Urizi, god of the harem.

Although Nammhani was one of the immediate successors of Ur-Bau he no longer made use of the huge cubit moulds (17 inches square) of the Agade period which had been adopted by Ur-Bau. The size introduced by him is a little more than a foot square, the mould subsequently employed by Gudea, and by the great builders of the last dynasty of Ur. From this we may infer that Ur-Bau lived shortly after Sharkalisharri and that Gudea belongs to a period not far removed from Ur-Bau. This in itself shows the impossibility of inserting a long period between the dynasty of Ur-Engur and the kingdom of Akkad. [209] Nammhani was killed by Ur-Nammu, the son of Kesed.

Ur-Bau had a daughter whose name was Ninalla. She was, therefore, the granddaughter of Ragau of the Bible. She married Gudea, who was the son of one of Ragua's sons, whose name is not known. Therfore, Gudea, was also a grandson of Ragau.

Chapter Fifteen

Gudea, Grandson of Ragau
(c. 2240 BC-2060 BC)

G udea reigned over Lagash after his father-in-law Ur-Bau, from 2141 BC to 2122 BC Gudea inaugurated the Sumerian renaissance and ruled Ur on behalf of the Gutian kings. His name itself indicates he was a Gutian. The fact that there was a Gutian who reigned, even briefly, in Sumer in this time period is extremely important. The reason for this will become more apparent farther down the line of history. To begin to catch a glimpse of the magnitude of the familial relationships involved here, let me just give a hint as to what is going to unfold. The father of Abraham, Terah, was originally aligned with this family and in fact was, for only 40 days, a Gutian King. His name was Tirigan (Terah in the Bible).

The Gutians ruled over Mesopotamia for nearly a century but the trade routes were open, and local governors seemed to be autonomous. One of these, in a city near the capital called Girsu was Gudea, governor of Lagash from 2197 to 2178 BC Lugalzagesi of Umma (a descendant of Kesed through his son Gilgamesh) had burned down Girsu, but Gudea rebuilt it with fifteen or more temples, inspired by a dream he had in which a man as tall as the sky

143

and as heavy as the earth told him to build a temple. A woman also appeared holding a stylus of flaming metal and a tablet with the good writing of heaven. To understand this, Gudea consulted his "mother," the goddess Gatumdug, and he went by boat to the temple of the goddess Nanshe, who interpreted dreams. Nanshe explained that the man was the god Ningirsu and the woman the goddess of science, Nisaba. The wisdom of Ningirsu, the son of Enlil, would reveal to him the plan of his temple.

We must stop momentarily in this narrative tale in order to under-stand just how Gudea fits in with the family of Shem more directly. Gudea called his mother Gatumdug, who was a goddess, the daughter of Anu and Nammu, the "father/mother gods". However, Gudea's father was a brother of Serug of the Bible (Sargon the Great). Yet Gudea distinctly called his mother "Gatumdug". I will address this when I deal with the relationship of the sons of Noah to the "gods".

Gudea obeyed his dream and tried to unite the people of Girsu "as sons of the same mother," (an apparent reference indicating that Gudea and Girsu were brothers) by purifying the city with encir-cling fires, putting clay in a pure place. Making bricks, he purified the foundations of the temple and anointed the platform with per-fume. The city was also purified morally: complaints, accusations, and punishments were to cease; mothers were not to scold their children nor should children raise their voices against their par-ents; slaves were not to be struck. Workers from Elam and Susa collected timber from their mountains and brought it to Girsu. Cedars were cut with great axes and like giant snakes were floated down the river. Stone was brought in large blocks, copper from Kimash, silver from distant mines, and red stone from Meluhha (possibly Ethiopia or the Indus). Construction took a year, and then the god could enter the temple. Statues of Gudea portray a calm and pious ruler, but in attaining all these building materials there was at least one war with the Elamites of Anshan.[210]

Gudea attempted to engage the classical Sumerian civilization in spite of his Gutian domination. He had trade relations with the whole known world and had Elamite craftsmen to help build his temples. But he also defeated Anshan, Elam's neighbor to the south. He eventually controlled Ur, which had been held by the descendants of Kesed for over 250 years. Kesed's son, Utu-Hegal, destroyed the attempts of Gudea, through a young relative named Tirigan (Terah of the Bible), to extend his control over southern Sumer.

Fig. 36 Gudea, King of Lagash

Gudea was also a father of the ziggurat, with the plan for the zig-gurat being revealed to him in a dream: "His most reable building was a great tower-temple of seven stages erected for his city-god Nimirrud [Nimrod]..., the plan of which - the origin of the later fashionable 'Ziggurat' temple-towers - was, he says, revealed to him in a dream. [Earlier small temple-towers of the pre-Sargonic period are found at Nippur and elsewhere."[211] Notice that by this time (21st century BC) Nimrod, the son of Cush had already been deified. Notice also that the name Nimmirud is quite similar to the name in the Bible, Nimrod.

Gudea was a contemporary of Ur-Nammu, the King of Ur, whose area he was not able to control because Ur-Nammu's brother had already repulsed his efforts.

The fact that Gudea was a contemporary of Ur-Nammu as King of Ur also means that he was also a contemporary of Terah and Abraham, Patriarchs of the Bible.

King Gudea left extant writings, exclusively Sumerian in language, which are of inestimable value.[212] He had the time, power, and means to carry out an extensive program of temple construction during his reign, and in a hymn divided into two parts and preserved in two clay cylinders 12 inches high, he describes explicitly the recon-struction of Eninnu, the temple of the god Ningirsu. Comprising 1,363 lines, the text is second in length only to Eannatum's Stele of Vultures among the literary works of the Sumerians up to that time. While Gudea forges a link, in his literary style, with his coun-try's pre-Sargonic period, his work also bears the unmistakable stamp of the period of Akkad. Thus, the regions that furnish him building materials reflect the geographic horizon of the empire of Akkad, and the ensi's title "god of his city" recalls the "god of Akkad" (Naram-Sin). The building hymn contains interesting par-ticulars about the work force deployed. "Levies" were organized in various parts of the country, and the city of Girsu itself "followed the ensi as though it were a single man." Unfortunately lacking are

synchronous administrative archives of sufficient length to provide less summarily compiled information about the social structure of Lagash at the beginning of the 3rd Dynasty of Ur. After the
great pre-Sargonic archives of the Baba temple at Girsu, only the
various administrative archives of the kings of Ur III give a closer
look at the functioning of a Mesopotamian state.[213][214]

Fig. 37 Eannatum's Stele of Vultures

Gudea considered himself the representative of the god Ningirsu.
After his death he was deified.

Gudea's only war was against the "City of Anshan in Elam." It is
to his buildings, his sculptures, above all to his writings, that we
owe our sense of his reality as a most unusual individual. Though
we must assume that he was dependent upon a king who ruled
elsewhere, yet he says not a word about such an overlord in all
his voluminous records. It is likely that his overlord was his father,
whose name, unfortunately, we do not have. The father was the son

of Ragau, whom I have shown was King of Lagash, so possibly this father of Gudea was also a king of Lagash. If he was living while Gudea ruled as "governor" of Lagash, then this would explain why Gudea was not the King. However, the fact that he accomplished so many building projects obviously meant that his overlord and he were very close and that he was given "free reign" to do what he wished. This would be normal if his father was his overlord.

Fig. 38 Gudea, King of Lagash

Gudea boasted that he made trips for building supplies to the outposts of civilization in such a way that scholars have mistaken them for military expeditions, and there is no hint that the Elamite campaign was carried out in the train of some conqueror.

The fact that historians have mistakenly taken his excursions as military expeditions led to the idea that the Gutians were ruthless people: "The Gutians practiced hit-and-run tactics, and would be long gone by the time regular troops could arrive to deal with the situation. Their raids crippled the economy of Sumer. Travel became unsafe, as did work in the fields, resulting in famine."[215] In fact nothing could be farther from the truth. However, the Sumerian King List does indicate that one king, Ur-Utu of Uruk, was defeated by the Guti around 2150 BC In addition, it is said that the Guti "swept down [and] defeated the demoralized Akkadian army [and] took Akkad, and destroyed it around 2115 BC However, they did not supplant all of Akkad, as several independent city states remained alongside them, including Lagash, where a local dynasty still thrived and left numerous textual and archaeological remains."[216] One would naturally ask why the Gutians didn't "finish the job". The answer is clear: the god Enlil had instructed the Gutians to destroy Akkad, and only Akkad, which they did. This instruction was given, and it was followed to the letter. The Gutians were not what history tells us they were. Gudea was a generally peaceful King, having only once ventured out to Elam territory, but then only for goods for his temple building!

Gudea was a grandson of Ragau. Terah (Tirigan) was a great-grandson of Ragau. Gudea was a "Gutian" just as Terah was. It was Terah, however, who finally extinguished the "Gutian" influence in Sumer. There was no Gutian dynasty. There was only another "sibling rivalry." When the Gutians were finally destroyed, it was not a very significant event. In fact, it was a "skirmish" between Terah (Tirigan), the great-grandson of Ragau, and Utu-Hegal, the son of Kesed, an "inter-familial" dispute.

Getting back to Gudea, his buildings were on a royal scale and must have required great wealth, yet he would have us know that it was not at the expense of the common people. Not until the very latest days of Sumer was there to arise another such governor to tell so much of himself. Measured by mere number of words, his inscriptions cover more ground than all the others. Even such a comparison is not quite fair to Gudea. The vast majority of these records are of the most monotonous character and have little to offer to the historian. On the other hand, those of Gudea have a real literary value, and they throw light upon almost every phase of the culture in which he lived. All the more strange is that they throw no light on the problems of the political history. Why? Because Gudea did not reign in a period of large conflict! His extended family ruled most of the Sumerian city-states.

Though he was one of the most illustrious of the Sumerian governors, Gudea remains a relatively obscure personage in terms of mainstream history. He was both priest-king and architect, a builder of great cities and temples, not unlike Nimrod. And it just so happens that Nimrod was Gudea's patron saint, as well as having been his ancestor. Gudea was like many of the Old Testament prophets in that he was prone to dreams and visions. In one such dream, Nimrod himself appeared to the king, revealing to him the blueprints of a temple he wished to be erected in his honor. Upon waking, Gudea lost no time setting in motion plans to construct the Temple of Nimrod, a structure that would eventually be seen as one of the most significant edifices of its day.[217]

In a well-known statue of Gudea, the base is emblazoned with the floorplan of this temple.[218] Other statues frequently depict him with Masonic architectural tools, such as squares, rulers, and so forth. The first priests were also the first architects. Their secret gnosis encompassed not only the sacred, but the functional as well. And they encoded their sacerdotal wisdom (sacred geometry, astronomy, etc.) into the structures they built, so that their shape, placement, and dimensions were all a reflection of divine principles. Looking further back in the past, we note that the Babylonian god, Marduk, is often depicted bearing a trowel. Though commentators have speculated that this may be an agricultural tool (as Marduk was thought to have taught man the science of agriculture), it is far more likely to be an architectural tool. And indeed it looks identical to the trowel which appears in so much Freemasonic ritual and symbolism. From all appearances, this would seem to constitute the tradition from which the Knights Templar and the Freemasons derived their creeds.

At any rate, the reign of Gudea witnessed a flourishing of culture and civilization in his region. He wandered the full length and breadth of Mesopotamia (and often beyond) to amass lumber, blocks, and precious metals for his many projects. He not only built new cities and temples, but rebuilt old ones. Ruling from his capitals of Lagash and Ur, he preferred not to be seen as a king, but rather as a priest and prophet. He was known simply as the "Good Shepherd", and may in fact have refused the title of king (although his name does appear in the King List.) Gudea is referred to as a king in an epic which was composed not more than two centuries after his death:

> I am lord; thou art made fit for my heroic arm.
> The king who will bequeath his name to life of
> far-off days,
> Who will fashion a statue for eternal days,
> In Eninnu, the temple which is filled with
> festivity,
> At the place of the mortuary libations.. fittingly
> may he set thee.[219]

In summary, it appears that Gudea was a good man who happened to have fallen in love with the daughter of Ur-Bau and nephew-in-law of none other than Sargon the Great (Serug of the Bible). As a good servant he knew his role and played it well. He knew where the power was, and he respected it.

Gudea was succeeded by his son Ur Ningirsu, who reigned as patesi at least three years. We know nothing of his life or works.

Fig. 39 Gudea, King of Lagash

Chapter Sixteen

Serug (Sargon the Great), Son of Ragau (2406 BC – 2198 BC)

Serug became the most powerful ruler over all of the lands of both the Shemites and the Hamites during his lifetime. He was known in history as Sargon the Great, King of Sumer and Akkad. Here is his story. The ancient *Book of Adam* indicates clearly that Serug and Sargon were the same person:

> And then Serug died, being two hundred and thirty years old, and Nâhôr, and Tarah, and Abraham his sons, buried him in Sarghîn, the city which he built after his own name.[220]

We see from this record that the name of Serug was also Sargon (Sarghin). According to the *Book of Jubilees* Saruch (Serug, Sargon) grew up in Ur:

> For this reason he called the name of Sêrôh, Serug, for every one turned to do all manner of sin and transgression. And he grew up, and

dwelt in Ur of the Chaldees, near to the father of his wife's mother, and he worshipped idols, and he took to himself a wife in the thirty-sixth jubilee, in the fifth week, in the first year thereof, and her name was Melka, the daughter of Kaber, the daughter of his father's brother. [221]

So how do we identify the "father of his wife's mother" from the quote above? First, we must find out who his wife was. His wife was Melka, as just quoted. Melka was the daughter of Kaber, and Kaber was the daughter of "his father's brother." That person was Ragau. Therefore, Melka was the great-granddaughter of Ragau, King of Lugash. The marriage of Melka to Serug (Sargon) was a "dynastic marriage." Since the rulership of the land passed through the women, a "matrilineal progression," this marriage was important for the family. In short, Melka made it possible for Sargon to claim the throne of "the family." Sargon the Great became the ruler of the world, as it was known then, yet he never destroyed his family relationships.

According to the *Book of the Cave of Treasures* we have this additional information about Sargon (Serug):

And Serug lived thirty years and begot Nâhôr, and all the days of his life were two hundred and thirty years. And in the days of Serug the worship of idols entered the world. And in his days the children of men began to make themselves graven images, and it was at this time that the introduction of idols into the world took place. For the children of men were scattered all over the earth, and they had neither teachers nor lawgivers, and no one to show them the way of truth wherein they should walk, and for this reason they became confused and fell into error. Some of them through their error adored

> the heavens, and some of them worshipped the
> sun, and moon and stars, and some of them the
> earth, and wild beasts, and birds, and creeping
> things, and trees, and stones, and the creatures
> of the sea, and the waters, and the winds.[222]

Serug (Sargon) learned the secrets of divining in Ur, where the
sons of Kesed ruled for 385 years, as I have shown. He was taught
by "the family". He passed that knowledge regarding idol wor-
shipping secrets to his son Nahor. Therefore, as I will show later,
Terah actually inherited directly the errant "secrets" of paganism
from his grandfather Serug (Sargon), who had received them from
the sons of Kesed, either Ur-Engur, Utu-Hegal, Ur-Nammu, or all
three! The city-state of Ur was the foundation of the "Kasidim," or,
the religion of Kesed. It became known as "Ur of the Kasidim" for
that very reason.

Serug settled for a while in what later was called "Padan-Aram". A
city called by his name, Serug, was found to exist, close by the cities
of Haran and Nahur (Nahor).

From the *Book of Jubiliees*:

> And he [Serug] grew up, and dwelt in Ur of
> the Khaldis, near to the father of his wife's
> mother, and he worshipped idols, and he took
> to himself a wife in the thirty-sixth jubilee, in
> the fifth week, in the first year thereof, and her
> name was Melka, the daughter of Kaber, the
> daughter of his father's brother. And she bare
> him Nahor, in the first year of this week, and
> he grew and dwelt in Ur of the Khaldis, **and
> his father taught him the researches of the
> Khaldis to divine and augur, according to the
> signs of heaven.**[223]

Tradition has held that Sargon first became cup-bearer to the king of Kish, whose name was Ur-Zababa.[224] Ur-Zababa was the son of Puzer-Suen, who was a Gutian King. However, he was also listed as the second king of the 4th Dynasty of Kish. This by itself should put to rest the idea that the Gutians were invaders into Sumer from the outside. Sargon later deposed Ur-Zababa at Kish, but later still installed his son, Zimudar, as a vassal king at Kish.[225] Puzer-Suen ruled 7 years, followed by Yarlaganda, for another 7 years, followed by Si'um for 7 more years. After him was Tirigan, the last Gutian king, whom I will show was Terah of the Bible. So let's go back to Ur-Zababa, the son of Puzer-Suen, a Gutian king. Somehow he became the second king of the 4th Dynasty of Kish. Yet we have been led to believe that the Gutians were barbarians and robbers who came in and "took over" Sumer for about 100 years. In fact, the Gutians were a part of the family!

So, we come back to Sargon, the "cup-bearer" to Ur-Zababa, the king of Kish, who was himself a son of a Gutian king. If Ur-Zababa was the son of Puzer-Suen, then that made him a brother of Yarlaganda, whose grandson was Tirigan (Terah), who reigned for a mere 40 days before being "shut down" by his ancestor Utu-Hegal for a supposed attempt at taking over Ur, the most prestigious city-state in the family. The point of this exercise is simple. The Gutians were not "barbarians" who came from the outside to invade Sumer. In fact, they were a part of the larger family of Shem, having been led by none other than Gudea, one of the most prominent of Sumerian kings. Serug (Sargon), who grew up in the family and very well may have been a "cup bearer" (similar to a treasurer) to his relative Ur-Zababa of Kish, eventually rose through the family hierarchy to assume a powerful position. This can now be seen to be a continuation of the dynasty of Shem playing itself out (in Serug's case through Eber, who clearly controlled the northern part of Sumer and into Akkad). Lugalzagesi, a descendant of Gilgamesh, son of Kesed, either dethroned or killed king Ur-Zababa before beginning a series of conquests. Sargon launched a surprise attack against Lugalzagesi's capital, Uruk, and destroyed its walls.[226]

Fig. 40 Serug (Sargon the Great)

The brother of Serug (Sargon) was King Ur-Bau of Lagash, who was overthrown by his father-in-law Ur-Nammu, King of Ur, the son of Kesed of the Bible.[227] Like Moses, there are legends that Sargon (Serug) was left adrift in a small basket only to be found and raised by some maiden. However, nothing could be farther from the truth. In fact, the life of Serug (Sargon) can be clearly delineated and shown to fall within the larger fabric of the families of Shem and Ham. Because of his final takeover of the Hamite lands of Sumer, it seems appropriate that we look at his role in these events from his perspective at this time. Serug (Sargon the Great) was the first king to unite the lands of his own ancestors of Assyria, northern Sumer, and Elam with the Hamite portions of Sumer, which included all of central and southern Iraq (today) under one rule. The Assyrian and northern Iraqi lands were known as Akkad. Therefore he became the King of Sumer and Akkad.

From the *Book of Jubilees* comes this amazing record:

> And the sons of Noah began to war on each other, to take captive and to slay each other, and to shed the blood of men on the earth, and to eat blood, and to build strong cities, and walls, and towers, and individuals (began) to exalt themselves above the nation, and to found the beginnings of kingdoms, and to go to war people against people, and nation against nation, and city against city, and all (began) to do evil, and to acquire arms, and to teach their sons war, and they began to capture cities, and to sell male and female slaves. And Ur, the son of Kesed, built the city of Ara of the Chaldees, and called its name after his own name and the name of his father. And they made for themselves molten images, and they worshipped each the idol, the molten image which they had made for themselves, and they began to make graven images and unclean simulacra, and malignant spirits assisted and seduced (them) into committing transgression and uncleanness.[228]

Here we have a religious record, although not from the Bible, that provides us with a significant link to a purely securlar occurrence. The name of "Ur" who built the city of Ara of the Chaldees, and called its name after his own name" is none other than Ur-Nammu, who indeed did build Ur [Ara] after its near destruction. We, therefore, have an historic linkage to the lineage of Abraham in the person of Serug and in the father of Ur-Nammu, namely Kesed of the Bible. Although the passage indicates that Kesed is the father of Ur it also says that the city of Ur was named "after his own name and the name of his father." The city of Ur of the Chaldees was also known as Ur of the Kasidim (Ur of Kesed's line). And, as I have just shown, Sargon (Serug) not only realized this but he was raised in it! From the secular records we know that Serug's father-in-law, Ur-Nammu, the dynasty's most illustrious king, inherited the reign over southern Sumer from his brother Utu-Hegal, but through his own military-campaigns gave Ur, his home town, its continuing great empire. All of the Sumerian city-states became his vassals, either by acknowledgement or by force. After Sargon's death in 2176 BC the control of Sumer passed to Ur-Engur, the son of Kesed, who continued the empire, passing it on to his brother Utu-Hegal. On Utu-Hegal's death, or overthrow, Sumer came to Ur-Nammu.

In the meantime Sargon's son, Ur-Nahor (Nahor of the Bible), had been placed as a High Priest in the temple at Nippur. Ur-Nahor was the father of three sons, among others: Shulgi, Dungi, and Turgi. Turgi is identified with Terah in the Bible, the father of Abram (Abraham). Turgi (Terah) was a Gutian through his relationship with Gudea, as I have shown. He had aspirations to become a king, but was also raised in the line of High Priests through his father, Ur-Nahor, High Priest at Nippur. We will take up Terah in due course.

Ur-Nahor was succeeded by his son, Shulgi. Shulgi was murdered by his brother Dungi, who usurped the throne in prejudice of his late brother's eldest son, Bur-Sin, who overthrew his uncle, and took the throne. Bur-Sin was succeeded, in turn, by his two brothers, Ama-Sin and Shu-Sin, after which their cousin, Gimil, the son of Dungi, their late uncle, usurped the throne in prejudice of the son of the late king Shu-Sin, namely, Ibi-Sin. Later, upon Gimil's death, Ibi-Sin, the rightful heir, took the throne. He was the last king of 3rd Dynasty Ur, whose idol-worship decayed the empire, which was conquered by Elam, which became the First Persian Dynasty. The news of the defeat and death of King Ibi-Sin of Ur, in battle against the King of Elam, sent the royal house of Ur in flight, along with thousands of refugees, many hundreds of miles to the north out of harm's way, and took up residence at Haran.[229] This historical episode is called the "Call of Abram" in the Bible, when God called Abram out of Ur; however, the Bible account omits many details. His father Terah [Turgi] remained a heathen who worshiped the pagan moon-god Nannar-Sin; however, Abram "crossed-over" to the worship of Yahweh, "The One True God," with whom he made a covenant, called the "Abrahamic Covenant."

In the book *Eblaitica*, we find a confirmation of another sort that Sargon and Serug were the same person:

> As for Nagar, [the name] appears (as NAGAR-Ki) in two administrative Sargonic tablets, and its name may be restored in a Sargonic tablet from Tell Brak, attributable, with other tablets of the same level, to the reign of Naram-Sin [son of Sargon]. It lists corvee workers from a number of towns, all of which were located in the eastern part of the Habur Triangle, close to Naram-Sin's palace at Tell Brak. The damaged second sign of the toponym was read hur by Kessler, thus yielding the name of the well-known city of Nahur in the northwestern corner of the Habur Triangle.[230]

Here we see clear evidence linking the name of Sargon (Serug) to his son, Nahur (Nahor), founder of the town of Nahor, which was named after himself. This is further confirmation that we are following the correct path of identifying the Patriarchs.

Sargon became king of Akkad, also called Agade. The transition is described in the historiographic poem *The curse of Agade* which strongly hints that Sargon was assisted by certain gods who conveniently cleared the road for him by destroying Kish and Uruk. In particular it was Enlil, the chief god of Sumer who came to his aid.

> After the frowning forehead of Enlil had killed [the people of] Kish like the Bull of Heaven, after he had ground the house of Uruk into dust, like a giant bull, after in due time, to Sargon the King of Agade from the lands above to the lands below, Enlil had given him lordship and kingship.[231]

The "Bull of Heaven" was a euphemism often used in the Sumerian legends for one of the special weapons used by the deities. It appears graphically in the legend of Gilgamesh, for example, when he and his companion Enkidu managed to destroy the "Bull of Heaven," a weapon sent by the goddess Ishtar.[232]

From the inscriptions preserved of Sargon, we know that he contolled (not conquered) all of northern Syria as far as Anatolia and up to the borders of Lebanon. It also provides the first recorded reference to Ebla in cuneiform: "Sargon the king prostrated himself in prayer before Dagon (Enlil) in Tuttul (now modern Hit). He gave him the upper regions: Marit, Iarmutu, and Ebla as far as the forest of cedar and the mountains of silver. Enlil did not let anyone oppose Sargon."[233]

There are several points of interest in Sargon's claims. He conquered Sumer and the upper valley and the lands to the west, up to the borders of Anatolia (the mountain of silver) and that of Lebanon (the forest of cedar). Elsewhere, he describes how he captured the cities of littoral Lebanon and the Bekaa Valley, as indicated in the self-laudatory poem "The Legend of Sargon" where he boasts: "The Sea Lands three times I circled. Dilmun my hand captured."[234]

Sargon's greatest achievement was to conquer areas outside of the traditional Shemite lands of Akkad and Sumer, which, as I have shown, were amalgamated into the Shemite dynasty over hundreds of years. He made great strides to the west, however. The cities of the coast of the Mediterranean were apparently captured by Sargon, cities which were usually referred to as the Sea Lands in the literature of Sumer. Although Sargon entered the sacrosanct valley between the mountains, he apparently caused no damage and was satisfied merely to place his brand on the land of Dilmun (today's Bahrain).[235] Sargon conquered the known world from Egypt to India and became known as a military genius, an imaginative administrator and builder, and one of the most capable political figures of the ancient East. Later legends and chronicles celebrating the exploits of Sargon suggest his conquests may have included the lands of Egypt, Ethiopia, and India as well.[236]

Unlike the rulers that followed, Sargon preferred to control and rule rather than conquer and rule his vast empire, one that encompassed the entire known world. This is manifest in the archives of Ebla which reveal that the city seemed to thrive under the administration of Sargon but was later destroyed by his grandson Naram-Sin.[237] Although he declared himself to be the "OINT of Anum" and the priest of Enlil, Sargon respected the religions and temples of the Sumerians. After taking Ur, he made his daughter Enheduanna the High Priestess of the Sumerian Moon-god Nannar-Sin. She served at the same temple in which Terah, the father of Abraham, was also serving. Ebla, Iamarti and Mari in the north gave him a large annual bounty.

Sargon's ambition did not end there -- he led his army in two campaigns into Elam (Persia/Iran) to subdue the two principalities of Awan and Warahshe (its ally). These towns are in southern Iran to the east of the Euphrates River and about parallel with Lagash, Umma, and Uruk in southern Sumer. The towns were sacked but not destroyed, again showing that Sargon recognized that these were Shemite territories, having come from Elam, the son of

Shem. Sargon made vassals of the two chiefs on receiving their surrender. Then he entered Susa, the chief city of Elam, and made it "the capital of Elam," leaving the power in the hands of its former viceroy, who was a descendant of Elam or Arphaxad. Using the numerous slaves that he had captured in his many campaigns, Sargon enlarged and maintained innumerable irrigation canals to cultivate cereals. In short, he was not interested in "conquering" these territories as much as "controlling" them. He knew his role: he was a Shemite!

The only way to understand this simple truth is to realize that the longevity of lifetimes allowed him to appreciate the reality of what had happened over the last 700 years. People like Kesed had "seen it all." There is no doubt in my mind that Serug (Sargon) had communicated with his great-grandfather Kesed on numerous occasions. The fact that he allowed every single Shemite city-state to remain, and be added to, while at the same time allowing the leadership to remain, is evidence that this is the case. Ur-Engur, for example, was allowed to call himself the "King of the Four Regions." How could he do this in the lifetime of Sargon, who also held that title? He did so, because this was his family.

Between Kish and Babilim (the future Babylon), Sargon (Serug) built his "new royal capital of Agade," with its huge palace and double ramparts of fortification. As this city was situated on the ancient trail of the Euphrates, he enlarged the port so that it could accommodate all the ships of that time. He started a system of permanent inspection and transfer of cavalry every 25 miles. Each of these posts was managed by a royal officer. According to legend, he took his armies to Creta, Cyprus and even as far as Anatolia (Turkey today).[238]

The latter part of Sargon's reign was troubled with rebellions, which later literature ascribes, predictably enough, to sacrilegious acts that he is supposed to have committed; but this can be discounted as the standard cause assigned to all disasters by Sumerians and

Akkadians alike. The troubles, in fact, were probably caused by the inability of one man, however energetic, to control so vast an empire without a developed and well-tried administration. There is no evidence to suggest that he was particularly harsh, nor that the Sumerians disliked him for being a Shemite. After all, the entire empire was Shemite by this time! On his death the empire did not collapse totally, for his successors were able to control their legacy, and later generations thought of him as being perhaps the greatest name in their history. Attributing his success to the patronage of the goddess Ishtar, in whose honor Agade was erected, Sargon of Akkad became the first great empire builder. Two later Assyrian kings were named in his honor. Although the briefly recorded information of his predecessor, Lugalzagesi, descended from Gilgamesh, the son of Kesed, shows that expansion beyond the Sumerian homeland had already begun, later Mesopotamians looked to Sargon as the founder of the military tradition that runs through the history of their people.

The basic Indo-European vocabulary in Akkadian is due to a process called linguistic alliance. This means that only when two different linguistic groups of people actually live together will their languages interpenetrate each other. Words embedded in Akkadian and so attested from the first appearance of Akkadian texts, confirm the tradition of the *King of Battle Epic* that Sargon's Akkadian Dynasty had Anatolian connections from the beginning. Since the Akkadian records start around the middle of the third millennium BC, the formation of the Akkadian language in linguistic alliance with Indo-Europeans in Anatolia [today's Turkey, where the Ark and Noah settled] must have taken place still earlier.[239]

Serug, known to history as Sargon the Great, died in 2176 BC His sons who reigned after him were born of a priestess of Inanna whose name is lost to history. Rimush served first but was assassinated by his servants. He was followed by the next younger brother, Man-ishtushu. He was the brother of Rimush. He started out by restoring order in the vassal states of Elam, which were trying to gain their independence. Using all his power, he decided to lead a campaign on the banks of the Arabian/Persian Gulf, where he put down the uprisings in two vassal cities: Ansham and Sherihum. Then, with a huge fleet, he conquered and pillaged "32 cities" which lay between Qatar at Magan to the country of Oman in Arabia. After killing the princes who reigned beyond the coastal mountains, he plundered their silver mines (ingots of silver served as money), and great black stones (diorite), from one of which was sculpted his own statue which he installed in the great temple of Enlil at Nippur. Clearly, Man-ishtushu did not rule as had his father, Sargon (Serug).

Man-Ishtushu reigned over Akkad from 2205 BC to 2191 BC Manishtushu was mostly preoccupied with trying to recover the distant colonies which had become mutinous. He, too, appeared to have died in a palace revolt. It is not clear if his son, Naram-Sin, killed his father in order to assume the mantle of kingship but in view of his subsequent activities it seems highly likely.

Naram-Sin, Grandson of Serug

He ruled Akkad from about 2190 BC to 2154 BC Next to the last king in the dynasty of Akkad was Naram-Sin. Naram-Sîn (Akkadian, meaning 'the lover of Sîn,' the Moon god) the grandson of Sargon had collected many feats of arms and had a comparable status and power as his grandfather. He called himself 'King of the Four Quarters' meaning the entire known world at the time. His empire was even larger than Sargon's empire. Naram-Sin was one of the first kings to deify himself. At some point in time during his reign, his name appeared with the determinative used in front of divine names. In a victory stela (now at the Louvre museum in Paris) he is depicted with a horned crown, an attribute reserved for deities. The period when his name appeared without the determinative for god was the period in which he had to deal with revolt and rebellion in his own country. In the group of texts when his name bore the divine attribute related to the end of his reign, Naram-Sin was concerned with fighting off a new enemy, among which were the people called Gutians who tried to penetrate from the north.[240] The Gutians were the relatives of Sargon, and of Naram-Sin. They realized that Naram-Sin had "crossed the line" and had begun to become an evil dictator, something that Sargon had never done.

Deification of a human by itself is not new. Rulers like Lugalbanda and Gilgamesh also appear in lists of gods, but in the case of the self-glorification of Naram-Sin, he called himself "god of Akkad," a title clearly belonging to the Akkadian goddess Ishtar (Inanna in Sumer). She was the city patron of Akkad and owned as such all properties and estates of the city. Naram-Sin's self-glorification may have been an act that disturbed the local priests and the leaders of the religious centers in the country, and mainly in Nippur, the "religious capital," where Kesed was the High Priest. Naram-Sin found himself running into an established dynasty that Kesed had developed hundreds of years before Naram-Sin was born. He really had no idea what he was up against, as his grandfather, Sargon, had realized early on. As a "voice box" for the gods, Kesed had Naram-Sin removed.

The story of Naram-Sin's downfall is as follows:

> In his anger, Enlil brought the Gutians down
> from the hills east of the Tigris, to bring plague,
> famine and death throughout Mesopotamia.
> To prevent this destruction, eight of the
> gods decreed that Agade (Akkad) should be
> destroyed to spare the remaining cities.[241]

However, we now know that it was not Enlil who ordered the murder of Naram-Sin and the destruction of his empire. It was the High Priest of Enlil, whose name was Nahor (of the Bible). As the High Priest of the Temple of Enlil he was the "voice" of the god. As the creator and sustainer of the dynasty of Sumer, he was also its secular ruler. Naram-Sin had become a liability that his grandfather, Sargon (Serug), would never have been, and wasn't. But Naram-Sin's megalomania was too much for Nahor. Therefore, as an "oracle-priest," Nahor pronounced, in the name of Enlil, that Naram-Sin, and his city, had to go.

Naram-Sin almost became a god. He left a famous victory stela from Sippar (modern Iraq) which was subsequently taken as war booty to Susa in Elam. Its date was close to the time of comet Hale-Bopp's passage. The stela is now in Paris' Louvre Museum. Naram-Sin died about 2154 BC His empire in Sumer and Akkad remained, and the sons of Kesed, Ur-Engur, Utu-Hegal, and Ur-Nammu, kept it intact. One can see on the stele that there are a pair of "suns" in the heavens above the scene. What do these heavenly bodies signify? It is not a Sun/Moon combination according to Dr. Edwin Krupp, noted archaeo-astronomer and director of the Griffith Observatory.[242] The two objects in the stela appear to be identical. The Moon and other planetary objects each had their own symbols. If the sculptor was intending to represent the Sun and Moon, he would have chosen a different symbol for the second object. The same would go for the Sun and Venus. According to Dr. Krupp, the twin suns of the Naram-Sin Stela are a bit of an enigma. The appearance of twin suns is uncommon in ancient symbolism. The stele which Naram-Sin erected was originally at Sippar, but was later found at Susa. It shows him climbing a mountain over the prostrate forms of his enemies. He faces a large conical object on top of a mountain with the star of Shamash overhead. Naram-Sin wears the horned headdress of a god.[243]

Let's see how the "mythology" of Naram-Sin measures up with the "history" that I just reported. There is a Sumerian composition known as *The Legend of Naram-Sin* which related his expedition to a mountain land where he destroyed a rebellious city, but also lost his whole army in the process. In addition, there is a long Sumerian historiographic poem called *The Curse of Agade, the Ekur Avenged,* which was composed soon after his death, perhaps as an exculpation for his destructive policies and his sacrilegious behavior in the plunder of the sacred Ekur, which led to the gods placing a curse on Naram-Sin and his city of Agade. The narrative of *The Curse of Agade* begins with the rise of Sargon to power with the support of Ishtar (Inanna), who made Agade her tutelary city. With Enlil's help, the empire of Sargon flourished until the advent of Naram-Sin to the kingship. Soon after he assumed power, the gods deserted the city and Ishtar removed her sponsorship, leaving the city weak and impoverished. At first, Naram-Sin accepted his fate with humility, but after seven years of this contrite behavior, he consulted the oracle of the Ekur and apparently was repulsed. His humility turned to defiance and he mobilized his army and attacked the Ekur, desecrated its holy places, and devastated the land. According to the legend, this brought down the wrath of Enlil who unleashed the barbaric tribes of the surrounding hills that spread devastation throughout the land of Sumer. The mythic tale goes on but the reality is already clear. Kesed, High Priest of the temple of Enlil, had Naram-Sin "taken out."

Fig. 42 The Victory Stele of Naram-Sin

The legends of the hero Gilgamesh were certainly known to Naram-Sin. In his overriding ambition he probably tried to emulate him, as well as duplicate the achievements of his grandfather Sargon (Serug). In declaring himself a god, it showed that there was apparently no limit to the excessive ambition of the egomaniac Naram-Sin. After his death, the control of Sumer went to the son of Kesed, whose name was Utu-Hegal, the brother of both Gilgamesh and Ur-Nammu. He is credited with the expulsion of Gutians and their organization of the cities under the 3rd (actually Second) Dynasty of Ur.

Next we return from Serug, whose other wife was Melka, and whose mother was Kaber, the daughter of one of the brothers of Ragau to their son, Nahor (Ur-Nachor) of the Bible.

Chapter Seventeen

Nahor (Ur-Nachor), the Son of Serug (2276 BC – 2028 BC)

N ahor's mother's name was Melka. It is likely that Nahor was a younger son of Serug since the empire that Serug had created fell to Man-ishtushu. However, the tradition in the family was that the royal line went through the women (matrilineal). Melka was the granddaughter of Peleg and the great-granddaughter of Eber, who had been an Emperor in his own right, conquering the majority of the Hamite territories and setting up the enormous kingdom that later became known as the "Kingdom of Akkad and Sumer."

From the apocryphal book of *The Cave of Treasures* comes the following:

> And Serug lived thirty years and begot Nâhôr, and all the days of his life were two hundred and thirty years. And in the days of Serug the worship of idols entered the world. And in his days the children of men began to make

themselves graven images, and it was at this time that the introduction of idols into the world took place. For the children of men were scattered all over the earth, and they had neither teachers nor lawgivers, and no one to show them the way of truth wherein they should walk, and for this reason they became confused and fell into error. Some of them through their error adored the heavens, and some of them worshipped the sun, and moon and stars, and some of them the earth, and wild beasts, and birds, and creeping things, and trees, and stones, and the creatures of the sea, the waters, and the winds. Now Satan had blinded their eyes so that they might walk in the darkness of error, because they had no hope of a resurrection. For when one of them died they used to make an image of him, and set it up upon his grave, so that the remembrance [of his appearance] might not pass from before their eyes. And error having been sown broadcast in all the earth, the land became filled with idols in the form of men and women. And then Serug died, being two hundred and thirty years old, and Nâhôr, and Tarah, and Abraham his sons, buried him in Sarghîn, the city which he built after his own name."[244]

As I have noted before, this passage confirms for us that Serug and Sargon (Sarghin) were the same person.

Not a few towns of biblical interest appear in the Ebla tablets, which preserve the earliest-known mention of the following names in written records. Ebla was the city that was ruled by the great-great-grandfather of Nahor. Well east of Ebla, on or near the Khabur River, Nahur is mentioned, a centre familiar from the Mari archives, which might also be the "city of Nahor."[245] Nahor was a relatively common name, found also for the grandfather and the brother of Abraham.[246] According to *The Chronology of Genesis*, by Neil Zimmerer and Jim Keith, Nahor was the Royal High Priest for the city of Nippur in Sumer. The source of this information is not given. However, it is highly likely that the authors are correct. As a younger son of Serug (Sargon), Nahor was not in line for kingship. At the same time, his great-grandfather-in-law, Kesed, was about to die. Kesed was the true High Priest Patriarch of the family of Shem. As his own death approached, it was likely that he would arrange for a son of the "true line" of Shem to succeed him. He had already placed all of his sons into postions of secular power quite successfully, even controlling his great-grandson Serug (Sargon) quite effectively. Therefore, making Nahor a High Priest was the next best opportunity for Kesed, and probably his last major political/religious act. Therefore, Nahor became the High Priest in the Temple of Enlil in Nippur, the holy religious city in Sumer, placing him in a similar position to that which had been held by his great-great-grandfather Kesed in the Temple of Ninsun. However, it needs to be noted here that his relationship to Kesed was not through the "biblical" line. Instead, it went this way: his father was Serug, Sargon the Great. Serug's mother was Ora, the wife of Ragau. Ora's father was Ur-Nammu, the King of Ur and all of Sumer in the late 21st century BC And Ur-Nammu's father was Kesed, High Priest of Ninsun at Nippur.

Now that we know just how Nahor was positioned, we will be able to appreciate the influence that he had on the rulers of Sumer, and in particular over Utu-Hegal and Ur-Nammu, the sons of Kesed. Nahor outlived both of these rulers of Sumer, having died in 2028 BC Utu-Hegal died in 2113 BC and Ur-Nammu died in 2095 BC Therefore, as Kesed was influential in the lives of each of the rulers of this dynasty of 385 years, Nahor, as his replacement, also exercised a great deal of influence. We must remember, this was a "matrilineal" form of inheritance, when it came to power. Nahor's wife, Napush, was a daughter of Ragau, whose grandfather was the great Eber, in whose name the Hebrews are now called.

Nahor had both a patrilineal claim to royalty as well as a matrilineal claim. On his father's side were Sargon, Emperor of Akkad and Sumer, and so on back to Arphaxad. His wife could make the same claim, being the daughter of Ragau, King of Lagash. On Nahor's mother's side he had as a grandfather the great king Ur-Nammu, King of Akkad and Sumer as well. But beyond that, he had the great High Priest Kesed, his great-great-grandfather, brother of Cainan, both sons of Arphaxad, the son of Shem. In taking over the High Priest position similar to that of Kesed, therefore, Nahor, while not a king himself, was the titulary "priest-king" of the family of Shem. In him the secular kingly line and the priestly line converged. In theory, his power was immense. In practice it appears that Nahor was not as influential as his ancestor Kesed had been. He did not maximize his position. However, he still had power, which he used in the priestly position. As the High Priest he was given access to the "holy of holies" in the temple, where communications with the god took place. It is likely that his father, Serug (Sargon the Great), had placed Nahor in this high position to be able to obtain "first hand" information from Enlil when needed. Since Kesed probably died prior to the end of Sargon's reign, it is likely that Nahor took his place as both the High Priest and the son of Sargon. This would have been a position that would have naturally fallen to a "second son" of the emperor, since Man-ishtushu, the first son, was the heir to Sargon's empire. It is important at this point to bring dates in again to make this perfectly clear.

Sargon (Serug) died when Nahor was 100 years old. We do not know when Kesed died, but we may reasonably presume that it was when Nahor was at least 50 (2226 BC). This would mean that Nahor, as both son of Sargon and as the High Priest of the Temple of Enlil in Nippur, would have 50 years to advise his father. Power is the focus here. The gods will be mentioned later. As Kesed had exercised enormous power in the religious realm, without a secular role, Sargon, by placing his son, Nahor, in Kesed's place, was enabled to exercise both a religious role and the secular role that he already had acquired. Recognizing that Kesed had made his own position possible, Sargon (Serug) had not bothered the sons of Kesed (Ur-Engur and Utu-Hegal). Instead, they were retained in exactly the same positions that Kesed had insisted that they hold.

Recognizing further the extreme power that the position of High Priest to Enlil held, Sargon wisely placed his own son in that position on the death of Kesed (say 2225 BC). In doing so, Sargon (Serug) was able, over the remaining 50 years of his own life, to extend his empire into the world empire that he created. He did so because his son, Nahor, was the "spokesperson of the god," Enlil. However, after the death of his father, Nahor found himself dealing with Man-ishtushu, his brother, and then Naram-Sin, his nephew. As Naram-Sin became more megalomanical, to the point of declaring himself a god, it was clear that Nahor would have to act. Therefore, as the "spokesperson" of the god Enlil, Nahor announced that Naram-Sin needed to be taken out. It was done. Naram-Sin was eliminated and his city of Agade was destroyed, never to be found again. Clearly the "priesthood" had powers that were, ultimately, greater than the kings.

Nahor's role as High Priest was passed on to his son Terah, who held that position in the temple of Nannar-Sin in Ur. Nahor's son was Terah of the Bible, whose name outside the Bible was Tirhu (according to Zechariah Sitchin) and Tirigan, or Turgi (King of the Gutians). Our narrative brings us to the lifetime of Abraham and his father. But first, I am going to go back in time to address the family of Ham. I will follow the descendants of Ham into this time period of Terah and Abraham.

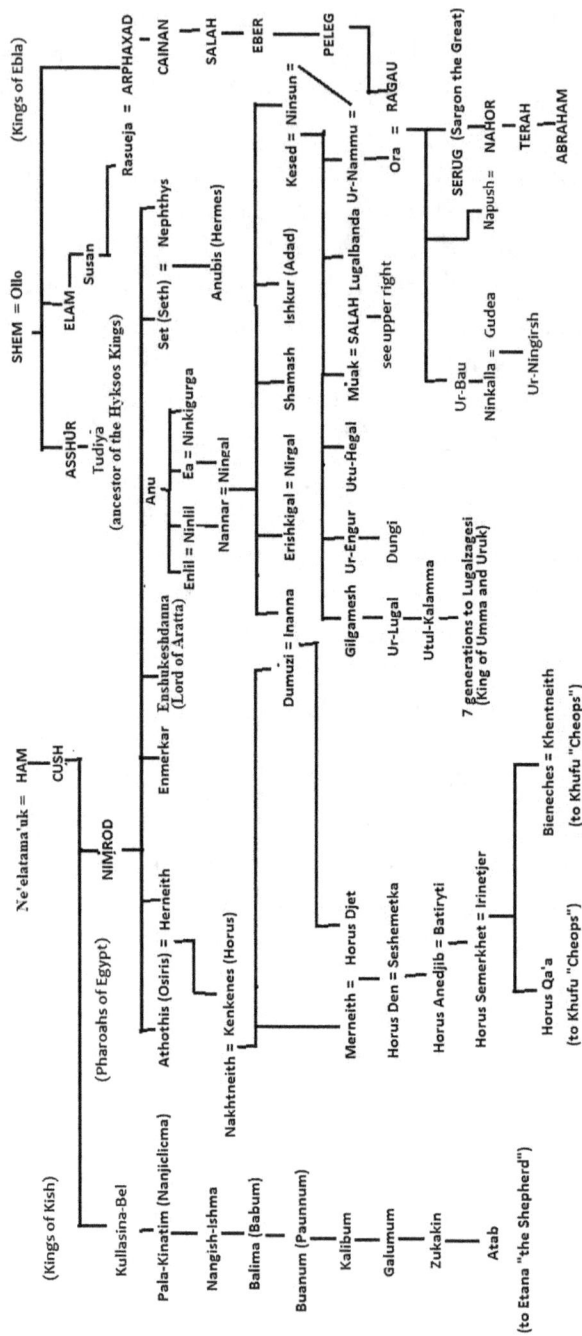

Fig. 41

Chapter Eighteen

Cush, the Son of Ham
(c. 3100 BC – c. 2615
and 2582 BC)

A s the family of Ham moved out of the mountains of Ararat, they began to settle in what is now central Sumer. The sons of Ham settled to the south of where Arphaxad was settling, in northern Sumer (Iraq) and Syria, and west of where Elam had settled in what is now Iran. Cush was probably the founder of the ancient city of Kish in Sumeria, one of the oldest cities in the world. It was named after himself (Cush = Kish). In the earliest known period, Sumer was divided into several independent city-states, whose limits were defined by canals and boundary stones. Each was centered on a temple dedicated to the patron god or goddess of the city and ruled over by a priest or king, who was intimately tied to the city's religious rites. Some of the major cities included Eridu, Kish, Lagash, Uruk, Ur, and Nippur. As these cities developed, they sought to assert primacy over each other, falling into a millennium of almost incessant warfare over water rights, trade routes, and tribute from nomadic tribes.[247]

The first ruler of Kish according to the Sumerian King List, which lists the rulers of Sumeria from before the Flood until the time of Abraham, and which is a non-biblical document, names the first ruler of Kish (Cush) as Jushur, or Ga-Ur, apparently the Sumerian name of Cush, son of Ham. In the name Jusher the "J" could equally be a "K" or a "G" as in Kusher or Gusher in the earliest cuneiform. Therefore, his name could equally have been Kusher which is reasonably similar to Cush.[248] More fascinating than the fact that Jushur (Kusher) was the first ruler of Kish, the first city built after the Flood, is the fact that the last ruler before the Flood was Ubar-Tutu, whom I have identified as Methuselah, the grandfather of Noah. Proof of this will be provided when I publish the Patriarchs Before the Flood, a sequel to this book. Therefore, the ruling of the world went, on a secular level, from Methuselah, grandfather of Noah, to Cush, grandson of Noah, in the line of Ham. This is a separate line from the "divinely appointed" line which went through Methuselah's son Lamech to Noah, and then to Shem.

Hence, it is in the Flood that God changes course, if you will, and history begins to be split into two distinct routes, one secular and one divinely appointed. The line of Ham, through Cush and his descendants, as well as through other sons of Ham, is the secular line. This is not to say that it was idolatrous, initially. In fact, it will become clear as we proceed that it was both the line of Ham and the line of Shem that fell into idolatry. Cush began by reigning as the first king of Kish, under his Sumerian name of Jusher (Kusher). He was the first son of Ham to enter the Sumerian valley and He did so in spite of the fact that Noah had given the area to the family of Shem. The result was to become the earliest history of the world. Kish was where Cush settled, naming the first post-Flood city-state after himself. However, he allowed his sons to do the same that he had done, and there is evidence to that affect. Amazingly, since Ham knew where the pre-diluvian city-states had existed, his descendants, led by Cush, founded new city-states in the same locations. Zechariah Sitchin has written a very convincing argument on this in his *Earth Chronicles*.

Kullassina-bel of Kish was the second king in the First Dynasty of Kish according to the Sumerian King List. He would almost certainly have been the son of Cush. On page 62 where I discuss longevity and dating, I have noted the descendants of Kullassina-bel down to Mesilim, also a king of Kish. As the name seems to be an Akkadian phrase meaning "All of them (were) lord," it has sometimes been suggested that the occurrence of this name on the list was intended to denote a period of no central authority in the early period of Kish. In a relatively short time, however, kingship was spread throughout Sumer, as I will show.

One of the first city-states formed after Kish was in the south of the Euphrates/Tigris valley and was known as Ur. **Meskalamdug** is the first archaeologically recorded lugal, or king (*Lugal* from *lu*=man, *gal*=big) of the city of Ur. He was succeeded by his son **Akalamdug**, and Akalamdug by his son **Meshannepada**.[249] It appears that Meskalamdug must have been a son of Cush. His grandson, Meshannepada, is also called the first king of Ur listed on the king list, and it says he defeated Lugal-kitun (abt 2475 BC-2363 BC) of Uruk, who was the last ruler of that dynasty. Lugal-kitun was a descendant of Gilgamesh, the son of Kesed, the High Priest. Meshannepada also seems to have subjected Kish, which would have been the city-state of his great grandfather, and thereafter assumed the title "King of Kish" for himself. This title would be used by many kings of the preeminent dynasties for some time afterward.[250]

His son was named Nanni, or **Ur-Nanshe**, or Ur-Nina. He was called the first ruler of the Second Dynasty of Ur, even though he was the son of Mesannepada. He is said to have ruled for 120 years. He was also the first ruler over another new city-state, namely Lagash. In the case of Ur-Nina, however, rulership became more than just secular. It also became religious. He also called himself the High Priest. He took the place of his own High Priest, Lugal-Suggur, to become the King-High Priest, combining the roles. In Sumerian he combined the Ensi (King) with the Lugal (High

Priest). After him the terms became interchangeable and it is difficult to determine who was a "king" and who was a "high priest." However, it is clear that politically speaking, the High Priest had the most influence. This is because he was the "voice of god," in whose temple he served. Therefore, kings who rose to power from a secular perspective always sought the ultimate power of the high priest as well. This led, eventually, to the concept of the "Sacred Marriage," in which the king would have intercourse with the goddess of the temple whose city-state he ruled. While the ceremony was initially politically motivated, it eventually represented a "reality," as I will show, and kings ended up having sons and daughters through these "Sacred Marriage" ceremonies. It did not take long before the high priests of Lagash made themselves kings, and a dynasty was founded there by Ur-Nina. In the ruins of a building, attached by him to the temple of Nina, terra cotta bas-reliefs of the king and his sons have been found, as well as lions' heads in onyx, that remind one of Egyptian work and onyx plates. These were "booty" dedicated to the goddess Bau. One inscription states that ships of Dilmun (Bahrain) brought him wood as tribute from foreign lands.

Eannatum

Eannatum was the grandson of Ur-Nina. He made himself master of the whole of the district of Sumer, together with the cities of Uruk (ruled by Enshakushanna, of the Sumerian King List), Ur, Nippur, Akshak, and Larsa. He also annexed the kingdom of Kish; however, it recovered its independence after his death. He also made Umma a tributary, a certain amount of grain being levied upon each person in it, that had to be paid into the treasury of the goddess Nina and the god Ningursu, or Ninurta.

The so-called "Stele of the Vultures," now in the Louvre, was erected as a monument of the victory of Eannatum of Lagash over Enakalle of Umma. On this stele, various incidents in the war are represented. In one scene, the king stands in his chariot with a curved weapon in his right hand, formed of three bars of metal bound together by rings, while his kilted followers, with helmets on their heads and lances in their hands, march behind him. Eannatum's campaigns extended beyond the confines of Sumer. He overran a part of Elam, took the city of Az on the Persian Gulf, and exacted tribute as far as Mari; however, many of the realms he conquered were often in revolt. During his reign, temples and palaces were repaired or erected at Lagash and elsewhere; the town of Nina was rebuilt, and canals and reservoirs were excavated.

En-anna-tum

He was succeeded by his brother, En-anna-tum I. During his rule, Umma once more asserted independence under Ur-Lumma, who attacked Lagash unsuccessfully. Ur-Lumma was replaced by a Priest-King, Illi, who also attacked Lagash.

Entemena

En-anna-tum's son then became his successor. Entemena restored the prestige of Lagash. Illi of Umma was subdued, with the help of his ally Lugal-kinishe-dudu of Uruk, successor to Enshakushanna and also on the king-list. This Lugal-kinishe-dudu seems to have been the predominant figure at the time, since he also claimed to rule Kish and Ur. He was also a descendant of Gilgamesh, the son of Kesed, the High Priest of Kullab. A tripod of silver dedicated by Entemena to his god is now in the Louvre. A frieze of lions devouring ibexes and deer, incised with great artistic skill, runs round the neck, while the eagle crest of Lagash adorns the globular part. The vase is a proof of the high degree of excellence to which the goldsmith's art had already attained. A vase of calcite, also dedicated by Entemena, was found at Nippur. After Entemena, a series of weak, corrupt priest-kings is attested for Lagash. The last of these, Urukagina, was known for his judicial, social, and economic reforms, and this may well be the first legal code known to history. [251]

The most infamous son of Cush was Nimrod, whose name in the Sumerian King list is Meshkiaggasar. Nimrod was born in Kish and, as we shall see, remained in Sumer for a large part of his life, extending his control over a large part of Sumer and Assyria. Cush apparently migrated into the area now known as Ethiopia where several of his children eventually ruled. Whether he went there ahead of Nimrod or with Nimrod is not known. However, as the first King of Kish it would seem that he would have remained there at least until Nimrod left for Egypt. Cush's brother, Mizraim, founded the land of Egypt.

Josephus gives an account of the nation of Cush, son of Ham and grandson of Noah: "For Ethiopians, over whom he reigned, are even at this day, both by themselves and by all men in Asia, called Cushites."[252] The existence of the historical Kingdom of Cush in what is now areas of southern Egypt, and Sudan cannot be reasonably questioned, although the term may later have been employed with some latitude. Explorer James Bruce, who visited the Ethiopian highlands around 1770, wrote of "a tradition among the Abyssinians, which they say they have had since time immemorial," that in the days after the Flood, Cush, the son of Ham, travelled with his family up the Nile until they reached the Atbara plain, then still uninhabited, from where they could see the Ethiopian table-land. There they ascended and built Axum, and sometime later returned to the lowland, building Meroe. He also states that European scholars of his own day had summarily rejected this account on grounds of their established theory, namely that Cush must have arrived in Africa via Arabia and the Bab el Mandab. Further, the great obelisk of Axum was said to have been erected by Cush to mark his allotted territory, and his son, Ityopp, is was said to have been buried there, according to the *Book of Aksum*, which Bruce asserts was revered throughout Abyssinia equally with the *Kebre Negest*.[253]

Although decisive evidence is lacking, it is still alleged by some that the several references to Cush in the Old Testament do not refer to

Ethiopia; however, its frequent inclusion with Phut and Mizraim strongly suggest that it was at least considered to be African. Views on their precise location generally depend on how willing certain scholars are to concede that Ethiopia could have enjoyed the prominence claimed for it by others. The rhetorical question "Can the Cushite change his skin?" in the biblical book of Jeremiah implies people of a decidedly different skin color from the Israelites, probably an African people; also, the Septuagint Greek translation of the Old Testament made by Greek-speaking Jews around 350 BC uniformly translates Cush as "Ethiopia." [254] [255] In any case, we lose Cush in favor of his most infamous son, Nimrod.

Chapter Nineteen

Nimrod, the Son of Cush (c. 3040 BC – c. 2085 BC)

An ancient tradition, not in the Bible, states that after the Ark landed Noah went on a voyage to distribute the world to his sons. About 120 years after his return from this voyage, Noah began to divide kingdoms and to erect monarchies in the world. The first was Nimrod, son of his grandson Cush the son of Ham. The area that Nimrod was to rule was around Babylon in central Sumer. The Kushite prince Nimrod, called the son of Aethiops in Greek Mythology, is said in ancient literature to have been a very charismatic young man who slew a dragon, which deed made him popular among the people of the Sumerian settlement of the post-Flood Hamites. He was described in ancient literature as big and strong and a very handsome, athletic "black man," (as his father, Cush, was apparently dark skinned as well) whose looks dazzled the eyes of his female admirers, and whose charisma spellbound his male followers.[256]

"Shinar" was the first of the royal cities which were extensively built and became the visible symbol of the unchallenged reign of Nimrod. It was this city after which the entire plain of Sumer was named. It was not Kish or Eridu. Its name was changed to Babel because of the events that occurred there. Nimrod's fame spread throughout the land, the symbol of kingship was placed upon his head, and the era of the god-kings was begun. Rather than give credit to the source of his power, he consolidated the power and glory unto himself:

> ...and all nations and tongues heard of his fame, and they gathered themselves to him, and they bowed down to the earth, and they brought him offerings, and he became their lord and king, and they all dwelt with him in the city of Shinar, and Nimrod reigned in the earth over all the sons of Noah, and they were all under his power and counsel. And all the earth was of one tongue and words of union, but Nimrod did not go in the ways of the Lord, and he was more wicked than all the men that were before him, from the days of the Flood until those days.[257]

The challenge for any population attempting to dwell in Iraq's arid southern Floodplain was to master the Tigris and Euphrates river's waters for year-round agriculture and drinking water. In fact, the Sumerian language is replete with terms for canals, dikes, and reservoirs, indicating that Sumerian speakers were farmers who moved down from the north after perfecting irrigation agriculture there.

The first post-diluvian attempt by the survivors of the Flood to institutionalize a government was made by Nimrod at Babel, in Sumer, where the main body of the Hamites had planted themselves. Nimrod had some success in overthrowing the Shemitic line, which according to the "Noahic Covenant," had been given a divine mandate to rule as a series of hereditary Patriarchs. However, Nimrod established in its place a Hamitic "monarchy," as the world's first king (after his father Cush) as well as the first "world-king" since the descendants of Noah were actually re-unified by his monarchy. Nimrod established a government at Babel (Babylon) over Sumer. Babylon was just west of Kish where his father ruled. Nimrod extended his rule over other human settlements, either by their consent or by force, and founded the world's first empire. He was the first person in world-history to make war on his own species, according to the ancient sources.[258]

He was a great builder of cities including the cities of Babel (Babylon), Uruk, Accad (Akkad), and Calneh, all in the Tigris and Euphrates River Valley or just to the west of there.[259] He also was the builder of the Tower of Babel in about 2500 BC[260] Nimrod may well have lived nearly as long as Methuselah, whom the Bible indicates lived 969 years. This extreme longevity for Nimrod would have enabled him to conquer the known world as the first "world emperor." From the land of Sumer Nimrod went to Assyria and built the cities of Nineveh, Rehoboth, Calah (modern Nimrud, after his own name) and Resen, and also moved into southern Sumer where he built Ur (Ir in the Bible).[261] Outside the Bible his name was Meshkiaggasar in the Sumerian King List.[262] Since the Bible tells us that Nimrod was the builder of Uruk, and the Sumerian King List says that Meshkiaggasar was the builder of Uruk, then we know that Meshkiaggasar and Nimrod are the same person. In fact, the name Nimrod was probably a pejorative nickname. In Hebrew, the name means "rebel," so his nickname was probably "The Rebel."[263]

Further evidence that Meshkiaggasar was the same as Nimrod comes from this entry in the Sumerian King List: "Meš-ki-aĝ-gašer entered the sea and disappeared."[264] Nimrod did enter the sea and disappear from Sumer forever. He went to Egypt, where he founded a new dynasty. Therefore, the Sumerian King List is ignorant of what happened to Nimrod. Nimrod became the first King of Uruk, the Biblical Erech, and was its builder, along with his son Enmerkar.[265] Nimrod reigned for 324 years, according to the Sumerian King Lists and was credited with building Uruk after the Flood.[266] He was also the High Priest of the Temple of An in that city. Because of this non-biblical record we know that he had given up his knowledge of the true God and had replaced Him with another god whom he knew as An, the father of the gods (Anu of the Sumerians). Anu is the supreme god of the Annunaki, more commonly known as the Nephilim, or "those who fell from Heaven to Earth."[267]

The walls of Erech (Uruk) were built on the foundation of a pre-Flood city. Gilgamesh claimed, from his reading of tablets engraved on Lapis lazuli and secreted in a "copper tablet box" loosened with "the ring-bolt made of bronze," that this pre-diluvian city was built by the seven sages or Patriarchs of the line of Cain and was not the city of his possessions.[268] Of course that original city was destroyed by the Flood. Given the last bit of information, does it make sense that the father of Nimrod, namely Cush, who was the son of Ham, who was born 100 years prior to the Flood, might have known the exact location of the pre-Flood city which was called Shinar, and then later called Babel (Babylon)? It does make sense; furthermore, Cush may well have been familiar with the locations of several of the pre-diluvian city-states. Therefore, he arranged to have them reconstructed as they were before the Flood, including his own city-state, Kish, which was named after himself. Zechariah Sitchen makes this claim in his famous series of books, *The Earth Chronicles*.

Fig. 43 The Great Temple of Enlil in Nippur

Meskiaggasher (Nimrod, "the Rebel") won control of the region extending from the Mediterranean Sea (Phoenicia) to the Zagros Mountains (Iran). He was succeeded by his son Enmerkar, who was also known later as Jupiter Belus (Baal). Nimrod had founded the First Dynasty of Uruk not long after the time of Etana of Kish, who may have been another son of Cush, the father of Nimrod. In the Sumerian King List Nimrod (Meshkiaggasher) is called the "Son of Utu" which must refer to his role as the High Priest rather than referring to his parentage. He and his immediate successors went by the title En, which means Lord, but it implies both secular and religious functions.

After establishing his kingdom in the Tigris/Euphrates region, Nimrod consolidated his power by establishing a state religion. He constructed a religion that included deification and worship of the King (himself), worship of the pantheon of gods in Sumer, and star-worship (corrupted from a pure ante-diluvian astronomy). An ancient Jewish document claims that Nimrod received his knowledge of astronomy from Yonton, a son of Noah, who had been born after the Flood.[269] A key unifying factor in his religion was to be an astronomical and astrological observatory built upon the pinnacle of a pyramid, or tower, at Babel. It has been suggested that Nimrod spent some time in Egypt and that while in Egypt he studied the Egyptian mystery religion perpetuated there from before the Flood by the wife of Ham, whom tradition takes to be a descendant of Cain. In fact, she was the daughter of Methusaleh and not of the line of Cain.[270] It is not likely that Nimrod got any secrets from Egypt because Egypt was not populated until Mizraim and Cush headed that way. Furthermore, as I will show, there is a direct line of descent from Nimrod to the Pharoahs of early Egypt, so if anything, the secret knowledge came from Nimrod to them, rather than the other way around. Nimrod got his religious views through a much more direct line of descent.

Fig. 44 Artist Rendering of the Tower of Babel

The commonly accepted view today is that the Tower of Babel was located near the much later city of Babylon, which is in central Sumer.

And the whole earth was of one language, and of one speech. And it came to pass, as they journeyed from the east, that they found a plain in the land of Shinar; and they dwelt there.[271]

Who is it that traveled to this plain, and where did they come from? It was the family of Noah, specifically Ham,[272] and they were coming from the region originally settled by Noah and his family after the Flood, which was in the mountains of Ararat region.

Fig. 45 Artist Rendering of the Tower of Babel

If we use a little common sense, it can help our understanding of this first "exodus" from the area where the Ark settled. The people leaving this region would have had flocks of animals as well as their families. To travel, they would have needed to follow a river to assure they would always have a sufficient water supply for both the people as well as the animals. The Biblical account says they traveled "from the east" and since the Euphrates flows from east to west here, we can trace this river to see where it goes. (Note: The Euphrates has 2 sources, one near Erzurum, now called Karas, and the other near Ararat, now called Murat.[273] I have traced their journey from the Ararat region, along the Murat.) We are told that they traveled until they "found a plain in the land of Shinar" and that they then "dwelt there." The region of Turkey that they traveled through is extremely mountainous until they reached the point where the Euphrates turns south near the present day Syrian border. Here the mountains end and the region flattens out into a plain. Following the river southward brings us into central Sumer, where Babylon is located next to Kish.

> Therefore, is the name of it called Babel; because the Lord did there confound the language of all the earth: and from thence did the Lord scatter them abroad upon the face of all the earth[274]

Fig. 46 Artist Rendering of the Tower of Babel

We next learn that it was from Babel that the people dispersed. The leader in the building of the tower at Babel was a son of Cush's named Nimrod.

> He was a mighty hunter before the Lord: wherefore it is said, Even as Nimrod the mighty hunter before the Lord. And the beginning of

> his kingdom was Babel, and Erech, and Accad,
> and Calneh,, in the land of Shinar. Out of that
> land went forth Asshur, and builded Nineveh,
> and the city Rehoboth, and Calah [Nimrud].
> And Resen between Nineveh and Calah: the
> same is a great city.[275]

Nimrod began establishing cities, and from this region, Shem's son, Asshur, who had apparently become enamored with his cousin, went out and also established some cities. They are Nineveh, Rehoboth, Calah and Resen.[276] Two of these cities have been located, Nineveh and Calah [Nimrud]. Nineveh is in the north in what is now Syria and Nimrud is also in the north. This agrees well with the statement that Asshur went out of the region of Nimrod's first established cities and built his own.

The fact that Calah [Nimrud] is mentioned as the principal city of the region over Nineveh testifies to its antiquity. Nimrod's memory may have been preserved in the Akkadian god of war and hunting, Ninurta, who was called, "the Arrow, the mighty hero."[277] It is interesting that by the time of Moses in the 15th century BC, Accad (or Akkad) was virtually unknown. This means that whatever documents Moses used to compile this section of Genesis (Chapter 10) were very ancient. Nimrod's name has been preserved in the area where he ruled. The ancient city of Calah which is mentioned in Genesis is the present city on the Tigris River which is named Nimrud.[278]

Fig. 47 City gate at ancient Nimrud (Calah),
built by Nimrod

There is a city southwest of Babylon named Birs Nimrud, and the oldest ruins of Nineveh are given the name of Nimroud. From this archaeological evidence we know of Nimrod's ancient influence, and yet it is interesting that the literature from Babylonia and Assyria as far back as 2300 BC do not mention Nimrod by that name. However, Nimrod was his nickname ("the Rebel") while his real name was Meshkiaggasher. Under that name there are substantial records of his existence.

Gudea, who was a King of Lagash in the 21st century BC, and who was a grandson of Ragau of the Bible, was also a great builder. Waddell had this to say about him:

> His [Gudea's] most remarkable building was a great tower-temple of seven stages erected for his city-god Nimirrud [Nimrod]..., the plan of which - the origin of the later fashionable

'Ziggurat' temple-towers - was, he says, revealed
to him in a dream. [Earlier small temple-towers
of the pre-Sargonic period are found at Nippur
and elsewhere.].[279]

Notice that by this time (21st century BC) Nimrod, the son of
Cush, was already deified.

Fig. 48 Sumer and Akkad

The descendants of Shem also became rulers in this area of Syria.
Arphaxad, Cainan, Salah, and Eber were all kings of Ebla and Awan,
cities in the north in Syria. We see then that as the families spread
out from the mountains of Ararat they settled first in Syria, at the
base of the mountains, and then at nearly the same time moved
into the Tigris/Euphrates plain into central Sumer. The tombs of
the famous heroes who founded Babel are located in Egypt. Egypt
early became the second center of civilization. One can now easily
understand why both Babylonians and Egyptians claimed to be the
first people in the world and how they also claimed their civiliza-

tion and their religious customs were the earliest. In Egypt we now trace the history of what occurred immediately after Babel.

Egyptian history opens with the First Dynasty. Its capital was Thinis in Upper Egypt. The names of the first four rulers of the First Dynasty are Menes, Athothis, Kenkenes and Uenephes.[280] The spelling of the names is from the Greek of Manetho. The early Egyptian forms vary slightly. Who were these famous individuals? Also known as Aha and Scorpion, Menes (Nimrod) was the first pharaoh of the First Dynasty in Egypt. He ruled from 3000 BC to 2850 B.C during the Protodynastic era of Egypt's history. This period was characterized by "firm political structure of the land which was unified by the pharaoh" (Ancient Egypt-Narmers Palette).[281]

Fig. 49 The Narmer Palette

Nimrod (Menes) was the first king to unify Upper and Lower Egypt into one kingdom.[282] Ancient Egypt's most predominant form of civilization began with his crowning. Flavius Josephus helps us in determining the date that Nimrod arrived in Egypt: "All the kings from Menes, who built Memphis, … until Solomon … was more than one thousand three hundred years."[283]

If we use the start of the reign of Solomon as our beginning date we can arrive at a rough date for the arrival of Nimrod in Egypt. Solomon started his reign in 971 BC By going backwards 1300 years from that date we arrive at 2271 BC as the time of Nimrod's arrival in Egypt. However, Egyptologist Ian Shaw, who has come up with dates for the pharaohs of Egypt, believed that the First Dynasty started about 3000 BC [284] [285] At this point it is not clear to me that it is possible to come to firm decisions regarding the dating of the First and Second Dynasties of Egypt. However, it also seems clear that Josephus is way too late in his statement. Nimrod probably left Sumer for Egypt shortly after the Tower of Babel incident, which I have estimated to have occurred around 2500 BC

Wilkinson describes the great work which entailed fame on Menes, who, he says, "is allowed by universal consent to have been the first sovereign of the country."[286] "Having diverted the course of the Nile, which formerly washed the foot of the sandy mountains of the Lybian chain, he obliged it to run in the centre of the valley, nearly at an equal distance between the two parallel ridges of mountains which border it on the east and west; and built the city of Memphis in the bed of the ancient channel. This change was effected by constructing a dyke about a hundred stadia above the site of the projected city, whose lofty mounds and strong embankments turned the water to the eastward, and effectually confined the river to its new bed. The dyke was carefully kept in repair by succeeding kings; and, even as late as the Persian invasion, a guard was always maintained there, to overlook the necessary repairs, and to watch over the state of the embankments."[287] Menes founded the city of Memphis, and chose as its location an island in the Nile, so that it would be easy to defend. He was also the founder of Crocodopolis where he built a temple to Ptah. During his time, the Egyptian army performed raids against the Nubians in the south and expanded his sphere of influence as far as the First Cataract.[288] His chief wife was Queen Berenib, though she was not the mother of his heir, King Djer, whose mother was Neithotepe (Inanna, or Ishtar), who, under the name Inanna, was another spouse of Nimrod in Sumer.[289]

Pharoah Narmer was also known as King Catfish, and was the last ruler of the Egyptian Dynasty 0 and was later recognized as the first pharaoh of the First Egyptian Dynasty. He contributed to the unification of Upper and Lower Egypt and this unification is shown both on the Palette and Macehead of Narmer. After the unification of the two Egypts, all later pharaohs were known as "ruler of the two lands" or "King of Upper and Lower Egypt."[290]

Fig. 50 Menes (Nimrod)

This warrior-god-king of either Thinite or Hieraconpolite origins brought about economic growth and political stability in Egypt. He fought against the Delta rulers, kept trade going with the near eastern colonies, and kept military control over Egypt's boundaries (Narmer). Narmer was married to a princess from the north called Nithotep. It is not known whether this princess was the same woman who was married to the Pharaoh Menes, or if Narmer and Nithotep had any children. Narmer reigned for at least 35 years and his tomb is at Abydos in the double grave of B17-18, which was excavated by Petrie in 1900.[291]

There is some controversy surrounding whether Narmer and Menes (Aha) are the same person or two or three separate people. The evidence that suggests they were the same man lies in two artifacts recovered at Nahal Tillah and in Umm el-Ka'ab. The first artifact discovered was the Narmer Palette found in Quibell. The palette shows King Narmer unifying Upper and Lower Egypt; on one end of the palette Narmer wears the red crown of Lower Egypt and on the other the white crown of Upper Egypt. At first glance it would appear that this is evidence of Narmer being a separate being from Menes. However, the Greek historian Herodotus had written in his work that Menes was the ruler that unified Egypt and the founder of the first dynasty.[292] One possible explanation of the two individuals being one ruler was found at the site Nahal Tillah. At this site a sherd was found with the serekh of king Narmer. This serekh had the Horus names of the Egyptian kings, showing that the Egyptian kings had five royal names, in this sherd also were the signs for mn (Menes) without further title but adjacent to the Horus name of Narmer. This would lead to the conclusion that Menes' royal name included Narmer. The same sherd contains the name Aha that could signify that Aha was part of King Menes' name. There is also the legend surrounding how Menes and Aha died. Both were said to have been attacked by a hippopotamus and killed. Whether a literal or representative hippo is not said but for both to have died in this same strange fashion seems highly unlikely. There is also the fact that both Menes and Aha have been credited with founding the city of Memphis.[293]

There is some evidence that Menes was the ruler of Lower Egypt at the time of the unification, Lower Egypt being the more civilized of the two halves. He is credited with building Memphis. Herodotus' history says that Menes (Min) was a great builder. Building Memphis required the damming of the Nile and the creation of a lake. He also built many temples in and around Memphis. Papyrus was invented during his reign, which led to the written evidence of his rule. His tomb has been located in Abydos with his mummy still intact.[294] This mummy, then, is the mummy of Nimrod, the son of Cush. Menes, like Nimrod of the Bible was called a "mighty warrior."[295] Narmer, Menes, and Aha were the same person. Narmer was Nimrod, who had left Babel after the confusion of languages, probably with his father Cush, and came to Egypt to set up a new kingdom.

There is one common element to Nimrod (who may have become identified with the Babylonian god Marduk) in all his manifestations and that is the symbol of the snake/serpent/dragon. Nimrod took the dragon as his personal emblem, so that from him sprang various dragon myths and their special association with apocalyptic events. Strikingly, the only favorable accounts of dragons are found among the Hamitic peoples of the world (like Nimrod) including the Egyptians, Ethiopians, Hittites, Chinese, Japanese, and so on.[296] That the worship of Nimrod and Semiramis (Ishtar/Innana) is the origin of all the pagan systems on earth is well documented by Alexander Hislop in his book, *The Two Babylons*, which contains many sound facts in spite of the author's anti-Roman-Catholic sentiments which appear to some readers as too strong.

The following is from the apocryphal *Book of Jasher*:

> And Cush the son of Ham, the son of Noah, took a wife in those days *in his old age*, and she

bare a son, and they called his name Nimrod. At that time the sons of men again began to rebel and transgress against God, and the child grew up, and his father loved him exceedingly, for he was the son *of his old age*. And the garments of skin which God made for Adam and his wife, when they went out of the garden, were given to Cush. For after the death of Adam and his wife, the garments were given to Enoch, the son of Jared, and when Enoch was taken up to God, he gave them to Methuselah, his son. And at the death of Methuselah, Noah took them and brought them to the Ark, and they were with him until he went out of the Ark. And in their going out, Ham stole those garments from Noah his father, and he took them and hid them from his brothers. And when Ham begat his first born Cush, he gave him the garments in secret, and they were with Cush many days. And Cush also concealed them from his sons and brothers, and when Cush had begotten Nimrod, he gave him those garments through his love for him, and Nimrod grew up, and when he was twenty years old he put on those garments. And Nimrod became strong when he put on the garments, and God gave him might and strength, and he was a mighty hunter in the earth, yea, he was a mighty hunter in the field, and he hunted the animals and he built altars, and he offered upon them the animals before the Lord. And Nimrod strengthened himself, and he rose up from amongst his brethren, and he fought the battles of his brethren against all their enemies round about.[297]

From *The Cave of Treasures*:

And when Nimrod went up from the east, and
began to practise the art of divining, very many
men marvelled at him. And when Îdhâshîr
(Ardeshir ?), the priest who ministered to
the fire that ascended from the earth, saw
that Nimrod was practising these exalted
courses, he entreated the devil, who appeared
in connection with that fire, to teach him the
wisdom of Nimrod. And as the devils were in
the habit of destroying those who came nigh
unto them by sin, the devil said unto the priest,
"A man cannot become a priest and a Magian
until he hath known carnally his mother, and
his daughter, and his sister." And Îdhâshîr the
priest did this, and from that time the priests,
and the Magians, and the Persians take their
mothers, and their sisters, and their daughters
[to wife]. And this Îdhâshîr, the Magian, was
the first to begin to study the Signs of the
Zodiac, and [omens concerning] luck, and
fate, and happenings, and motions of the eyes
and eyelids, as well as all the other arts of the
learning of the Chaldees [family of Kesed]. Now,
all this learning is the error of devils, and those
who practise it shall receive, together with the
devils, the doom of the Judgment. And because
this art of divination, which was employed by
Nimrod, was taught to him by Yôntôn, none of
the orthodox doctors have suppressed it; nay,
they have even practised it. Now the Persians
call it "Gelyânâ" (i.e. "Revelation") and the
Romans "Estrômîôn" (i.e., "Astronomy"). But
that [knowledge] which the Magians have, viz.
astrology, is sorcery and the teaching of devils.

There are some who say that it doth indeed
[teach concerning] luck, and happenings (i.e.
future events), and fate, but these are in error.
Now Nimrod builded strong cities in the east,
Babel, and Nineveh, and Râsân (Râs ʿAin)
[Resen], and Selîk: (Seleucia), and Ctesiphon,
and Âdhôrbaighân; and he made three
fortresses.[298]

According to the *Book of Jubiliees* it took 43 years to build the
Tower of Babel.[299]

In the *Book of Jasher* also comes this note:

And Nimrod dwelt in Babel, and he there
renewed his reign over the rest of his subjects,
and he reigned securely, and the subjects and
princes of Nimrod called his name Amraphel,
saying that at the tower his princes and men fell
through his means.[300]

Amraphel was not another possible name for Nimrod later. I will
address this after dealing with the descendants of Nimrod.

Chapter Twenty

Descendants of Nimrod, the Pharaohs

Athothis (Osiris), Son of Nimrod

A thothis, the son of Nimrod, was born around 3020 BC He was born in Babylon prior to Nimrod's move to Egypt. We know this because Damuzi Damu, his grandson, the son of Kenkenes, was the King of Uruk prior to Gilgamesh in about 2650 BC The father of Athothis, and Egypt's first king, was Menes. His name means "The Establisher,"[301] or "The Everlasting."[302] Menes was the first to establish himself as king in place of the Everlasting God. Menes, the father of Athothis, is Nimrod of the Bible: "And Cush begot Nimrod, he began to be a mighty one in the earth."[303] His son, Athothis, was the brother of Enmerkar of Ur.

Athothis, Egypt's second king, was also known as Osiris. The tomb of Athothis at Abydos was "the sepulchre of the god Osiris, and, as such, became the shrine to which millions of pilgrims made their way."[304] The Egyptian god Osiris was the Baal of the Phoenicians. Osiris was also associated with Marduk of the Babylonians and Tammuz of the Shemites. Osiris became upset with the ambitions of the sons of Naphtuhim (Neptune), descendants of Mizraim. The giants, sons of Neptune, held a judicial council, with the support of their father Neptune, and put Osiris to death. This event was a cause of great lamentation that was regularly observed in the religion of ancient Egypt, and the practice was passed on to the Greeks and Romans who lamented the death of Bacchus (Osiris). The reality was that the son of Nimrod, Athothis, apparently died at the hands of the descendant of Mizraim, who was a brother of Nimrod's father Cush.[305]

The Cairo fragment of the *Annals of Dynasties I-V* preserves a name of the mother of Athothis. She is Hept, meaning "the veiled one." This is a designation of Isis, the Sumerian goddess. The Assyrians called Isis (or Hept) Ishtar or Semiramis. In the Bible she is called Ashtoreth. This woman was originally the queen of Meni (Menes, Nimrod), Egypt's first king. She became Athothis' queen and wife after the death of Meni (Menes, who is Nimrod). Later, Athothis himself was slain in the 28th year of his reign in Egypt, according to Plutarch.[306]

Fig. 51

Athothis (Osiris) in the middle flanked by
his son Kenkenes (Horus) on the left and
Isis (Inanna of Sumer) on the right

The wife of Athothis, who goes by the name Hept, Isis, Ishtar, Semiramis, and Ashtoreth is actually Inanna, the goddess of Sumer. I will now present again the quote that was included above: "the devil said unto the priest, 'A man cannot become a priest and a Magian until he hath known carnally his mother, and his daughter, and his sister.'" I deal with Inanna at the end of this book and will show that the "religion" that was created was essentially based upon a sexual relationship with Inanna, or Ishtar. She had many names, but she had sexual relations with several of the descendants of Noah, thereby almost destroying the "royal" lineage leading to Jesus. This issue is so profound that it must be presented in its entirety later.

Another name that Athothis was called was Hor-Aha, short for Horus Aha. Hor-Aha (or Aha) is therefore also considered the second pharaoh of the First Dynasty of ancient Egypt in current Egyptology.[307] He lived around the thirty-first century BC The commonly used name Hor-Aha is a rendering of the pharaoh's "Horus" name, an element of the royal titulary associated with the god Horus, and is more fully given as Horus-Aha.

For the Early Dynastic Period, the archaeological record refers to the pharaohs by their Horus names, while the historical record, as evidenced in the Turin and Abydos kings' lists, uses an alternative royal name, the "nebty" name. The different name elements of a pharaoh were often used in isolation, for brevity's sake, although the choice varied according to circumstance and period. The majority of Egyptologists follow the findings of Petrie in reconciling the two records and connect Hor Aha (archaeological) with the nebty name Ity (historical). The same process has led to the identification of the historical Menes (a nebty name) with the Narmer (a Horus name) evidenced in the archaeological record (both figures are credited with the unification of Egypt and as the first pharaoh of the First Dynasty) as the predecessor of Hor Aha (the second pharaoh). We now know that Menes/Narmer was, in fact, Nimrod of the Bible. Hor-Aha's chief wife was Benerib, whose name was "written alongside his on a number of [historical] pieces, in particular, from tomb B14 at Abydos, Egypt." Tomb B14 is located directly adjacent to Hor-Aha's sepulchre. Hor-Aha also had another wife, Khenthap, with whom he became father of Djer. She is mentioned as Djer's mother on the Cairo Annals Stone.[308]

Kenkenes (Horus), son of Athothis

Kenkenes was born around 3000 BC, in Babylon. We know this because his son, Damuzi Damu, was the King of Uruk prior to Gilgamesh, meaning that he ruled there about 2650 BC The third name in the First Dynasty of Egpyt is Kenkenes, a Greek form of Kenken, meaning "The Terrible."[309] He was born, according to Egyptian tradition, after the death of Osiris (Athothis). His mother placed him on the throne, claiming he was the reincarnation of Osiris, or Athothis; hence, he is at times called Athothis, or Itit in early fragments, although that was his father. (These various names may be found in Sir Alan Gardiner's *Egypt of the Pharaohs* and in Weigall's *A History of the Pharaohs*). He was also named Horus, the son of Isis. Enmerkar was his uncle, the brother of Athothis. Every one of these famous men of old had many names. Of Nimrod, we read in the Epic of Creation: "As for us, by however many names we call him, he is our god. Let us then proclaim his fifty names ...."[310]

It was about 57 years after Nimrod (Menes) had come to Egypt, and after his death, that his widow Uenephes (or Isis) came back to Egypt with a son, Kenkenes (or Horus). Four years later she began a co-regency with him on the throne of Egypt. Isis (or Uenephes) thus temporarily triumphed over those who were responsible for the execution of Nimrod.[311] Eight years later, or 42 years after the death of Nimrod, the son Kenkenes (Horus) became supreme ruler as his mother turned over to him the reins of government. Horus (or Kenkenes) reigned altogether 39 years, alone for 31 years, the remainder with his mother. Uenephes, therefore, reigned, after her return from exile, for 12 years (four years alone and eight years with her son). Afterward, she returned to the throne again for 11 years following the departure of Kenkenes (Horus) for Sumer, making a total of 23 years.[312]

Manetho, the legendary Egyptian historian, regarded Kenkenes as a scholar, and credited him with an anatomy text book that apparently still existed in Greek times.[313] It has been suggested that he made a military campaign deep into Nubia since at Wadi Halfa his inscription was found. One of the king's regnal years was named, "The Year of Smiting the land of the Setjet." Setjet was a word identified with Syria-Palestine, and we also believe that he sent forces into the Sinai. There is also evidence that he made excursions into Libya to the west. These are the first recorded military campaigns outside of the "Two Lands" of Egypt.[314]

Kenkenes was also known by the name Horus Djer. Tradition provides that Djer's successor was Djet (Uadji), but there is evidence provided by large tombs at Saqqara (3503) and Abydos (Tomb Y) that there might have been a consort of Djer who may have ruled prior to Djet. Her name was Merneith, and a seal from Abydos that was recently found seems to confirm this, giving the order of early kings beginning with Narmer and referencing her as the King's Mother.[315] Djer's tomb lies at Umm el-Quab, at Abydos. It was a subterranean brick structure containing a wooden inner chamber, much more elaborate than those of his predecessors Aha (Athothis) and Narmer (Nimrod) and other kings from Dynasty 0 so far known. Djer's burial area also includes 300 retainer graves, more than do the earlier ones. Fragments of at least a dozen vessels of Syro-Palestinian origin were found in the tomb, confirming trade contacts between Egypt and its neighbors.[316] Although the tomb had been robbed, Flinders Petrie discovered an arm near the entrance, still wearing four bracelets. Three of these were composed of gold, amethyst, turquoise and lapis beads, the fourth consisting of 13 gold and 14 turquoise alternating plaques, with a pair of gold cone end pieces. The arm has been lost, but the bracelets are now in the Cairo Museum.[317]

Ivory and wood labels are best direct evidence for the existence of Djer, since writing was still in its early stages. One example is an ivory label found at Saqqara. A Horus-falcon surmounts the serekh containing the king's name. Small figures advance to the serekh carrying offerings, while a mummy, or perhaps a statue, follows. Others carry a fish, a bird and a great spear to the falcon. At the other end of the label, two figures are shown, one whose arms appear to be drawn back or pinioned, and another apparently plunging a knife into the first. The figure wielding the knife also holds some sort of vessel, perhaps to catch the flowing blood.[318] Another ivory label includes characters for two ships, the sign for "town" and Djer's name in the serekh. The label may record a visit to the Delta cities of Buto and to Sais.[319]

The son of Kenkenes by his mother/consort Inanna was Damuzi Damu.

Damuzi Damu (Tammuz), the Son of Kenkenes

Semiramis (Inanna) became the consort of her son Kenkenes. They had a son whom she named Damu (from the Sumerian "dam," or blood), which in the later Babylonian language became Dammuzi, and in Hebrew Tammuz. Semiramis assumed the regency for her infant son, and ruled as absolute monarch over Babylon for 42 more years. She was not unopposed in her arrogation of the regency, however, or her rule as a woman. The military arm of the government was divided into two camps for and against her, and a short war ensued which ended when the populace (roused by the priesthood) not only refused to support the "rebels" but actively opposed them. During this war, however, the opposition got so close that Semiramis was forced to build a system of walls, towers, and gates around Babylon to defend herself. She was thus the first to build fortifications and her crown afterwards was in the form of the turreted walls of Babylon in Sumer. To aggrandize herself, she had herself declared the mother of the god Damu (since only a god can beget a god) , and installed as

"The Queen of Heaven" pictured in the constellation Cassiopeia, which the ancients had intended as a corporate representation of those people faithful to God who will be enthroned by Him after the end of the age.

Enmebaragesi, according to the Sumerian King List, was a king of Kish who subdued Elam and reigned 900 years, but was captured single handedly by King Dumuzi "the fisherman" of Uruk, predecessor of King Gilgamesh of Uruk, the son of Kesed. In the Sumerian King List Dumuzi the Fisherman appears as the king whose city was Kua, and who reigned 100 years, the third king of the first dynasty of Uruk, reigning between Lugalbanda and Gilgamesh. In other texts Dumuzi is always a shepherd, not a fisherman.

After the Tower of Babel incident, around 2500 BC, Nimrod and Inanna took the family, including Athothis (who had Inanna his mother as his consort), Kenkenes (who had Inanna his grandmother and his mother as his consort), and Dumuzi and they departed Babylon for good and went to Egypt where they continued the empire that Nimrod had started. Inanna, amazingly, also had relations with her son Dumuzi. Unfortunately, in spite of her affairs with her children and their children, she also sowed the seeds of her own destruction. As she raised her son Dumizu, she imbued him with divinity in the eyes of the priests and people as the means of retaining control as the divine mother without seeming to aggrandize herself too far. As Damuzi grew he became used to having every whim instantly gratified by a subservient populace. For safety's sake he had a personal bodyguard constantly at his side which formed an elite corps of soldiery loyal and accountable to him alone. Upon coming to maturity and demanding of his mother to be installed as king, she refused him this because she saw him as a challenge to her own rule. She therefore slated him for the same death she had meted to his father Kenkenes. Damu realized her scheme, and pre-empted his "assumption into heaven" by slaying his mother with his own sword, and putting down any priestly protests by purging the hierarchy of all who would not vow allegiance to him. Thus, Semiramis (Inanna the goddess, daughter of Nannar) died after reigning as queen over Egypt.

These events laid the groundwork for the pagan religious systems of antiquity, as well as many alive today. Semiramis was the model and original of every goddess and female cult figure in the ancient and modern worlds (either directly or by derivation); thus, it is essential to know her story to discern what is factual legend and what is merely myth. Dumuzi is the Sumerian form of the Semitic name Tammuz, a god of vegetation, fertility, and the underworld. He is called "the Shepherd" and "lord of the sheepfolds." As the companion of Nigizzida "to all eternity" he stands at the gate of heaven. In the Sumerian story "Descent of Inanna" he is the husband of the goddess Inanna, the Sumerian counterpart of Ishtar. Dumuzi was originally a mortal ruler whose marriage to his mother Inanna ensured the fertility of the land and the fecundity of the womb.

Chapter Twenty-One

Enmerkar, the Son of Nimrod
(c. 2820 BC – 2057 BC)

E nmerkar, who lived about 760 years, is also called the "son of Utu."[320] This comes from an ancient story called *Enmerkar and the Lord of Aratta*. While it is not the case that he was born of Utu, a Sumerian god, it is a sign that claims to divinity were beginning to develop shortly after the sons of Noah spread over the lands. By claiming himself as a "son of Utu" he was essentially claiming divinity for himself.

Enmerkar was the "builder of Uruk" according to the Sumerian King lists, although his father Meshkiaggasar is also named as the builder of Uruk. Since the Bible indicates that the builder of Uruk was Nimrod, then Nimrod would be Meshkiaggasar, the "first" builder of Uruk. Enmerkar, his son, made substantial improvements to the city. He reigned for 420 years according to that list.[321]

Enmerkar's mother was Inanna the goddess. Therefore, he was in fact "semi-divine." Enmerkar was also the lover/husband of his mother Inanna, thereby fulfilling the command made to his father, Nimrod (Meshkiaggasar): "The devil said unto the priest, 'A man cannot become a priest and a Magian until he hath known carnally

213

his mother, and his daughter, and his sister.'" Here is confirmation of the age-old tradition that Enmerkar, like Nimrod, married his own mother, and from this union came an offspring, Lugalbanda. This theme will be more fully developed when I discuss Inanna and her many consorts.

> "In a Sacred Marriage–related text from the Ur III period of Mesopotamia, Ensuhkesdanna, Lord of Aratta, challenges his rival, Enmerkar, King of Uruk, by claiming to be the true husband of the goddess Inanna. As Inanna is particularly the patroness of Uruk and the ritual "bride" of its king, Enmerkar takes the challenge seriously and reacts with great anger, condemning Ensuhkesdanna and asserting his right to Inanna. The King of Aratta sends a magician to Eres, a town near Uruk, where he dries up the milk of the sacred stables. The shepherds in the area beg the god Utu for help, and suddenly Sagburru, a wise crone from Eres, comes on the scene and challenges the sorcerer of Aratta to a contest involving the transformation of objects. Both magicians throw metal objects into the river. The man's turns into a carp, the woman's into an eagle that eats the carp. Then the man's ewe and lamb are eaten by the woman's wolf, and so it goes until the man gives in and the old woman throws him to his death in the river. Upon hearing the news, Ensuhkesdanna agrees that Enmerkar is the true bridegroom of Inanna."[322]

Aratta was originally thought to be the Sumerian city Shuruppak, but that is no longer seen to be the case. Although Aratta is known only from these ancient stories, which are often thought to be myths, some archaeologists have speculated on possible locations where Aratta could have been, using criteria from those myths. This was done to find the ancient city of Troy successfully, using Homer's *Illiad*, which, until Troy was discovered in the late 1800s, was considered to be "mythological."

The criteria used to find the land of Aratta include the following:

1. Land travelers must pass through Susa and the mountainous Anshan region in Elam to reach it. We know this to be east of Sumer.

2. It is a source of, or has access to valuable gems and minerals, including lapis lazuli, that are crafted on site. This would tend to indicate a mountainous region, thereby eliminating the valley east of the Tigris River in what is now known as Iran but before the Zagros Mountains.

3. It is accessible to Uruk by watercourse, yet remote from Uruk. Uruk lies on the Euphrates River. If one traveled south on that river it would join the Tigris River at the lower end of Sumer. Traveling then up the Tigris River one would first reach the Karheh River. However, this is still in the valley region and there were no gems found in the valley. Moving farther north there are, however, two more rivers that feed the Tigris. The first, roughly parallel to Babylon in central Sumer, is not large enough to have been the river in question. The next, called the Diyala River, forks off to the east above Sumer's Sippar and gradually goes northeast around the top of the Zagros Mountains. It has several tributaries in the upper plains.

4. Finally, it is close enough for a twenty-seventh century BC Sumerian army to march there. Since Sumer consists of an enormous valley through which both the Tigris and Euphrates rivers flow, it is evident that an army could easily move to Sippar, situated roughly midway between the rivers in central Sumer. From there it would move up the Diyala River basin until it reached Aratta.

Therefore, we may safely conclude that the "mythical" Aratta was in fact an ancient city-state in what is now Iran just at the northern end of the Zagros Mountains, north and east of Sippar in central Sumer. This would place Aratta in the upper plains area of today's northern Iran near what is now known as Arak. The area is surrounded by the mountains and would have met all the criteria named above, including the ability of an army from Sumer to get there in the twenty-seventh century BC Aratta is, then, the ancient northern Iranian civilization which was started around 2800 BC Inanna, having established the culture and civilization there, had become bored with it and desired to come to Mesopotamia where her fellow "gods" had worship centers and where there was more activity. It was shortly after her return from Aratta that she joined Nimrod, the son of Cush and grandson of Ham, in Egypt where they both were eventually worshipped.

Enmerkar, the son of Nimrod and Inanna, sent emissaries to Aratta, using every possible argument in a "war of nerves" to force Aratta to submit because "the lord Enmerkar who is servant of Inanna made her queen of the House of Anu." Although Inanna did move to the "House of Anu" in Uruk in the flatlands of Sumer, she continued to remain the goddess of the mountainous Land of Aratta.

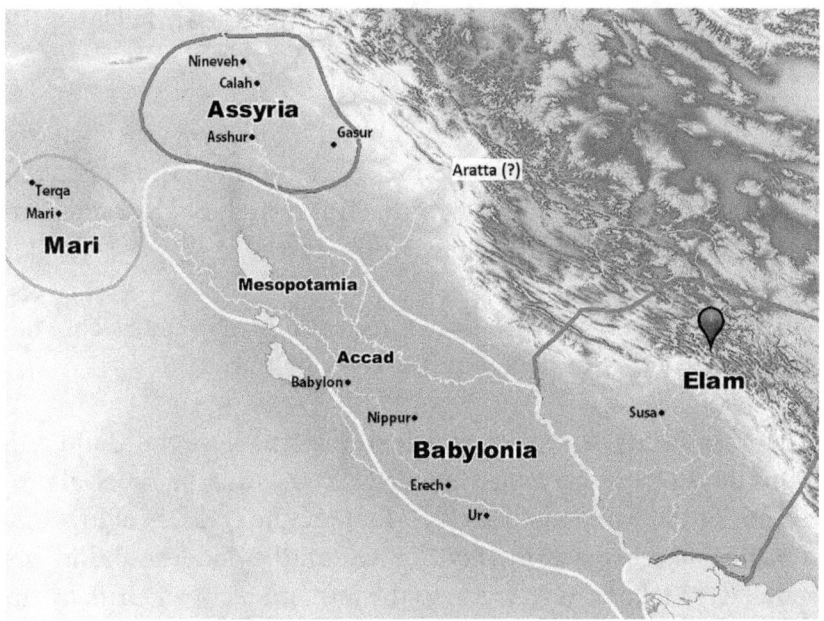

Fig. 52 Map showing possible location of Aratta

It was during the reign of Enmerkar that Sumerian tales say that the confusion of the languages of men occurred, estimated to be around 2500 BC This is a second confirmation that Enmerkar is related to Nimrod, who also was ruler of Babylon when the languages were confounded. Here is a quote from the epic poem *Enmerkar and the Lord of Aratta:*

> Once on a time there was .. no hyena, .. terror,
> Man had no rival.
> In those days, .. the land having all that is appropriate (?),
> .. resting in security,
> **The whole universe, the people in unison (?)**
> **To Enlil in one tongue [spoke]. ...**
> **(Then) Enki, the lord .. (whose) commands are trustworthy, ...**
> **Changed the speech in their mouths**, [brought (?)] contention into it,

Into the speech of man that (until then) had
been one.[323]

This is consistent with the Biblical statement in Genesis:
"Therefore its name is called Babel, because **there the Lord confused the language** of all the earth; and from there the Lord scattered them abroad over the face of the earth."[324]

The timing of the latter part of Enmerkar's reign is consistent with
the timing of the confusion in the days of Nimrod.

Aratta was a city-state with which Sumer had close trade and religious ties in the third millennium BC It was under the special protection of the Sun god's daughter, Inanna, the goddess of love and
war. In *Enmerkar and the Lord of Aratta*, the goddess and/or her
statue were taken from Aratta to the Sumerian city of Uruk by the
ruler of Uruk, who was Enmerkar. He then apparently believed
himself to have the goddess' protection, so he challenged the lord
of Aratta, who just happened to be his brother! How do we know
this?

The Iranic or Irano-Afghan race has dominated the plains of
Mesopotamia since Sumerian times, as the learned American
anthropologist Prof. C. S. Coon notes: "The Irano-Afghan race,
prominent since Sumerian times in Mesopotamia, is the chief population element in the entire highland territory from the western
border of Iran to northern India." [325]

Indeed, Iranic populations appear to have entered the ruling caste
of Sumer even prior to the Gutian invasion. Thus, Izady notes, "A
startling fact came to light when the Sumerologist S.N. Kramer
translated a Sumerian tablet revealing that **Enmerkar himself was
a brother of the king of Aratta**, and therefore, presumably a native
of the Kurdish mountains."[326] (emphasis mine)

Enmerkar, then, ordered his own brother, Enshukeshdanna (or Ensuhgir-ana), to send Sumer precious metals, precious stones, building materials and the craftsmen to transform them into shrines. The lord of Aratta was willing to provide the materials if Enmerkar would send him large amounts of barley. When the barley arrived in Aratta, however, the King of Aratta unexpectedly refused to fulfill his part of the agreement. After ten years, Enmerkar again sent his herald to his brother, the King of Aratta. This time, the lord of Aratta challenged Enmerkar to select one of his champions to fight in single combat with one of Aratta's champions. Enmerkar accepted. Because his response was lengthy and his herald was "heavy of mouth," Enmerkar inscribed his message on 20 clay tablets and sent them to Aratta with his herald. However, at this point the famine, which apparently had been plaguing Aratta, lifted and Aratta's King took courage, believing that Inanna had not really abandoned him. Although the ending of this "myth" is fragmentary, Aratta eventually seems to have provided the materials and craftsmen to Enmerkar.[327]

Aratta is mentioned again in a second briefer story known as "Lugulbanda and Enmerkar." In this story, Enmerkar of Uruk was under military attack from the Martu people. Enmerkar desperately sent his messenger, Lugulbanda, to Aratta to the goddess Inanna, here called his sister [!]. Inanna's response is unclear. However, it appears that Aratta again supplied Enmerkar with metals, precious stones, and craftsmen; and there is a suggestion that the materials were transported to Uruk by river. Finally, Aratta appears in a fourth story, "Lugulbanda and Mount Hurum." Enmerkar and his army were traveling to Aratta to make it a vassal state. En route they stopped at Mount Hurum where Lugulbanda became ill and "died." His comrades placed his body on Mount Hurum, intending to retrieve it after their war in Aratta. However, Lugulbanda was not really dead. After praying to the sun, moon, and the star Venus, he emerged from his trance and wandered the highlands. Unfortunately, the ending of this story is lost.[328]

The stories outlined above portray Aratta as a wealthy and militarily powerful state with which Sumer had relations from very early times. It was located some distance from Sumer and protected by its forbidding mountains, but it was not so distant as to prevent trade relations. Aratta had building materials, precious stones, metals and craftsmen skilled in their transformation. Aratta also had primacy regarding the religion of the mother goddess, Inanna, who resided in Aratta, who was the patron of that state, and who was taken or lured south to the Sumerian city of Uruk. Uruk and Aratta, also, were in contest for military superiority, each demanding the submission of the other.

Fig. 53 Artist Rendering of the Eridu
Temple, built by Enmerkar

The King Enmerkar of Uruk promulgated a confederated system in which all the lesser ensis (kings, or sub-kings) of cities in Sumeria would get one vote in joint policy making and Enmerkar would get 35, to balance the other votes. City-states normally had wide ranging freedom, especially in defense matters. This made for an unstable government and many times Sumerian cities united to install a new Lugal. In fact, Mesilim was installed by an allied army for Kish, Uruk, and Lagash which overthrew the Lugal of Larsa.[329] Enmerkar is credited with building one of the largest temples in Sumer at Eridu. Some scholars suspect that this temple may have been where the original Tower of Babel was located, although that is not the general consensus.

Lugalbanda, the Son of Enmerkar

Sumerian literary tradition states that Lugalbanda, in his own right, was a god-king of the city of Uruk.[330] He is sometimes held to be Gilgamesh's father although Gilgamesh's parents were Ninsun and Kesed of Kullab. In fact, Lugalbanda was the son of Inanna and Enmerkar, the king of Uruk. Zechariah Sitchin provides the details:

> This habit of Inanna [of having sexual encounters with a king and then with his son] may have begun with Enmerkar himself, a sexual union of which the next ruler of Uruk, a demigod known as "divine Lugalbanda, a Righteous Supervisor," was the progeny. Of Lugalbanda, who, as of Enmerkar, several epic tales have been found. Inanna, it seems, wanted him to reside in her stead in Aratta; but Lugalbanda was too restless and adventurous to stay put.[331]

We know of Lugalbanda from a story found among the ruins entitled "Lugalbanda in the Mountain Cave." At the time of this adventure Lugalbanda seems to have been a young officer in Enmerkar's army commanding a division of Uruk's troops. Enmerkar was the son of Nimrod in the Bible. Again in this "myth," we have Aratta (in northern Iran) as the city rival to Uruk, and a bizarre adventure that took place on the road from Uruk to Aratta. The story states that halfway along the mountain road to Aratta, Lugalbanda was stricken with a strange overpowering fever that baffled his companions. The best they could do, as his teeth chattered in the cold, was to find him a dry cave in which to shelter. There Lugalbanda lay deeply unconscious for so long that his companions feared that he might pass away while they went in search for help. They prepared the crude cave as if for a funeral, laying out food and drink in the traditional Sumerian manner and placing Lugalbanda's weapons beside him. If he lived, so much the better: he would have sustenance to give him strength. If he died, he would do so with dignity among the funerary goods and his companions would retrieve his body on their return from the campaign. With tears and lamentations, they left him to his fate.

But Lugalbanda did not die. After days laying unconscious in a coma he awoke. He was still feverish, and his barren surroundings appalled him. Brought up in the rich cities of Mesopotamia, the hostile mountains seemed to him a place of horror, so he prayed to the sun god Utu (Shamash) and this god's twin sister, Inanna (Ishtar), the Great Goddess of Love and War: "In the mountain cave, the most dreadful spot upon the Earth, let me be ill no longer! May my limbs not perish in the mountains!"[332] Lugalbanda, nevertheless, need not have feared for his life. Utu and Inanna heard his pleas, and, as a sign, sent him a complex dream in which Lugalbanda found himself wandering through the mountains by moonlight. In this dream, the god Zangara came to him in the form of a bull and hinted that he should capture the wild goats and, more importantly, the great bull of the mountains and offer them in sacrifice. "Who will melt their fat for me?" asked the god, "He should take my axe of tin, and my dagger, which is iron."[333] When Lugalbanda awoke, his fever had gone but the dream remained with him. As instructed in the dream, he hunted a wild bull of the mountains and offered it in sacrifce. The sacrifice was enough to restore Lugalbanda's health in full measure. Here the text breaks, although a retelling of the myth suggests that he received an invaluable gift from the fierce Anzu bird, from whom he had gained approval having fed the bird's chicks. However, Lugalbanda was, indeed, saved from the brink of death by the gods, who have fed him as one of their own, one of those "who have a place in Inanna's heart....who stand in the battle."[334]

Chapter Twenty-Two

Enshukeshdanna, Son of Nimrod and Lord of Aratta (c. 2820 BC)

Enshukeshdanna was the brother of Enmerkar. Both were the sons of Nimrod. He was obviously a younger brother of Enmerkar, since the Sumerian King List states clearly that Enmerkar was the founder and builder of Uruk. However, Enshukeshdanna is listed as the first King of Uruk in the Second dynasty of that city-state. Being the brother of Enmerkar, the founder of Uruk, he was actually a part of the First dynasty of that city-state. He probably took over the rulership of Uruk when his brothers, Enmerkar and Athothis, left Sumer with their father, Nimrod, after the Tower of Babel incident. Earlier, he was the King of Aratta. He reigned over Uruk about 2500 BC Under Enshukeshdanna, Uruk conquered Hamazi, Agade, Kish, and Nippur to claim hegemony over all of Sumer. He also threw the Elamites out of Awan. He was the first ruler known to take the Sumerian title *en ki-en-gi ki-uri*, or "lord of Sumer and Akkad." Despite his own conquests, he was briefly subject to Eannatum of Lagash.[335]

Enmerkar was the priest-king of Uruk, and, as such, the ritual husband of the Great Goddess Inanna, upon whose favour the city's prosperity depended. But the city of Aratta, in the snow-capped mountains that border Mesopotamia, was also under the protection of the Goddess, and ruled by a priest-king devoted to her as well. To please the gods, Enmerkar planned to build a lavish temple in Uruk which would be the first of its kind. There was only one big problem: Enmerkar had none of the precious stones and metals he needed to decorate the temple. But Aratta, located in the mountains, was famous for its gold and precious stones, and it was to the lord of Aratta that Enmerkar turned. He sent a messenger to the city of Aratta, saying that the Goddess Inanna preferred Uruk and himself, Enmerkar, over Aratta and its ruler, his brother Enshukeshdanna. In case Aratta refused to submit to Uruk, war was going to be declared and Uruk swore to pursue the utter destruction of the other city.

But despite the threats from Uruk and the famine that threatened to afflict Aratta, Enshukeshdanna was firm in his resolve not to submit to Uruk. Indeed, even knowing that the goddess might have abandoned him to his luck, he proposed to his rival a series of three tasks, all impossible for Enmerkar to achieve. First, Enshukeshdanna requested Uruk grain to ease the famine in Aratta, but to test Enmerkar he insisted that the grain be delivered in open nets, not in sacks. Enmerkar quickly found a solution, for not only Inanna, but Nisaba, the Grain Goddess, decided to side with Enmerkar. On the Goddess Nisaba's advice, Enmerkar sent to Aratta grain that was so swollen with fermentation that it would not fall through the nets. With the grain he sent a message demanding that Aratta accept, in a well-understood gesture of submission, a sceptre from Uruk. "So be it," agreed Enshukeshdanna, but only if the sceptre were a unique one. "Let it be not wood, or called by the name of wood..." and he continued with a long list including every material known to him. Once more, Enmerkar found an answer, thanks to the intervention of Enki, the god of magic and of wisdom. On Enki's advice, Enmerkar grew a sceptre from a type of reed, the like of which had never been seen before in Sumer. His rival was baffled again. A last challenge was then issued. The matter should be decided by a single combat between champions from the two cities. Enmerkar's champion, nevertheless, had to be dressed in colors that were not black, white, nor brown nor green nor any hue at all. This time Enmerkar found the answer without divine aid: his champion was going to wear undyed cloth of no named color.

The tale omits details of the combat, but we do have another composition that deals with the combat of two sorcerers from both lands, the champion of Uruk being a sorceress. The sorceress from Uruk beat up the sorcerer from Aratta. But while victory in the magical battleground is given to Uruk, rain returned to water the dry fields of Aratta, thus saving the year's harvest. There was no need for Aratta to bow to Uruk as in utter subjection, despite that Enmerkar had won the magical contest. Who was the victor, who the loser? Apparently, the battle between the two brothers ended in a standoff. The epic finished with the coming of an old woman now transformed into a maiden out of the mountain (a symbol for the Underworld), and this maiden espoused Enmerkar, the first in Inanna's heart. Aratta, nevertheless, was not destroyed, because it had a harvest, famine was over, and in the end, Inanna never intended for Aratta to be destroyed. Enmerkar, on the other hand, never really stood a chance of destroying Aratta to build his temples. Why so? Because no temple can be built upon an unstable foundation, and this was one of the unstated lessons he had to learn. On Aratta's side, it had to help Uruk build the temple, lending its precious metals and craftsmen, but the city itself did not starve and continued as free and independent as ever.

Legends state that when the gods first came down to the Earth, they built the city of Aratta on the highest mountaintops to be nearer to Heaven. The mountain range, today's Zagros Mountains, was called the Land of the Gods. The gods lived in the city of Aratta with their servants, human mortals, nearby. Later, after the gods abandoned the city and moved down to the plain of Sumer, humans took over the city. When the other gods left, a young goddess named Inanna, who had been born on the Earth and had therefore not been assigned a mission, took it on herself to take charge of Aratta. She remained its tutelary goddess, until Anu, the father of the gods, named her to be the Queen of Heaven. As Inanna, she followed the other gods down to the plain of Sumer, where she took over the city of Zabalam on the Iturungal Canal. The Lord of Aratta pleaded for Inanna to return, but to no avail. The mountainlands grew lawless and became the home of bandits. They were, thereafter, called the Hursag and regarded as both foreign and hostile.

Aratta is located in the Zagros Mountains, possibly at the archaeological site of Godin, six miles east of Kangavar in southern Kurdistan in Iran.

I found the following article so fascinating that I decided to include it in its entirety. The article will conclude this chapter.

Kurdistan, Where Credit is Due
By Dr. Mehrdad R. Izady

In correspondence with the prestigious British scientific journal, *Nature* Vol.360,5, (Nov. 1992): p.24, Rudolph Michel of the Museum of Applied Science, Center for Archaeology, Patrick McGovern of University Museum of Archaeology and Anthropology, University of Pennsylvania and Virginia Badler, Department of Near Eastern Studies, University of Toronto, provide archaeological and laboratory evidence regarding the world's oldest existing trace of the production of barley beer. Their investigations took place at the archaeological site of Godin, six miles (10 kilometers) east of Kangawar in southern Kurdistan in Iran. It was at this same site where, a few years earlier, evidence of the earliest grape wine production (also dating between 4000-4500 years ago) was found by the Royal Ontario Museum of Canada team that originally excavated the site.

The disturbing, but not surprising, element in their report is that they attribute the development of beer making technology to the far off Sumerians, just as several years earlier winemaking technology was similarly attributed to the Sumerians. Yet for the past three generations it has been in Kurdistan where archaeologists have been excavating to find evidence for the invention and development of the technologies that transformed man-the-hunter into man-the-farmer and ultimately into man-the-civilized. It is as if the Kurdish mountains and their inhabitants could not possibly have been the site of technologies of such significance, despite irrefutable evidence that they themselves unearthed. Almost instinctively, archaeologists have been reluctant to attribute origins to the original inhabitants of Kurdistan. Instead, they continue to search for external originating sources, at times with a measure of desperation. When such a source eludes them, they tend to list the originating culture as "unknown." By contrast, when evidence is found in other loci of civilization, as in Mesopotamia, Egypt or Greece, for example, it is automatically attributed to these cultures until proven otherwise.

The reverse is true in treating cultures of the Kurdish Mountains. The irony is that, as in the case of beer and wine discoveries, the argument supporting Sumerian involvement is based on evidence that is not only indirect but of later date (i.e., from seal impressions). Kurdish hard evidence deriving from actual fermentation vats complete with dried calcium oxalate sediments (beer residue), is dismissed. Yet Michel et. al. admit that the carbonized remains of barley used in preparation of the beer was also found first at Godin, as were grapes used for wine making. A brief but close examination of the archaeological evidence and the relationship that existed between Kurdish mountain societies and the Sumerians indicate both the direction of influence and the reasons behind it.

Godin was by no means the isolated incidence of technological sophistication in an otherwise culturally and technologically barren region that would justify the search for an external civilizing influence. In fact, the mound of Godin (or Gawdin) is located in one of the world's richest archaeological regions stretching for one hundred miles from Shahabad, one of the capitals of the ancient Elamites, to Hamadan, the capital of the ancient Medians. In this region the problem for the archaeologist is not where to excavate but which to choose from the literally hundreds of mounds, temples, palace complexes and cave habitats. Here one finds some of the earliest evidence of the domestication of cereals (e.g., barley and wheat), livestock (e.g., goats and sheep) and development of other basic technologies dating back 11000 years (Braidwood et al, 1960). Additionally, in the same region are found remains of the world's oldest glazed pottery at Seh Gabi (Levine, 1974; Vandiver, 1990), earliest experiments with writing and accounting at Godin and Ganj Dara (Schmandt-Besserat, 1986; Nissen, 1986; Green, 1981), and now, wine and beer. At a time when most of the rest of the world inhabited caves, Godin appears to have been a major city with well planned and solidly constructed buildings, a city contemporaneous with the oldest cities of Sumeria and Akkadia. Today Godin can be seen as an imposing mound on the eastern horizon if one stands on the remains of its 2300-year-old grand staircases and the vast colonnaded temple platform of the Goddess Anahita at Kangawar.

This entire archaeological region straddles the old Silk Road which is predated by millenia by other important commercial arteries of the ancient world connecting East to West over the Iranian Plateau, lowland Mesopotamia and the Levant. As such, the region boasted a commerce oriented civilization that exported many of its technological achievements and products and now holds the remains of artifacts and raw materials imported from far away sources and cultures.

About 4500 years ago, this region served as the heartland of the native empire of the Qutils [Guti], who were among the Hurrian, Palaeo-Caucasic ancestors of the modern Kurds before their Arianization by immigrating

Indo-European tribes: Medes, Sagarthians and Scytho-Alans. Qutil [Guti] military might soon have expanded from their capital of Aratta and the Kurdish mountains to subdue every neighboring region including Sumeria and Akkad. In light of the discovery at Godin of many well constructed buildings, a wealth of artifacts and new technology, the city is the strongest candidate for the site of ancient Aratta.

The Qutil [Guti] general, Merkar [Enmerkar], declared his independence from the mountain domains of the Qutil [Guti] Federation, whose king was his own brother [Ensukushsiranna]. Having broken away from Aratta, circa 2500 BC [this should be 2800 BC], Merkar succeeded in establishing a separate Qutil dynasty that ruled independently over Sumerian and Akkadian city-states. Merkar took the reknowned Uruk (Erech-Kullab) of Gilgamesh for his capital. The Qutils actually settled and flourished in large numbers in Sumeria, populating, among others, the twin city of Kesh-Adab (Kramer, 1987). Conversely, there has never been any evidence to indicate that the Sumerians expanded, let alone settled any part of the far off Kurdish highlands.

It is absolutely extraordinary that to this day, tablets have survived that record the correspondence between the Qutil ruler in Aratta and the rebellious Merkar (commonly known as Enmerkar, after he took up the Sumerian royal title of En). These now represent some of the most valuable written records of the history of the Kurdish highlands in ancient times. Fortunately, S. Noah Kramer, the foremost Sumerialogist, has translated this correspondence establishing that there was a good deal of commercial and political contact between Aratta and Uruk. In none of this correspondence is there a hint that the society at Aratta (Godin?) was less sophisticated or perceived as such by the Uruk of Sumeria.

Since the Kurdish mountains are the natural habitat of wild barley, wheat and many other cereals and evidence points to domestication there and not in the Sumerian marshlands and deserts where domesticated cereals were introduced from the highlands at a much later date one can logically conclude that the fermented product of barley for beer making also originated in the same highlands. Recent archaeological evidence alluded to above only reinforces this logic. In fact, the beer and wine discovered at Godin date from the precise time period of the Qutil takeover of Sumeria and could have been introduced by the group which gave rise to Enmerkar in Sumeria. Indirect Sumerian evidence from sealings depicting people drinking beer through straws from a common vat post-dates the Qutil dynasty of that land.

Moreover, the Sumerian tablets also record another introduction into Sumeria by the Qutil, Enmerkar, the cult of the birdgod Anzu, still worshipped by the Yezidi Kurds as the bird icon Anzul (or Anzal).

In the Yazidi belief system, God created the world and it is now in the care of a *Heptad* of seven holy beings, often known as angels or *heft sirr* (the Seven Mysteries). Preeminent among these is Tawuse Melek (frequently known as "Melek Taus" in English publications), the Peacock Angel. According to the *Encyclopedia of the Orient*,

> The reason for the Yazidis reputation of being devil worshipers is connected to the other name of Melek Taus, Shaytan, the same name the Koran has for Satan.[336]

Furthermore, the Yazidi story regarding Tawuse Melek's rise to favor with God is almost identical to the story of the jinn Iblis in Islam, except that Yazidis revere Tawuse Melek for refusing to submit to Adam, while Muslims believe that Iblis' refusal to submit caused him to fall out of Grace with God, and to later become Satan himself.[337]

Tawuse Melek is often identified by Muslims and Christians with Shaitan (Satan). Yazidis, however, believe Tawuse Melek is not a source of evil or wickedness. They consider him to be the leader of the archangels, not a fallen angel. They also hold that the source of evil is in the heart and spirit of humans themselves, not in Tawuse Melek. The active forces in their religion are Tawuse Melek and Sheik Adi.

The Kiteba Cilwe "Book of Illumination," which claims to be the words of Tawuse Melek, and which presumably represents Yazidi belief, states that he allocates responsibilities, blessings and misfortunes as he sees fit and that it is not for the race of Adam to question him. Sheikh Adi believed that the spirit of Tawuse Melek is the same as his own, perhaps as a reincarnation. He is believed to have said:

> "I was present when Adam was living in Paradise, and also when Nemrud threw Abraham in fire. I was present when God said to me: 'You are the ruler and Lord on the Earth'. God, the compassionate, gave me seven earths and throne of the heaven."

Yazidi accounts of creation differ from that of Judaism, Christianity, and Islam. They believe that God first created Tawuse Melek from his own illumination (*Ronahi*) and the other six archangels were created later. God ordered Tawuse Melek not to bow to other beings. Then God created the other archangels and ordered them to bring him dust (*Ax*) from the Earth (*Erd*) and build the body of Adam. Then God gave life to Adam from his own breath and instructed all archangels to bow to Adam. The archangels obeyed except for Tawuse Melek. In answer to God, Tawuse Melek replied, "How can I submit to another being! I am from your illumination while Adam is made of dust." Then God praised him and made him the leader of all angels and his deputy on the Earth. (This likely furthers what some see as a connection to the Islamic *Shaytan*, as according to the Koran he too refused to bow to Adam at God's command, though in this case it is seen as being a sign of Shaytan's sinful pride.) Hence the Yazidis believe that Tawuse Melek is the representative of God on the face of the Earth, and came down to the Earth. Yazidis argue that the order to bow to Adam was only a test for Tawuse Melek, since if God commands anything then it must happen. (*Bibe, dibe*). In other words, God could have made him submit to Adam, but gave Tawuse Melek the choice as a test. They believe that their respect and praise for Tawuse Melek is a way to acknowledge his majestic and sublime nature. This idea is called "Knowledge of the Sublime" (*Zanista Ciwaniye*).

One of the key creation beliefs of Yazidism is that all Yazidis are descendants of Adam rather than Eve.[338] Yazidis believe that good and evil both exist in the mind and spirit of human beings. It depends on the humans, themselves, as to which they choose. In this process, their devotion to Tawuse Melek is essential, since it was he who was given the same choice between good and evil by God, and chose the good, according to their faith.

The followers of the Yezidi religion, who have variously referred to themselves also as the Yazidi, Yazdâni, Izadi, and Dasna'i, have often been pejoratively referred to by outsiders as "devil worshippers." They constitute less than 5% of the Kurdish population. At present they live in fragmented pockets, primarily in northwest and northeast Syria, the Caucasus, southeast Turkey, in the Jabal Sanjâr highlands on the Iraqi-Syrian border, and regions north of the Iraqi city of Mosul.

From Yezidi religious writings: "In the beginning created the White Pearl out of his most precious Essence; and He created a bird named Anfar. And he placed the pearl upon its back, and dwelt thereon forty thousand years. On the first day [of Creation], Sunday, He created an angel named ʿAzâzil, which is Malak Tâwus, the chief of all...."

In one account of the fall of the angels in the *Book of Enoch*, Azazel (Asaʾel as in the Qumran texts) is the leader of the Watchers who educates humankind of heavenly secrets that lead humankind to sin. These teachings include making weapons of war and preparing cosmetics, which enabled the women to seduce the angels.

The angels then charge Asazel before the Lord with crimes of revealing the heavenly secrets which mankind was not supposed to know. Raphael was then assigned to punish Asazel by binding him hand and foot and throwing him into the darkness among the sharp and jagged rocks, where he would remain until the day of judgment when he would be hurled into the fire. The story then claims that "the whole earth has been corrupted by [Asazel's] teachings of his (own) actions; and write upon him all sin." It was because of Asazel's teachings that God sent the Flood to destroy the evil in the world including even the souls of the giants, so that all evil will be wiped away from the face of the earth.

The *Apocalypse of Abraham* also associates Azazel with Hell. Abraham says to him "May you be the firebrand of the furnace of the earth! Go, Azazel, into the untrodden parts of the earth. For your heritage is over those who are with you." (14:5-6) There is also the idea that God's heritage (the created world) is largely under the dominion of evil. It is "shared with Azazel." (20:5) Azazel is also identified with the serpent which tempted Eve. His form is described as a dragon with "hands and feet like a man's, on his back six wings on the right and six on the left." (23:7)

Finally, the Apocalypse of Abraham says that the wicked will "putrefy in the belly of the crafty worm Azazel, and be burned by the fire of Azazel's tongue." (31:5) Here again, there is another reference to Azazel as being Hell.

Chapter Twenty-Three

Terah, the Son of Nahor and Father of Abraham (2242 BC – 2037 BC)

In Zechariah Sitchin's book, *The Wars of Gods and Men*, he identifies the source of the name Terah:

> In this regard the name of Abraham's father, Terah, is of great interest. Seeking clues only in the Semitic environment, biblical scholars regard the name, as those of Haran and Nahor, as mere toponyms (names that personify places), holding that there were cities by such names in central and northern Mesopotamia. Assyriologists searching the Akkadian terminology (being the first Semitic language) could only find that *Tirhu* meant "an artifact or vessel for magical purposes." But if we turn to the Sumerian language, we find that the cuneiform sign for *Tirhu* stemmed directly from that of an object called in Sumerian DUG.NAMTAR – literally, a 'Fate Speaker' – a Pronouncer of Oracles![339]

The city's patron deity was Nanna, the Sumerian moon god. The site is marked by the ruins of the Great Ziggurat of Ur, which contained the shrine of Nanna, excavated in the 1930s. The temple was built in the 21st century BC, during the reign of Ur-Nammu whom we have shown was the son of Kesed of the Bible. Terah was a member of the royal family of Ur. He was the great-great-grandson of Ur-Nammu, the King of Ur. He was also the grandson of Sargon the Great (Serug, Saruch), King of Akkad and Sumer. He was an oracle-priest and a descendant of Arphaxad and the sixth generation of the Nibiru-Ki priests. He was also called, in the apocryphal Book of Jasher, quoted in Joshua in the Bible, the "captain of the host of King Nimrod."[340]

The father of Terah was Nahor, whom I have shown was the High Priest of the "religious capital" of Sumer located in Nippur. The temple there was the temple of Enlil, supreme god of the Sumerians. Therefore, Terah was almost certainly born in Nippur and his father, Nahor, was a very powerful "oracle priest" who was a "go-between" between the gods and the kings of Sumer. As such, Nahor would have been consulted regularly by the Kings of Sumer for advice from the gods. Terah took up a similar position as the oracular priest at the Temple of Nannar in Ur, during the reigns of Utu-Hegal and Ur-Nammu (Ur-Nammu was his great-great-grandfather). It was Utu-Hegal, his great-great-uncle, who assigned him to that position after he had defeated him in battle.

Terah was married to Yawnu, whose father was Avram and whose mother was a daughter of Serug (Sargon the Great). On her father's side she was the granddaughter of Heraclim, who was the son of Peleg. On her mother's side she was the granddaughter of Serug (Sargon the Great) and Melka, whose mother, Kaber, was the daughter of another brother of Serug, as I have shown earlier.

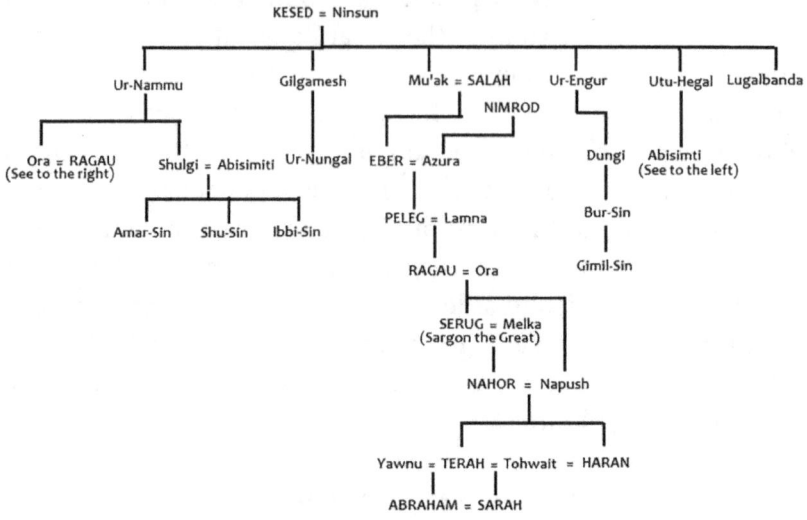

Fig. 54 Genealogy of Kesed's Descendants

Serug (Saruch, Sargon the Great), the grandfather of Terah, either held contol of the land of the Gutians, which I have identified as Aratta, or contended for that position. His grandson, Tirigan (Terah), was made a king of Guti. The Gutians allowed kings to reign only for a year to 3 years, evidence of which comes from the Sumerian King List. Terah was the last Gutian king. He held the position for only 40 days before his great-great-great-great uncle, Utu-Hegal, destroyed the Gutian kingdom, taking Terah as his prisoner and making him a High Priest in the Temple of Nannar-Sin in Ur. In scholarly circles there has been an error made in discussions about the Gutian Empire. The capital of the Gutian Empire was Aratta, and its first king was Enshukeshdanna, the son of Nimrod. Enmerkar, the brother of Enshukeshdanna, was a general in Aratta as a Gutian before he became the King of Uruk. Therefore, the Gutians were actually descendants of Cush through his son Nimrod, and Nimrod's sons Enmerkar and Enshukeshdanna. We do not have the names of these descendants since the rulership of Guti (Aratta) was not passed from father to son. Therefore, the Gutians were not hoards of barbarians from the mountainous regions as reported in the scholarly journals. They were, in fact, in the line of Ham and very closely so, being started by Ham's descendants through Cush, his son, and Nimrod, his grandson, and Enmerkar and Enshkeshdanna, his great grandsons.

Terah was assigned to be a king of Guti. The *Book of Jasher* called Terah the "captain of the host of King Nimrod." Nimrod was alive when the Gutians invaded Ur under Utu-Hegal. Clearly, it was Nimrod who had raised Terah (Tirigan) to the position of King of the Guti, or King of Aratta. When Utu-Hegal defeated him, he humiliated Terah by placing his foot on his head as he was laid prostrate on the ground. However, this was the sum of the punishment for Terah. Being a member of the larger royal family and a great-great-great-grand nephew of Utu-Hegal a solution was found. Terah was made the High Priest of the Temple of Nannar in Ur, where Utu-Hegal ruled.

Why would Terah receive the position of High Priest of this major Temple? Again, the answer is not difficult to determine. Members of the royal family were either kings or priests, or both. These positions were the control points. However, to become a priest in a major temple, you had to know the "magic" that made these positions work. In the case of Terah he had not one but two sources of training for his role as a High Priest. As the "captain of the host of King Nimrod" he had a direct connection to Nimrod, who had been taught the secrets of the religion by Yonton, the son of Noah. In addition, however, he also had connections to the family and sons of Kesed, including Utu-Hegal and Ur-Nammu. In fact, he may well have known Kesed himself who was a High Priest at Nippur, the religious capital of Sumer.

Therefore, Terah was the perfect candidate for this key religious position. He was a dependable soldier to Nimrod and, even though defeated by Utu-Hegal, he would have no problem exchanging his alliegiance from Nimrod to Utu-Hegal given this "plum" opportunity. This point is extremely important for the understanding of

Terah and Abraham. Therefore, I will summarize the important aspects of the article from the last chapter that I included. That article was *"Kurdistan, Where Credit is Due,"* by Dr. Mehrdad R. Izady. The following is a summary of the import of this article to the life of Terah:

> The Guti general, Enmerkar, declared his independence from the mountain domains of the Guti Federation, whose king was his own brother Ensukushsiranna. Having broken away from Aratta around 2500 BC, Enmerkar succeeded in establishing a separate Guti dynasty that ruled independently over Sumerian and Akkadian city-states. Enmerkar took the reknowned Uruk (Erech-Kullab) of Gilgamesh for his capital. The Gutis actually settled and flourished in large numbers in Sumeria.

The story of "Enmerkar and the Lord of Aratta" is then actually a correspondence between two Guti kings, Enmerkar and Ensukushsiranna, his brother.

In none of this correspondence is there a hint that the society at Aratta was less sophisticated or perceived as such by the people of Uruk.

In fact, Aratta, the Guti capital, became the breadbasket that fed much of Sumer. In addition, the Gutians were the original producers of beer. The beer and wine discovered at Godin (Aratta) date from the precise period of the Gutian takeover of Sumer and could have been introduced by the group which gave rise to Enmerkar in Sumer. Finally, the Sumerian tablets also record another introduction into Sumer by the Gutian Enmerkar. That was the introduction of the cult of the bird-god Anzu, still worshipped by the Yezidi Kurds as the bird icon Anzul (or Anzal) today. As I noted earlier, Kesed was the High Priest at the Temple of Kullab, a portion of Uruk. We are now finally able to put all of the pieces of this puzzle together.

Terah is the name of an ancient Semitic moon god as well. It is possible that his name was changed to reflect the fact that he was a High Priest of Nannar-Sin, the Sumerian moon god. He was chosen by Enlil (Sumerian God) to provide the seed for a great nation of earthlings. Enlil had been visited in a dream by the prophet Galzu and had been warned that there would soon come a period of great evildoing and bloodshed, brought about by Marduk (another Sumerian God). Enlil was told that in three celestial portions the Ram of Marduk would replace Enlil's own Bull. This referred to the "precession of the equinoxes" which was causing Taurus to give way to Orion in the celestial sphere. Galzu warned Enlil to be aware that Marduk, having once delcared that he was the supreme Annunaki God, would spread war and devastation to make that claim come true. Enlil was instructed to choose an earthling, as Ziusudra (Noah) had previously been chosen, in order to preserve the seed of the earthlings.

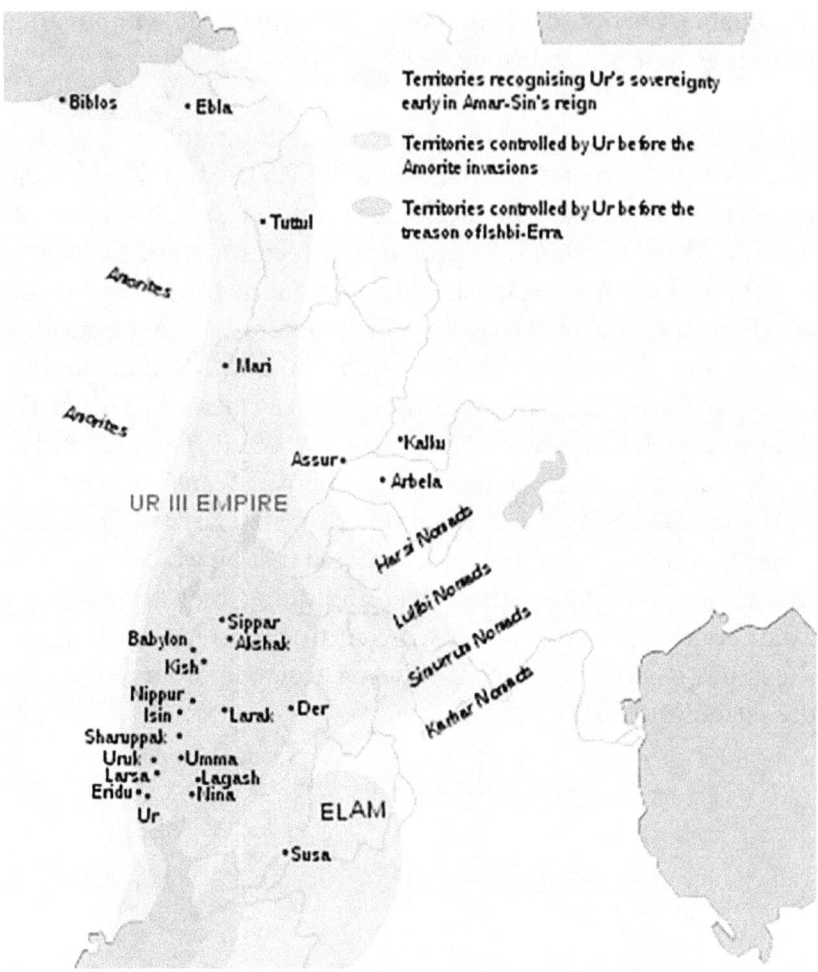

Fig. 55 Ur during the lifetime of Terah

Enlil instructed his son, Nannar-Sin, to build a city in the land between the Tigris and Euphrates Rivers to be named Haran, in whichTerah would be established as the Priest-Prince. The temple was built and Terah was made the Priest-Prince of that temple. He fulfilled his role well, in fact so well that "king and the princes loved him, and they elevated him very high… and dignified him above all his princes that were with him."[341]

We know that Terah's father, Nahor (Ur-Nachor), was the high priest in the Temple of Enlil at Nippur. Therefore, we can now see the connection between Enlil and his choosing Terah for the great task of running the Temple at Haran as a Priest-Prince. According to the *Book of Jubilees*, Terah was a High Priest in the Temple of Nannar-Sin, the Sumerian moon god. This temple was in Ur, where his great-great-grandfather Ur-Nammu reigned as king after Ur-Nammu's brother, Utu-Hegal, died in a drowning accident in 2113 BC His movement from Ur to Haran coincides with the movement of the major Temple center of Nannar-Sin from Ur to Haran as well. He may also have moved due to the difficulties arising from the loss of favor of the royal family on the death of Ur-Nammu, whom Terah would have known personally. The fact that people lived longer in those days than they do now makes it possible for these relationships between families to exist.

Fig. 56 Ruins of Ur, with Ur-Nammu's Ziggurat in the rear

Haran was nearly a duplicate of Ur in terms of its worship of Nannar-Sin. Ur had lost the favor of Nannar-Sin, so it stands to reason that he would move his temple worshippers, including his priests, from Ur to Haran.

Terah's son, Abraham, was 27 years old at the time that the Lord instructed Abraham to leave Ur and go to Haran. The most detailed and fascinating story of Abraham's early life is found in *The Book of the Apocalypse of Abraham*. The Slavonic *Apocalypse of Abraham*, as it is sometimes called, is dated to the first century A.D. and probably originated in Hebrew in Palestine. It was completely lost to the Western Christian Church until the eleventh century, having been preserved in Old Slavonic. In this document, Terah is described not only as an astrologer but also an idol-maker. With his son's help, Terah ran a workshop that manufactured idols for the temples of the Mesopotamian cities as well as for sale to private citizens for home use. These were made of different materials - stone, wood, iron, copper, silver, and gold, with their value determined by the substance and workmanship. These idols were presumably the *teraphim* of the Old Testament.

Fig. 57 The probable handiwork of Terah

Abraham's father was not just an ordinary priest. According to the Haggadah, he "was a Prince and magnate in the house of the king."[342] The king, at this time, was presumably Utu-Hegal; thus, the fate of Terah and Abraham was intimately connected with the fortunes of this ruling house. Utu-Hegal was the King of Ur and he was also Terah's great-great-great grand uncle. Based on the quote above, Terah lived in the palace of the king, the same king who defeated him when he was the young "king" of the Gutians for 40 days! Terah moved with his family, including his son Abraham, to Haran, where he continued his role as a High Priest in the Temple of Nannar-Sin. Terah died in Haran at the age of 205 when Abraham was 75 years old.

Fig. 58 More probable works of Terah

The following is taken from:

The Babylonian Empire
by A. T. Olmtead

> The long agony of Babylonia under the sway of the barbarian [sic] Guti was brought to an end by the Sumerian Utu-hegal. In an inscription unique for freshness of expression among the royal records of early Babylonia he tells us of his operations. Gutium is the "dragon of the mountains, the enemy of the gods, which had ravished the wife from her husband, their

infants from the parents, and caused woe and evil in the land." Utu hegal, the king of Uruk, the king of the Four World Regions, prayed to Inanna for aid, since Enlil had granted to him that the kingdom of Sumer should be independent. Meanwhile the Guti king, Tirigan [Terah], had thought, "No one will come against me, the Tigris has Flooded the country, below in Sumer it has covered the fields, it has covered the roads, the roads of the land are covered with torn-off plants." From Uruk, Utu-Hegal sallied forth and moored his boat at the temple of Ishkurra, whence issued his proclamation to the people, informing them that Enlil had given him Gutium, that the lady Inanna was his aid, that the old hero of Uruk, Gilgamesh [the brother of Utu-Hegal], had given him protection. To the people of Uruk and Kullab [where Kesed, his father, was High Priest] he brought joy of heart; his city like one man marched behind him; to the same purpose they turned their face. From the temple of Ishkurra he weighed anchor. In five days he came to the dam of Ilitabbeka, where the lieutenants of Tirigan [Terah] arrived with a message and were captured. On the sixth day Utu-Hegal anchored at Muru; the wall of Gutium he broke through; soldiers he brought within. Tirigan, alone and on foot, fled to his fortress of Dubrum. The people of that town, knowing that Utu-Hegal was the king to whom Enlil had given the might, gave not the hand to Tirigan [Terah]. Through the messenger of Utu-Hegal they made Tirigan, his wife, and his children prisoners in Dubrum; on his hands they placed fetters. Utu-Hegal took him. Prostrate before his conqueror the Guti king threw himself, and Utu-Hegal placed his feet on his neck. So Utu-Hegal established Sumer in its independence and began the fifth and last dynasty of Uruk (2500+ BC). Yet it was Tirigan [Terah] and not Utu-Hegal who was remembered a thousand years hence as the founder of a city.

Gutian kings employed Iranian names. For instance, the name of the last Gutian king was Tirigan [Terah]. Tirigan is clearly an Iranian and Indo-European word, as Waddell notes:

In the Runes, significantly, this archaic arrow-head form survived, and the letter is therein called Tyr, which evidently preserves its Sumerian name of Til - l and r being always freely interchangeable dialectically as we have seen. Moreover, Tyr is the Gothic god of the Arrow or god of War, whose name survives in our Tues-day or Tys-day, just as Thurs-day derives from Thor. And Tir is the common Indo-Persian word for 'arrow.'[343]

We now can see that Terah (Tirigan) was initially groomed to become a king of the Gutian lands whose capital was Aratta, and from which place Enmerkar, the Gutian king, became a King of Uruk around 2500 BC Not surprisingly, the Gutian Empire also gave us Ur-Bau, the son of Ragau, who was the brother of Terah's grandfather, Serug (Sargon the Great). Therefore, Ur-Bau was Terah's great-uncle. As the picture unfolds we see that Terah was the "premiere" royal. It is for this reason that Terah was granted the last kingship of the Gutians. He was a member of the family. As it turns out, however, his other relative, Utu-Hegal, had grander schemes and deposed his descendant summarily, after only 40 days as the King of Guti (Aratta). However, even though Utu-Hegal placed Terah under his heel at the ceremony of his victory, he still rewarded his young relative with a High Priesthood in the Temple of Nannar-Sin in Ur. Terah was wed to Yawnu, also known as Amthelo, the daughter of Cornebo. To this union was born a son, Abram. In celebration of his birth, a great party was thrown and the guest list included heads of state (wise men) and conjurors. The evening of the party, they witnessed an exploding star which came from the east which caused a vast luminescence and rapidly spread and covered the whole night time sky on the Sumeria delta. This spectacular celestial scene prompted the wise men, the Magi, to give their oracular interpretation to Nimrod that Terah's son, Abram, would become powerful and kill all the kings of the earth, an international dynastic coup.[344] Nimrod offered Terah a bribe to purchase Abram, which included gold and silver enough to fill Terah's house, with the knowledge that Abram would be killed. A three day waiting period was given for consultation, and during that time, a son of Terah's servant was substituted for Abram. The king immediately threw the child down and dashed his head against a stone, secure in his mind that a future political coup had been prevented.[345]

Abram was secreted out of the city to a rural cave hideout with his mother and a nurse and they lived there 10 years in exile and isolation. At the onset of puberty, Abram left his family and traveled north near the site of the Ark, south of the mountains of Ararat, where some descendants of Noah and Shem apparently were still living. There he "learned the instruction of the Lord and his ways, …and Abram served Noah and Shem his son [sic: they had been dead for over 700 years] for a long time," isolated from the city-state center of "higher learning" of Sumer.[346] Within the foothills of the mountains or Ararat, and within the political influence of the tribal mountain people, the Khaldini of Urartu, whose name stemmed from Kesed (the Kasidim, or Chaldees), son of Arphaxad, Abram received the instruction and wisdom of the original faith in Yahweh. This wisdom had passed from Adam to Lamech, and then, directly to Noah. It remained among some of the Patriarchs, but was lost in the time of Salah and Ragau.

Through this sojourn to the "source" of their true faith, the religion of "Yahweh" was once again given to Abram.

In the meantime, the priestly dynasty and its secrets were almost certainly passed down through the daughter of Ur-Nammu, whose name was Ora. She had become the wife of Ragau and was the mother of Nahor, the grandfather of Abram. The traditions were then passed on to Terah, and from Terah to Abram. The oracular mysteries were confined within the dynasty of Terah's family, where his role as Priest-Prince was secure. The power and social acclaim were his birthright. After moving to Haran, although we have no direct records of Terah's role there, we may safely assume that Terah continued as High Priest to Nannar (who had moved his temple there, the reason why Terah went there), and that although he wanted to influence his now adult son, his influence decreased significantly because Abram, who was to become Abraham, had been called by Yahweh.

Chapter Twenty-Four

Abraham, Son of Terah, Son of the Promise (2167 BC – 1992 BC)

T he name Abraham (Abram), apparently comes from the Akkadian Abu-Ramu, which is also a name of the moon god (Nannar-Sin) in the city of Ur.[347] Akkadian was the original Shemitic language, the language of Arphaxad who lived in Akkad (Ebla being its capital then). Therefore, Abraham was apparently named after the god whom his father Terah served in the Temple of Nannar-Sin in Ur and then later in Haran. Nannar-Sin was one of the important Sumerian gods. In Sumerian, the name of Abraham was AB.RAM, according to noted Sumerian linguist Zecharia Sitchin.[348]

Nannar-Sin is commonly designated as *En-zu*, which means "lord of wisdom." During the period (c. 2600 BC-2400 BC) that Ur exercised a large measure of supremacy over the Euphrates valley, Nannar was naturally regarded as the head of the pantheon. It is to this period that we must trace such designations of Nannar-Sin as "father of the gods," "chief of the gods," "creator of all things," and the like. The "wisdom" personified by the moon-god is likewise an expression of the science of astrology, in which the observation of the moon's phases is an important factor.[349] Therefore, the role of Abraham's father as the High Priest of the Temple of Nannar-Sin in Ur and later in Haran was extremely important. It is not an exaggeration to state that Terah was the "go between" between the people and the god himself. Furthermore, it would also follow that he was a "go between" between the god and the King of Ur. Terah, as we have shown, held this position under both King Utu-Hegal and King Ur-Nammu, the former being his great-great-great grand uncle and the latter his great-great-great grandfather. It is in this environment that Abraham, then known as Abram (or Abu-Ramu), grew up.

Abram was named after his grandfather on his mother's side, who was Abram, the son of Heraclim, who was the son of Peleg. Therefore, Abram was descended from two sons of Peleg, both Heraclim on the female side, and Ragau on the male side. This is very important to know, since the family of Shem was largely matrilineal in its descent in terms of royal connections. I only use the term "largely" here because we do not know all of the names of the females in the line from Shem, or how they were related. Jewish tradition states that Abraham was hidden away old by his own mother, Yawnu, or Edna, or Amthelo, and kept in a cave from his birth until he was 10 years, because she feared that Nimrod (c. 3040 BC – 2085 BC) would seize the young lad and kill him. It is worth noting here that Nimrod was in the same generation as Cainan and was, therefore, 8 generations older than Abraham. Therefore, the Jewish tradition not only had no problem with the great longevity of the Patriarchs; it actually incorporated that longevity into its non-biblical memories as well as in the biblical stories. This is another confirmation that the Patriarchs lived long lives. The tradition also states that Abraham lived among the descendants of Noah and Shem for the next several years out of the same fear of his mother that Nimrod would attempt to take his life. Through this experience, Abraham may have come to understand the nature of the true God and have become a believer in the same.

An ancient non-biblical book called *The Cave of Treasures* has this interesting addition to the story of the life of Abraham. It was written around the time of the life of Jesus, but may well have been based on a much older tradition. Flavius Josephus used a portion of this story in writing his *Jewish Antiquities*.

> When still a boy, Abraham had no belief in idols, and, according to the Kebra Nagast (chapter xiii), 'when he was twelve years old his father sent him to sell idols. And Abraham said, "These are not gods that can make deliverance"; and he took away the idols to sell even as his father had commanded him. And he said unto those unto whom he would sell them, "Do ye wish to buy goods that cannot make deliverance, things made of wood, and stone, and iron, and brass, which the hand of an artificer hath made?" And they (the people) refused to buy the idols from Abraham because he himself had defamed the images of his father. And as he was returning he stepped aside from the road, and he set the images down, and looked at them, and said unto them, "I wonder now if you are able to do what I ask you at this moment, and whether you are able to give me bread to eat or water to drink?" And none of them answered him, for they were pieces of stone and wood; and he abused them and heaped revilings upon them, and they spake never a word. And he buffeted the face of one, and kicked another with his feet, and a third he knocked over and broke to pieces with stones, and he said unto them, "If you are unable to save yourselves from him that buffets you, and you cannot requite with injury him that injures you, how can you be called 'gods'? Those who worship you do

so in vain, and as for myself I utterly despise you, and you shall not be my gods.'" Then he turned his face to the East, and he stretched out his hands and said, "Be Thou my God, O Lord, Creator of the heavens and the earth, Creator of the Sun and Moon, Creator of the sea and the dry land, Maker of the majesty of the heavens and the earth, and of that which is visible and that which is invisible; O Maker of the universe, be Thou my God. I place my trust in Thee, and from this day forth I will place my trust in no other save Thyself." And then there appeared unto him a chariot of fire which blazed, and Abraham was afraid, and fell on his face on the ground; and God said unto him, "Fear thou not, stand upright."

On the day of the birth of Abraham the house shone with a bright light. Many people fell down, and there was a cry in a loud voice, which said, "Woe is me! Woe is me! For he who shall crush my kingdom hath been born." And he who cried out wept, and described the events which should take place, saying, "It is he who shall burn down my abode." And there were among the people certain men who said, "Kill this child forthwith," and those who spake thus knew well that grace would be given to Abraham. And God set mercy in the heart of the father of Abraham, and he said to the Satans, "Whence come ye, O ye who tell me that I should kill my son who is a gracious gift of God?" And he reared the child . . . . . And Abraham was circumcised by the hand of Gabriel and Michael, who helped him.[350]

According to the *Book of Jubiliees* Abraham moved out of his father's home at the age of 14:

> And the child [Abraham] began to understand the errors of the earth that all went astray after graven images and after uncleanness, and his father taught him writing, and he was two weeks of years old [14], and he separated himself from his father, that he might not worship idols with him. And he began to pray to the Creator of all things that He might save him from the errors of the children of men, and that his portion should not fall into error after uncleanness and vileness. And the seed time came for the sowing of seed upon the land, and they all went forth together to protect their seed against the ravens, and Abram went forth with those that went, and the child was a lad of fourteen years. And a cloud of ravens came to devour the seed, and Abram ran to meet them before they settled on the ground, and cried to them before they settled on the ground to devour the seed, and said, 'Descend not: return to the place whence ye came,' and they proceeded to turn back. And he caused the clouds of ravens to turn back that day seventy times, and of all the ravens throughout all the land where Abram was there settled there not so much as one. And all who were with him throughout all the land saw him cry out, and all the ravens turn back, and his name became great in all the land of the Khaldis [Kasidim, sons of Kesed]. And there came to him this year all those that wished to sow, and he went with them until the time of sowing ceased: and they sowed their land, and that year they brought enough grain home and

ate and were satisfied. And in the first year of the fifth week Abram taught those who made implements for oxen, the artificers in wood, and they made a vessel above the ground, facing the frame of the plough, in order to put the seed thereon, and the seed fell down therefrom upon the share of the plough, and was hidden in the earth, and they no longer feared the ravens. And after this manner they made (vessels) above the ground on all the frames of the ploughs, and they sowed and tilled all the land, according as Abram commanded them, and they no longer feared the birds.[351]

From the *Book of Jubilees* we find out how Abrahm was involved in his brother Haran's death:

"And it came to pass in the sixth week, in the seventh year thereof, that Abram said to Terah his father, saying, 'Father!' And he said, 'Behold, here am I, my son.' And he said, 'What help and profit have we from those idols which thou dost worship, and before which thou dost bow thyself? For there is no spirit in them, for they are dumb forms, and a misleading of the heart. Worship them not: worship the God of heaven, who causes the rain and the dew to descend on the earth and does everything upon the earth, and has created everything by His word, and all life is from before His face. Why do you worship things that have no spirit in them? For they are the work of (men's) hands, and on your shoulders do you bear them, and you have no help from them, but they are a great cause of shame to those who make them, and a misleading of the heart to those who worship them: Worship them not.'

"And his father said unto him, 'I also know it, my son, but what shall I do with a people who have made me to serve before them? And if I tell them the truth, they will slay me; for their soul cleaves to them to worship them and honor them. Keep silent, my son, lest they slay you.'

"And these words he spoke to his two brothers, and they were angry with him and he kept silent. And in the fortieth jubilee, in the second week, in the seventh year thereof, Abram took to himself a wife, and her name was Sarai, the daughter of his father, and she became his wife. [Note that he married his own step-sister, as tradition would expect]

"And Haran, his brother, took to himself a wife in the third year of the third week, and she bare him a son in the seventh year of this week, and he called his name Lot.

"And Nahor, his brother, took to himself a wife. And in the sixtieth year of the life of Abram, that is, in the fourth week, in the fourth year thereof, Abram arose by night, and burned the house of the idols, and he burned all that was in the house and no man knew it. And they arose in the night and sought to save their gods from the midst of the fire. And Haran hasted to save them, but the fire flamed over him, and he was burnt in the fire, and he died in Ur of the Khaldis before Terah his father, and they buried him in Ur of the Khaldis."[352]

There is another tradition that states the situation somewhat differently. Rashi cites Chazal who explains that the meaning of "Haran died in the lifetime of Terah his father, in his native land, in Ur Kasdim" is that Haran died in the kiln of Kasdim because of his father. Because Abraham had espoused monotheism and had broken his father's idols, along with his brother, he was taken by his father, Terah, to Nimrod the king. Abraham was given an ultimatum to either bow to the idol or be thrown into the kiln (of Kasdim). Abraham chose to die and went into the fire. He emerged miraculously unscathed. Haran, Abraham's brother, was also given the same ultimatum to bow or be thrown into the fire. He decided that if his brother Abraham emerged from the fire he would not bow to the idol either. However, if Abraham was consumed by the fire he would bow. Since Abraham did not die, Haran chose not to bow and thus was cast into the kiln. God did not spare Haran. This is the meaning of "Haran died in the lifetime of Terah his father."[353] All of these events occurred before Abraham, at 27 years of age, left Ur with his father to head for Haran. So these events happened before 2140 BC We need not concern ourselves as to which story is correct. What is important, however, is the note that Nimrod was still alive at this time and was a King. Nimrod lived until Abraham was 82 years old.

Four years earlier he had left the dwelling of the descendants of Noah and Shem in 2144 BC Then, at 27 years of age in 2140 BC, Abraham received a message from God Himself.

> Now the LORD had said unto Abram, Get thee
> out of thy country, and from thy kindred, and
> from thy father's house, unto a land that I will
> shew thee.[354]

The verses relating to God's call to Abraham to leave his home and go into Canaan must be examined out of their order in the Bible to get the entire picture. He is called to leave his "country," his relatives (kindred) and his father's home. In other words, he is called to leave the place where his entire family had established their residence. This didn't imply one "house" but one area. However, we learn that his father had originally set out with Abraham to enter Canaan:

> And Terah took Abram his son, and Lot the son
> of Haran his son's son and Sarai, his daughter in
> law, his son Abram's wife; and they went forth
> with them from Ur of the Chaldees, to go into
> the land of Canaan; and they came unto Haran,
> and dwelt there.[355]

Terah had also been instructed to leave Ur for Haran, so the two left together, stopping at Haran on the way to Canaan. According to the record: " .. Terah died in Haran."[356]

Terah, the father of Abraham, was a High Priest in the Temple of Nannar-Sin, the Sumerian god, in Ur of Sumeria. It is from there that he left. His position was extremely important and he had gone there under the direct orders of Nannar to become the High Priest of the new temple of Nannar at Haran. There have been questions raised as to the location of Ur where Abraham and Terah dwelt before they went to Haran. There are reasons to believe that Ur, the realm of the King Ur-Nammu, is where Abraham was born.

The term Chaldees does not refer to the Kaldis of Haran. A search of the biblical term Chaldees will show that it was also known as Ur of the Kasidim. Kasidim comes from the name of Kesed, the ancestor of Abraham (Terah, Nahor, Serug, Ragau, Peleg, Eber, Salah, Cainan). Cainan's brother was Kesed, who was a High Priest in the Temple of Kullab. In addition, the King of Ur in the south at the time of Terah and Abraham was Ur-Nammu, who was the son of Kesed. Therefore, calling the city Ur of the Kasidim, or Ur of the family of Kesed was recognition of the King of Ur, Ur-Nammu. Abraham left Ur in his twenty-seventh year [2140 BC] under a direction from the Lord. He went with his family, including the wives, two brothers, and his father Terah to Haran at the north-western edge of the Tigris and Euphrates River Valley. He remained there with his father, childless, for another 50 years! In Abraham's seventy-fifth year, 2092 BC, he was again instructed by the Lord Yahweh to move, this time to Canaan.

Abraham went to Egypt to buy grain due to the famine in Canaan and the surrounding areas, at that time. Genesis relates that there were 3 sister/wife stories regarding an Abraham, Gerar, and the Pharaoh of Egypt. Only two deal with Abraham, and only one deals with Abraham and a Pharaoh of Egypt. The other deals with Abraham who came "down" to Gerar, which is in south-central Israel today, clearly an indication that Abraham was not living in Egypt based on that story. Since it does not deal with a Pharaoh but instead with a King of Gerar, somewhat north and east of Egypt, we need not concern ourselves with this story. However, it should be noted that if Abraham were a Pharoah of Egypt, as has been suggested by Ralph Ellis,[357] he could not go "down" to Gerar, since Gerar is north and east of the very northeast corner of Egypt.

Here is the story, starting at Genesis 12:9: "Then Abram traveled south by stages toward the Negev."[358]

"The Negev Desert comprises approximately 12,000 square kilo-meters (4,633 square miles), more than half of Israel's total land area. Geographically it is an extension of the Sinai, forming a rough triangle with its base in the north near Beersheba, the Dead Sea, and the southern Judean Hills, and it has its apex in the south-ern tip of the country at Eilat."[359] Since the Negev Desert is totally within Israel, and since Abraham moved "south" toward the Negev, it is clear that he was located within Israel (Canaan at that time) and, in fact, north of Beersheba, which is the most northern part of the Negev Desert. In other words, Abraham lived in Canaan (now Israel) and not in Egypt. He was, therefore, not the first Hyksos King of Egypt, as Ellis asserts, since he didn't even live in Egypt.

We will now deal with the sister-wife story in more detail. Here are the verses:

> At that time there was a severe famine in the land, so Abram went down to Egypt to wait it out. As he was approaching the borders of Egypt, Abram said to Sarai, 'You are a very beautiful woman. When the Egyptians see you, they will say, "This is his wife. Let's kill him; then we can have her!" But if you say you are my sister, then the Egyptians will treat me well because of their interest in you, and they will spare my life. And sure enough, when they arrived in Egypt, everyone spoke of her beauty. When the palace officials saw her, they sang her praises to their king, the pharaoh, and she was taken into his harem. Then Pharaoh gave Abram many gifts because of her--sheep, cattle, donkeys, male and female servants, and camels. But the Lord sent a terrible plague upon Pharaoh's household because of Sarai, Abram's wife. So Pharaoh called for Abram and accused him sharply. 'What is this you have done to me?' he demanded. 'Why didn't you tell me she was your wife? Why were you willing to let me marry her, saying she was your sister? Here is your wife! Take her and be gone!' Pharaoh then sent them out of the country under armed escort--Abram and his wife, with all their household and belongings.[360]

In normal biblical exegesis there is a simple principle: if the plain sense makes sense, don't look for any other sense. That principle should be applied here. First, it is clear that Abraham was in fear of his own life. Regardless of just how powerful he was in the sense that he was born of royalty, he feared for his life, and his actions were a direct result of that fear. At the same time he knew that he needed grain for his people, so he devised a plan to allow him to get the grain. The plan was obviously agreed to by his wife, Sarah.

Because the couple had royal ancestry, it seems obvious that they would be aware of the ceremonial concept of "the Sacred Marriage", called *herios gamos* later by the Greeks, but also known to the Egyptians and Sumerians at the time of Abraham. This concept involved a ritual marriage, sometimes but not always consummated. It was based upon a Sumerian "Sacred Marriage" in which the "marriage" took place between the king of a Sumerian city-state and the High Priestess of Inanna. Based upon Abraham's upbringing under his father, the High Priest of the Temple of Nannar (sister of Inanna), it seems obvious that he would be aware of this political/religious technique. However, it is also clear that he would not believe that the "marriage" would have any value, since Abraham had already recognized only one God. The Pharaoh was hardly a "god" in his eyes. Being practical people it seemed that the idea of allowing this "Sacred Marriage" would be the best possible way to acquire the grain they needed for their people to survive. Therefore, they agreed to the plan. It should be noted that Sarah obviously agreed to the plan as well, since she became a part of the Pharaoh's harem.

In addition, Abraham found himself not only in the possession of the grain that he wanted. The Pharaoh showered him with even more gifts. I will re-quote the story: "Then Pharaoh gave Abram many gifts because of her--sheep, cattle, donkeys, male and female servants, and camels."[361] At this point Abraham was committed and had to continue the ruse. He had already been granted significant gifts from the pharaoh. Therefore, he and Sarah had to ride out the scenario, in spite of the fact that this was not their preference.

Now the story relates that the Lord sent a plague on Pharaoh's household because of what he had done with Sarah. This may indicate that Abraham and Sarah were in Egypt during this period.

The statement that the Lord sent the plague may or may not be the case. It is not seminal to the point of the story. The fact is that the Pharoah figured out what Abraham and Sarah had done. At this point, the Pharaoh would have had several options. He could have summarily killed Sarah. He could have killed Abraham. He could have killed them both. Yet he did none of these things. Instead, he returned Sarah to Abraham and then had an armed escort remove them from his lands, along with their household and belongings, which, presumably, included the gifts that the Pharoah had given Abraham upon taking Sarah as his wife.

It seems that this situation must have lasted several months, at least. It is unlikely that the Pharoah would lavish such great wealth on Abraham just because he allowed his "sister" to be a part of the Pharaoh's harem. Instead, it seems likely that Abraham also brought something else to offer to the Pharaoh, something that has not been included in the biblical narrative. There is a tradition that Abraham brought the knowledge of astronomy/astrology from Sumer to Egypt during this event. We must remember that Abraham was not ignorant of the tradition of his father, and his ancestors, all the way back to Nimrod and Kesed, regarding the "secrets" of their religion. Even though he himself may have rejected them, it seems that he may have passed them on to the Pharaoh. That gift alone would have been sufficient to lead the Pharaoh to show Abraham favor, even after he found out about the deceit.

Flavius Josephus wrote that Abram and his wife were honored by Pharaoh himself, at a place where he is said to have taught the Egyptian Court mathematics and astronomy which he had learned from the Chaldeans (Kasidim, descendants of Kesed, who got the learning from his brother Cainan].[362]

In a similar manner, it may well be that Abraham's actions with the Pharoah were "legal" in that they technically fulfilled a law of the land at that time. While morally it was not "legal" from today's standards, still it would appear that Abraham and Sarah found a "legal" way to get what they wanted (grain) and not lose their lives in the process. It would also now seem that this interpretation is correct. What they did was technically "legal." Had it been otherwise the Pharoah would have had them both executed. Instead, following the law, he banished them, but he did not punish them. He allowed them to leave with their household and goods. This means that what they did had given the Pharaoh something important! Recognizing that he had been legally duped, while at the same time realizing that he had been given the "secrets" of the religion of Sumer, he was left with only one recourse.

In no case is it necessary to make Abraham a Pharaoh of Egypt for this story to have validity. What it does require is that Abraham must have been astute about the legalities of royal life and the "secrets" of the Sumerian religion. As the son of a High Priest and a descendant of royalty himself, we may safely assume that Abraham knew how to "play the game" among the royals. He did so, and did so very well. He played his ace, namely his wife Sarah, perfectly. She must have cooperated in the plan since it clearly had to have occurred over several months. Once found out, however, knowing that what they had done was legal in terms of the culture of that time, they left. But they also left with their entire household of servants and slaves, cattle, and goods. It is not necessary, or appropriate, for us to impose a "moral obligation" scenario into this event. We are still over 500 years prior to the life of Moses, who was given the Law regarding the morality of an issue such as this. Therefore, it does not apply. Abraham was a shrewd man; of that we may rest assured.

Abram was his original Sumerian name. It meant "Father's Beloved." In his ninety-ninth year [2067 BC], Yahweh changed his name to a Semitic one, Abraham, which means "Father of a Multitude of Nations."[363] Similarly, his wife's name was changed from the Sumerian Sarai ("Princess") to Sarah, which also means "Princess." Abraham's sister-in-law, Milkah, also had a royal name meaning "Queenly." Abraham's family were directly related to the kings of Ur. Abraham was the great-great-great grandson of Ur-Nammu (c. 2675 BC – 2096 BC), King of Ur, through Ora, the daughter of Ur-Nammu, who was the wife of Ragau (2438 BC – 2099 BC). More importantly, he was the great-grandson of Sargon the Great (Serug, Saruch) (2406 BC – 2176 BC), one of the greatest rulers of Mesopotamia. He was therefore of royal lineage! It should be noted that Abraham lived 77 years while Ragau was still alive.

His great-grandfather, Sargon the Great (Serug in the Bible), died the same year that Abraham was born. We may safely assume that his parents, and grandparents, had told him stories of the wondrous things that his great grandfather had done during his lifetime.
When his father, Terah, died in 2037 BC, Abraham had his final links to his royal lineage cut. There was no going home from that point on. Yet, he still had royal blood in himself from his ancestors, as well as priestly blood from his High Priest father, although his father had been a pagan. This helps to explain the fact that Abraham was instrumental in the War of the Kings. Abraham had "connections" that went way back. Since people in his era lived throughout several generations (over 200 years on average), he was able to call in favors from his ancestors as needed. He formed a small army, and he formed alliances as an equal, at least.

The Sumerian texts state that Enlil, the Sumerian god, called upon Ibru-Um (Abraham), the eldest son of Tirhu (Terah), and instructed him to travel from Haran to Canaan to protect the sacred sites at the "Place of the Celestial Chariots" in the Sinai Peninsula so that the Annunaki chariots might continue to make safe take-offs and landings. This is a non-biblical confirmation of the same story in Genesis.[364] The major difference between this story and the Sumerian tale is the name of the god who gave the order. Enlil was the head of the gods of Sumer. Yahweh was (is) god alone. We need not question this further at this point. Faith will determine for each person what to believe. However, according to Zechariah Sitchin, this is attested in a non-biblical source, a Sumerian tablet.

Abram married Sarah, his half-sister. Abram and Sarah had not had any children together yet, so when he was 85 Abram had a son (Ishmael) by his wife's Egyptian servant, Hagar.[365] When he was 99, Abram formed a covenant with God by which Abram would serve and glorify God as the one and only God, and God would make him the father of many nations and tribes. God told Abram to change his name to Abraham which means "Father of Many Nations."[366] When he was 100, Abraham was visited by divine messengers who told him that he and his wife would soon have a son. Because of their age (Sarah was 90), Abraham and Sarah were incredulous. However, the angels were correct, and Sarah gave birth to a son, Isaac, who became the second of the Patriarchs of Israel and who became the father of Esau and Jacob. God used Isaac to test Abraham's faith by ordering Abraham to kill his son Isaac as a sacrifice. Abraham obediently attempted to do this, but was prevented from killing Isaac by an angel, who revealed that God had been testing Abraham, and did not really want him to kill his son.[367] Abraham died at the age of 175 after having lived a faithful life to his sole God.

There is no evidence whatsoever that Abraham was ever a Pharaoh of Egypt. Quite the contrary, while he was of royal blood through his ancestral kings, as shown above, he had, in fact, rebuked the high priesthood that would have been his inheritance from his father, Terah. In the next chapter I will identity the Pharaoh with whom Abraham made the deal to buy grain. The genealogical chart will help the reader to understand the relationships that led to the identifications of the Patriarchs in non-biblical records.

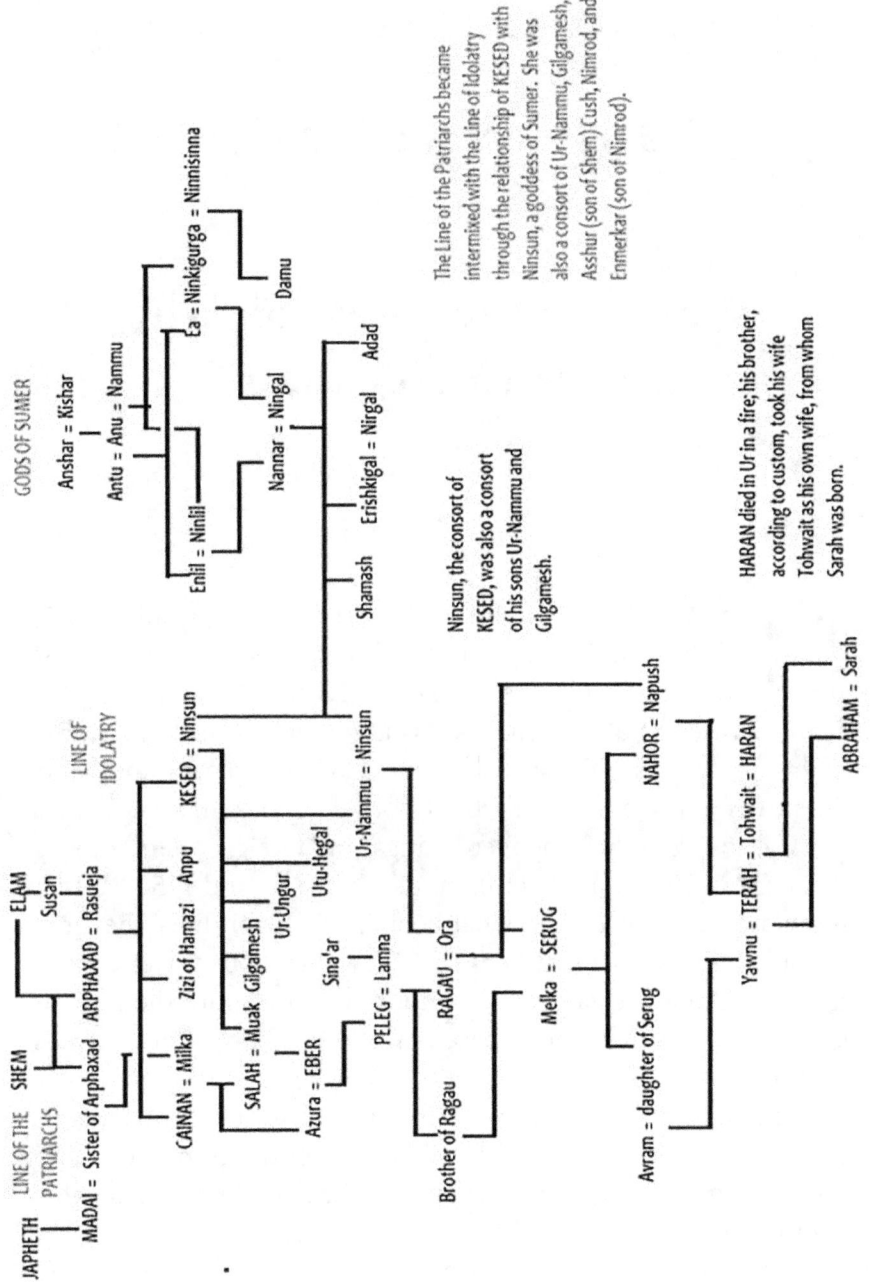

Fig. 59 Lines of Connection

Chapter Twenty-Five

Who was the Pharaoh who met with Abraham?

R alph Ellis wrote a book about 10 years ago called *Jesus, Last of the Pharaohs.* In this book, Ellis presents his view that Abraham was actually a Hyksos Pharaoh of northern, or Lower Egypt. He makes this argument through a number of interpretations of the story in Genesis. He also places Abraham's life in the era of about 1750 BC in order to make his case, since the Hyksos were the "Shepherd Kings" or "foreign rulers" during this period. However, if Abraham didn't live around 1750 BC but, instead, somewhat earlier, what happens to Ralph Ellis' thesis? It should be noted that the dates that I have developed with consistency for Abraham fall several hundred years before the Hyksos period in Egypt. Therefore, based on this evidence alone, there is no way that Abraham could have been a Pharaoh of the Hyksos, who came into Egypt around 1750 BC This can be proven simply. I will also show exactly where the Hyksos did come from, and how they are related to the ancient Israelites, although not directly. Terah, Abraham's father, died in 2092 BC in Haran. God called Abraham to leave Haran in that same year, and he went to Canaan. Abraham was 75 years old at that time, according to Genesis 12:4.

The record continues in Genesis:

> And Abram took Sarai his wife, and Lot his
> brother's son, and all their substance that they
> had gathered, and the souls that they had
> gotten in Haran; and they went forth to go into
> the land of Canaan; and into the land of Canaan
> they came. And Abram passed through the
> land unto the place of Sichem, unto the plain
> of Moreh. And the Canaanite was then in the
> land. And the Lord appeared unto Abram, and
> said, "Unto thy seed will I give this land": and
> there builded he an altar unto the Lord, who
> appeared unto him. And he removed from
> thence unto a mountain on the east of Bethel,
> and pitched his tent, having Bethel on the west,
> and Hai on the east: and there he builded an
> altar unto the Lord, and called upon the name
> of the Lord. And Abram journeyed, going on
> still toward the south.[368]

While we cannot determine the exact year that Abraham journeyed "going on still toward the south, we can definitely place Abraham in Canaan, working his way toward the south. At the outside he might have taken a full year to get settled in Canaan before he began his journey south to Egypt. Assuming this is about correct, then in about 2091 BC Abraham left Canaan to travel to Egypt. "And there was a famine in the land: and Abram went down into Egypt to sojourn there; for the famine was grievous in the land."[369]

Notice that the Bible record says that Abraham went "down" into Egypt. Ellis says that he had to be in Egypt to go "down" into Egypt. But if he was already in Egypt, how could he go "down" into Egypt? On the other hand, if he were somewhere "above" Egypt, as in Canaan, going "down" (south and west) would get him to Egypt. It is at this year of 2091 BC, that we must look for the Pharaoh who had contact with Abraham and Sarah.

Who was the King of Egypt in 2091 BC? According to scholars the Ninth and Tenth dynasties of Egypt lasted from 2160 BC to 2025 BC[370] Therefore we should look to these dynasties to find the Pharaoh who met with Abraham. Dynasty Nine was founded at Herakleopolis Magna and Dynasty Ten continued there. It was the capital of Lower Egypt (the northern part) from 2185 BC to 2060 BC, so we know that we are in the right time frame. [371] At this time Egypt was not unified, and there is some overlap between these and other local dynasties. The Turin Canon lists eighteen kings for this royal line, but their names are damaged, unidentifiable, or lost. One King whose name is on the list is Neferkare III. Neferkare III is sometimes numbered VII, VIII, or IX, but he is the third pharaoh of the Ninth dynasty of ancient Egypt, around 2140 BCE (during the First Intermediate Period).[372]

This ruler of Herakleopolis Magna is identified by various scholars with the king named Neferkare, mentioned in the biographical text *Ankhtify*, who is the nomarch of Herakleopolis and prince of Moala, which is situated about 25 miles to the south of Thebes. *Ankhtify* led a coalition of his nome and Edfu against Thebes, the capital of Upper Egypt (southern Egypt).[373] The text describes it thus: Neferkare, in alliance with the nomarchs Hotep and Ankhtify, tried to destroy the power of the Theban princes in Upper Egypt. Given by Ankhtify the job of deposing and substituting for the prince of Edfu, Jui, allied with Intef I (of the contemporary 11th dynasty), in Thebes. Ankhtify, with the help of the prince of Elephantine, attacked the governor of Thebes and his ally the prince of Qift. But the operations were finally suspended, given that the country was paralyzed by a period of drought and famine. Since the record makes a distinction between Neferkare and Ankhtify we may safely assume that they are not the same person.[374] Neferkare is not included on the Abydos King List or the Saqqara King List.

In the south the ruler was Intef I. He ruled in Thebes, near what is later known as Luxor. It lies in the middle of the country and was the capital of Upper (southern) Egypt.[375] Here is what is known about this ruler:

Intef I was a local Egyptian ruler at Thebes, and a member of the Eleventh dynasty during the First Intermediate Period. He was the first of his dynasty to assume the title of Pharaoh, with the Horus name of Sehertawy, ('He who has brought calm to the Two Lands'). Intef I was the son of Mentuhotep I. His authority was contested by the other nomarchs of Egypt, chief among them being the Tenth dynasty at Herakleopolis Magna and Ankhtifi, the well known nomarch of Hierakonpolis who was a faithful follower of the Herakonpolitan dynasty. On his accession to the throne, Intef probably ruled little more than the surrounding areas of his capital but he had gained control over Koptos, Dendera, and the three nomes of Hierakonpolis by the end of his reign after apparently winning a victory over Ankhtifi or this nomarch's successor.[376] His reign's length is unknown but must have been less than 16 years since the damaged Turin Canon papyrus assigns this figure to the combined reigns of both Mentuhotep I and Intef I. He was succeeded by his brother Intef II. Intef I died in 2118 BC, so he was not the Pharaoh of Egypt who met with Abraham and Sarah.

Intef II, the brother of Intef I, was a Pharaoh of the Eleventh dynasty during the First Intermediate Period. His capital was also located at Thebes. At this time Egypt was split between several local dynasties. After the death of the nomarch Ankhtifi, before 2118 BC, Intef II united the southern nomes down to the First Cataract which is near Aswan today, close to the southern border of Egypt today. After this he clashed with his main rivals, the nomarchs of Herakleopolis Magna for the possession of Abydos. Abydos is about in the center of the country, in a north/south direction. The city changed hands several times, but Intef II was eventually victorious, extending his rule north to the thirteenth nome, which meant that he controlled most of the country with the exception of the Nile Delta area at the far north of the country.

After these wars, more friendly relations were established and the rest of Intef's reign was peaceful. The discovery of a statue of Intef II, wrapped in a *sed* festival robe, in the sanctuary of Heqaib at Elephantine suggests that this king's authority extended to the region of the First Cataract and, perhaps, over part of Lower Nubia by his thirtieth year. This impression would appear to be confirmed by an expedition led by Djemi from Gebelein to the land of Wawat (i.e.: Nubia) during his reign. Consequently, when Intef II died, he left behind a strong government in Thebes which controlled the whole of Upper Egypt and maintained a border just south of Asyut. However, the First Cataract is back at Aswan, which is far south of the "thirteenth nome," indicating that during his reign he lost control of the majority of the center of the country.[377] The earliest attested dating of the god Amun at Karnak occurs during his reign. The surviving sections of the Turin Canon for the Middle Kingdom with Intef II assigns this king a reign of 49 years. Therefore, having taken over from his brother in 2118 BC and having reigned for 49 years, he must have died in 2069 BC We may now state with confidence that Intef II was the King of Thebes at the crucial year of 2091 BC when Abraham and Sarah came there for grain. But is he the Pharaoh/King with whom Abraham and Sarah met? At this point in time he is the best candidate for that role. In summary, the King of Egypt with whom Abraham made a deal for grain was Intef II, a nomarch of an area somewhere between the border of Egypt to the south (and possibly including parts of Nubia south of there), on the one hand, and the "thirteenth nome" to the north, which was at the border of the delta region of the Nile itself.

Fig. 60 Intef II

We must now address the question as to whether Abraham was a King of Lower Egypt at this time. As noted above, Abraham was born in 2167 BC He died in 1992 BC The earliest Hyksos King took power in about 1650 BC Therefore, in spite of Ralph Ellis' attempt to make Abraham a Hyksos King, he was off by at least 300 years. Instead, Abraham and Sarah probably met Intef II, a fairly successful king of Upper (southern) Egypt who, throughout his long reign of 49 years, saw his empire ebb and flow, only to become miniscule at his death around 2069 BC, some 22 years after Abraham and Sarah met him. There is some evidence that there were severe famines and shortages during this period, covering over 50 years. The rival of Intef II proudly expressed how he had fed the people, even of Intef's father's control during his lifetime due to his judicious planning. We know that the famine of his time, one generation removed from Abraham and Sarah, was so great that it completely dried up a lake in the area, causing significant crop failures. It is not unreasonable to suspect that the lake did not regain capacity and because of that the famine continued until Abraham came to acquire grain from Intef II.

Because Intef II had conquered his rival Ankhtify, who had been an amazingly adept person in seeing that preparations for the upcoming famine were necessary, it is likely that Intef II learned from his adversary who, almost assuredly, submitted to the overlordship of Intef II. We know this because Ankhtify built himself a huge tomb near the end of his life, after acceding to the reign of his overlord, Intef II. Yet, it was Ankhtify who had all the grain stored away for such tough times. He died in 2113 BC, so it is unlikely that his grain was still around in 2091 BC when Abraham and Sarah arrived. However, it is quite likely that Intef II, heir to his father who had conquered Ankhtify, had learned the secrets of proper planning, and maintained his control over his lands because he controlled the grain. So we may safely determine that it was Intef II who was the King of Egypt who took Sarah into his harem.

Let's now move to Isaac, who, some long time later, also had to go to another land to obtain grain. We do not know the year in which this incident occurred. However, we know that Isaac was born in 2067 BC and died in 1887 BC Let's assume that this incident occurred at least halfway through his life, or, say, around 1997 BC This is almost 100 years after the incident recorded about Abraham and Sarah, which occurred in 2091 BC Furthermore, and this is very important, the incident between Isaac and a king was dealing with Abimilech, the King of the Philistines, and not a King of Egypt. In case there is any question left, let's look at the Isaac story. It is in Genesis:

And there was a famine in the land, beside the first famine that was in the days of Abraham. And Isaac went unto Abimelech king of the Philistines unto Gerar. And the Lord appeared unto him, and said, "Go not down into Egypt; dwell in the land which I shall tell thee of. Sojourn in this land, and I will be with thee, and will bless thee; for unto thee, and unto thy seed, I will give all these countries, and I will perform the oath which I sware unto Abraham thy father. And I will make thy seed to multiply as the stars of heaven, and will give unto thy seed all these countries; and in thy seed shall all the nations of the earth be blessed. Because that Abraham obeyed my voice, and kept my charge, my commandments, my statutes, and my laws." And Isaac dwelt in Gerar: and the men of the place asked him of his wife; and he said, "She is my sister": for he feared to say, "She is my wife; lest, said he, the men of the place should kill me for Rebekah; because she was fair to look upon." And it came to pass, when he had been there a long time, that Abimelech king of the Philistines looked out at a window, and saw, and, behold, Isaac was sporting with Rebekah his wife. And Abimelech called Isaac, and said, "Behold, of a surety she is thy wife: and how saidst thou, She is my sister?" And Isaac said unto him, "Because I said, Lest I die for her." And Abimelech said, "What is this thou hast done unto us? one of the people might lightly have lien with thy wife, and thou shouldest have brought guiltiness upon us." And Abimelech charged all his people, saying, "He that toucheth this man or his wife shall surely be put to death." Then Isaac sowed in that land, and received in the same year an hundredfold: and the Lord blessed him."[378]

Not surprisingly, there are significant differences between this story and the one involving Abraham and Sarah. First, Rebekah is not the sister, or half-sister of Isaac. In fact Isaac only says that she is in fact his wife. As noted above, the scene is now the kingdom of the Philistines headed by Abimilech, and not Egypt, where marrying a sister was considered a pharoah's right. And most important, Isaac "sowed in that land" and prospered, as opposed to Abraham, who left, according to Ellis, to "save his skin." In short, the differences between these two stories outweigh the similarities. I am amazed that Ellis would see one story, over 100 years separated from the other, as a "carryover" by a scribe.

Let's now move to Jacob, who lived almost 200 years later than Abraham. Ralph Ellis would have us believe that Jacob was a King of Egypt, as had been his grandfather Abraham, and that he was a Hyksos King. However, I have already shown that the Hyksos were 300 years removed from the time of Abraham. Therefore, since Abraham was not a Hyksos king, should we expect that Jacob was a Hyksos king? Unfortunately, for Ellis, the answer is "no." Ellis would have us believe that he has found Jacob in the Hyksos king Yacobaam.[379] Unfortunately, Yacobaam reigned for only about 5 years from 1565 BC to 1560 BC[380] On the other hand, Jacob died in 1860 BC, so he could hardly have been the same person as Yacobaam. The problem for Ellis is that this thesis, that Abraham, Isaac, and Jacob were kings of Egypt, and Hyksos kings in particular, the "shepherd kings" or "foreign rulers" fails because of dating problems. His thesis fails because it is off by over 300 years. If he is off on this point, is there any validity to the rest of his work? You be the judge.

Let us start with Ellis' identification of some of these Patriarchs from outside the Bible. This list is found on pages 39 and page 75 of his book. I will summarize a few of them here. He identifies Cainan with Khyan, the fourth Hyksos king of the Fifteenth Dynasty. I have shown that Cainan lived from 3020 BC to 2620 BC Standard Egyptologists, however, say that Khyan reigned from about 1610 BC to 1580 BC[381] Ellis probably accepts the standard dates for his reign. However, if my thesis is correct there is no way that Cainan of the Bible could be equated with the Hyksos king Khyan. Furthermore, Ryholt notes that the name, Khyan, generally has been "interpreted as the Amorite *Hayanu* (reading *h-ya-a-n*) which the Egyptian form represents perfectly, and this is in all likelihood the correct interpretation."[382] Therefore, Khyan was not even of the line of the Patriarchs. He was an Amorite usurper into Egypt. His descendants had Amorite origins, not Caananite. Khyan was in fact a descendant of Tudiya, who was the son of Asshur, the son of Shem. However, this family line was not involved with the Patriarchs leading to Abraham (Arphaxad, Cainan, Salah, Eber, etc.)

He identified Yakubher with Eber of the Bible. I have shown that Eber lived from 2602 BC to 2198 BC Standard Egyptologists show that Yakubher reigned shortly after Khyan, which would place him around 1580 BC to, say 1550 BC[383] However, standard Egyptologists state that Yakubher was preceded by Sheshi, whom Ellis has identified as Abraham. Ellis then reveals another Jacob (Yakubher) whom he calls Yacobaam. This places Yakubher 8 generations before where Yakubher should be located.

He identified Apepi with Ragau of the Bible. Then another Apepi he has identified with Serug of the Bible. Irrespective of the dating issue, let me move on to a more important point. While some Egyptologists once believed that there were two separate kings who bore the name Apepi, namely Auserre Apepi and Aqenenre Apepi, it is now recognized that Khamudi succeeded Apepi I at Avaris and that there was only one king named Apepi or Apophis.[384] Therefore Ellis is incorrect on this. There were not two Apepi pharaohs, so they could not have been Ragau and Seruch. Khamudi, the successor of the only Apepi of Avaris was himself conquered by Ahmose. Khamudi was the last pharaoh of the Fifteenth Dynasty.

Nehesy has been identified by Ellis as the next Hyksos pharaoh, and he has equated him with Terah, the father of Abraham. However, Nehesy was a pharaoh of the Fourteenth Dynasty, not the Fifteenth Dynasty. Therefore, his actual existence preceded that of Apepi and Khamudi rather than succeeded either of them. Finally, Nehesy was called "the black Pharaoh" because he was a Nubian.[385] Ellis neglected to mention that. Nehesy could not have been Terah, the father of Abraham.

Ellis identifies Sheshi with Abraham. Once again, Ellis has moved Sheshi from his proper place in time. The Danish Egyptologist, Kim Ryholt, has suggested that Sheshi was a Fourteenth Dynasty Asiatic king.[386] This would place Sheshi before Kyhan, named above, and would certainly remove him as a candidate for Abraham.

Chapter Twenty-Six

The Goddesses of Sumer

Ninsun

In Mesopotamian religion Ninsun was the city goddess of Kullab. Known as "the great wild cow" and the great queen, Ninsun was considered wise, "knows everything" and she was an interpreter of dreams. She offered incense and drink to her brother Shamash and questioned his decision to send Gilgamesh against Humbaba. When doing so, she would wear a circlet on her head and an ornament on her breast. She adopted Enkidu as her own son prior to the quest against Humbaba. Worshiped especially by herders in southern Mesopotamia, she was originally represented as a cow and was considered to be the divine power behind all the qualities that herders wanted in their cattle. She was also represented in human form and could give birth to human offspring. Her son was the wild bull Dumuzi, whom she lamented in a yearly ritual. In this sense she is also seen as possibly the same goddess as her sister, Inanna, about whom I will write shortly.

She enticed Kesed, the son of Arphaxad, to be her consort. Kesed was a High Priest in her Temple of Kullab, a part of Uruk. Kesed must have handled his job well. Ninsun stayed with him and they together had five sons and a daughter. The sons were Ur-Nammu, Gilgamesh, Ur-Engur, and Utu-Hegal. The daughter was Mu'ak, who became the wife of Salah and the parents of Eber. As a divine being, therefore, these children were semi-divine. We are all familiar with the story of Gilgamesh and his great strength. We must assume that the other siblings shared the same added qualities that Gilgamesh had due to having a divine mother.

When they became adults, their mother, Ninsun, became a consort to Ur-Nammu, and Ur-Engur as well. Therefore, the sons of Ur-Nammu and Ur-Engur became 2/3 divine, having a divine mother and a semi-divine father. This includes Shulgi and Ora, the son and daughter of Ur-Nammu, as well as Dungi, the son of Ur-Engur. Finally, since Mu'ak was semi-divine, the son of her marriage to Salah, who was Eber, would have had at least some advanced genetic material as well.

From this we can see that through Kesed's relationship with Ninsun, the Patriarchal line was infused with divine genetics. As noted Mu'ak had Eber. In addition, Ora married Ragau and they had Serug (Sargon the Great). There is no way to know just what this infusion of divine genetics did to these people. We have the *Epic of Gilgamesh* that gives us a hint, however.

In the Epic, it is said that "King Gilgamesh's strength and lust left him with no rivals, so the gods prevailed on the goddess Aruru to make him a brother, which she duly did. Thus, Enkidu was created. Enkidu was brought up in the wild, eating grass in the hills. He was the strongest man in the world." Enkidu came to Gilgamesh to fight him and "Gilgamesh threw him aside. Enkidu acknowledged Gilgamesh's strength, and they became friends."[387]

On the death of Ur-Nammu, her son, Ninsun bemoaned his fate in a tablet that has been found: "The mother, miserable because of her son, the mother of the king, holy Ninsun, was crying: 'Oh my heart!' Because of the fate decreed for Ur-Namma, because it made the trustworthy shepherd pass away, she was weeping bitterly in the broad square, which is otherwise a place of entertainment. Sweet sleep did not come to the people whose happiness ......; they passed their time in lamentation over the trustworthy shepherd who had been snatched away."[388]

We have no record of when Kesed died. However, through his relationship with Ninsun the divine genetics entered into the family of Shem. Ninsun's father was Nannar-Sin. The temple in Ur that Ur-Nammu built for Nannar was therefore built for his own father-in-law.

Inanna

Inanna is the Sumerian goddess of sexual love, fertility, and warfare. She is known by many different names, including Innin, Ennin, Ninnin, Ninni, Ninanna, Ninnar, Innina, Ennina, Irnina, Innini, Nana and Nin, commonly derived from an earlier Ninana "lady of the sky."[389] Her Akkadian counterpart is Ishtar.[390] In Canaan she was known as Ashtoreth or Astarte.[391] In Egypt she had several names, including Isis, Hept, Semiramis, and Neith.[392] Inanna's name is commonly taken from Nin-anna "Queen of Heaven" (from Sumerian NIN "lady," and AN "sky").

As early as the Uruk period, which began immediately after the Flood (ca. 4000 BC to 3100 BC), Inanna was associated with the city of Uruk. The famous Uruk Vase, found in a deposit of cult objects of the Uruk III period, depicts a row of naked men carrying various objects, bowls, vessels, and baskets of farm produce, and bringing sheep and goats, to a female figure facing the ruler, ornately dressed for a "divine marriage," and attended by a servant. The female figure holds the symbol of the two twisted reeds of the doorpost signifying Inanna behind her, while the male figure holds a box and stack of bowls, the later cuneiform sign signifying En, or high priest of the temple.[393]

Seal impressions from the period of 3100 BC to 2900 BC show a fixed sequence of city symbols including those of Ur, Larsa, Zabalam, Urum, Arina, and probably Kish. It is likely that this list reflects the report of contributions to Inanna at Uruk from cities supporting her cult. A number of similar seals were found from the slightly later Early Dynastic I phase at Ur, from about 2900 BC to 2600 BC, in a slightly different order, combined with the rosette symbol of Inanna, that were definitely used for this purpose. They had been used to lock storerooms to preserve materials set aside for her cult.[394]

Along the Tigris and Euphrates rivers were many shrines and temples dedicated to Inanna. The Temple of Eanna, meaning "house of heaven" or "house of An" in Uruk, was the greatest of these, where "sacred prostitution" was a common practice. The god of this fourth-millennium city was originally An or Anu. After its dedication to Inanna, during the reign of Enmerkar, the son of Nimrod, as shown earlier, the temple seems to have housed priests and priestesses of the goddess. The High Priestess would choose for her bed a young man who represented the shepherd Dumuzi, consort and son of Inanna, in a "hieros gamos" or "Sacred Marriage," celebrated during the annual Akitu (New Year) ceremony, at the spring Equinox. Samuel Noah Kramer, in *The Sacred Marriage Rite*, states that in late Sumerian history (end of the third millennium, around 2000 BC) kings established their legitimacy by taking the place of Dumuzi in the temple for one night on the tenth day of the New Year festival. [395]

Inanna figures prominently in one of the earliest legends, *Enmerkar and the Lord of Aratta*, in something like a kingmaker role, transferring her personal abode and favor, and thus hegemony, from the court of Aratta's king to that of Uruk, whose king was Enmerkar, the son of Nimrod. I dealt with this earlier when writing about Enmerkar and his brother, Enshukeshdanna, the King of Aratta. Inanna had apparently become disenchanted with Aratta, since it was not the center of Sumerian activity. She preferred to become the patroness of Uruk instead.

In one story, Inanna tricked the god of culture, Enki, who was worshipped in the city of Eridu, into giving her the Mes. The Mes were documents or tablets which were blueprints to civilization. They represented everything from truth to weaving to prostitution, granting power over, or possibly existence to, all the aspects of civilization (both positive and negative). Inanna traveled to Enki's city, Eridu, and by getting him drunk, she got him to give her seven Mes, which she took to her city of Uruk. She was given the "Me" for "Lordship….Godship, the Exalted and Enduring Tiara, the Throne of Kingship," and "the Exalted Scepter and Staff, the Exalted Shrine, Righteous Rulership."[396]

When Enki recovered from his hangover the next day he realized his mistake and made efforts to recover the "Mes." He eventually did so, but not until after Inanna had declared herself the "Queen of Heaven." It was probably at this time that she had gone to the King of Babylon, Nimrod, and asked him to build her a temple in his kingdom. They had had two sons, Enmerkar and Enshukeshdanna, almost certainly as a result of the "Sacred Marriage" ceremony of Inanna and Nimrod. He consented to having Enmerkar make a temple for Inanna at Uruk. Enmerkar's brother, Enshukeshdanna, was angry, because Aratta had traditionally been Inanna's "home." Enmerkar succeeded in getting Inanna situated in her new temple at Uruk. He, too, as King of Uruk, engaged in a "Sacred Marriage" with Inanna, the result of which copulation was their son Lugalbanda.

Once again, then, we see that the "religion" of Nimrod and Inanna was being carried out. One of the basic tenets of the religion was that Inanna would have sexual relations with her husband and then their son. In her case, she did this for several generations of sons (Cush, Nimrod, Enmerkar and Athothis [brothers], and Kenkenes. With the tales written in the Sumerian tablets that have been discovered, it is clear that the gods and goddesses of Sumer took on normal human traits. Zechariah Sitchin has discussed this at length, and believes that they were all "real" people.[397] We will probably never know just where these Sumerian gods came from, but it seems clear to me that they were not just "made up" only to become "mythology." In fact, as I have shown, key players mentioned in this book talk about Inanna and Ninsun as their "mother" or the "mother of their son."

While it is not within the purview of this book to deal with this in great detail, the Bible does give us a possible place to look: "And it came to pass, when men began to multiply on the face of the earth, and daughters were born unto them, that the sons of God saw the daughters of men that they were fair; and they took them wives of all which they chose."[398] The reference here is to male gods cohabiting with female humans. However, if the male gods could make wives of the daughters of men, then why couldn't the female gods make husbands out of the male humans as well? It would appear that this not only occurred to Inanna and Ninsun. Even more importantly, they made an entire religion out of it. The High Priest of the temple, a human male, or even the king of the city-state, would engage in a "Sacred Marriage" with the goddess of the temple. In some cases, there were also priestesses who would take the place of the goddess, but the tales that I have referred to are specific in that it was the goddess herself who engaged in the "Sacred Marriage." Thus, for instance, both Gilgamesh and Ur-Nammu are on record as having called Ninsun their "mother." Similarly, Inanna was claimed to be the mother of several persons as well (such as Lugalbanda, for instance).

The concept of a Sacred Marriage, initially formed by Nimrod and Inanna, presumably, was carried forth for many generations. It became a "state religion" and was eventually honored by a ceremony of the "Sacred Marriage" on New Year's day (and night) each year. I have shown an example of this in the Appendix.[399] When we come to the line of the Patriarchs, we see that Inanna was engaged with the sons of Ham in various capacities (see the genealogical chart in this chapter). Similarly, for the sons of Shem we see that Ninsun was active as well. However, in one case that is particularly interesting, Inanna's progeny left the line of Ham to join with the line of Shem.

Nimrod and Inanna had a daughter, Azura, who became the wife of Eber, the Patriarch. Through this means, then, the genetic influence of Inanna was infused into the Patriarchal line. However, Eber's father, Salah, had married Mu'ak, who was the daughter of Kesed and Ninsun. This, then, meant that Peleg had even more divine blood in him. His grandmother was Inanna on one side, and his great grandmother was Ninsun on the other side. In the next generation, the situation became even more compounded, since Ragau married Ora, who was both the daughter and the granddaughter of Ninsun. Of course, Ragau was the great-grandson of Inanna on one side and the great-great-grandson of Ninsun on the other.

It is in the next generation that we see this genetic influence coming to a head. Serug, the son of Ragau and Ora, was Sargon the Great of history, the Emperor of Sumer and Akkad. He obtained this position because of the matrilineal descent that was so powerful in Sumer and later in Akkad. Here is the way this lays out clearly. From Inanna, Sargon was her great-great-grandson. From Azura, Sargon was the great-grandson. From Mu'ak, Sargon was the great-great-grandson. From Ora, Sargon was the son. From Ninsun, Sargon was the grandson and great-grandson, and great-great-great-grandson. These women all had divine blood, either from Inanna or from Ninsun, or from both of them. Therefore, Serug (Sargon the Great), was full of royal blood, the blood of the gods. Is it any wonder that he was so successful? I think not. The son of Serug was Nahor, who was also a High Priest at the Temple of Enlil at Nippur. If he engaged in "Sacred Marriage" ceremonies, it would have been with a priestess in the temple, since Enlil was a male god. However, his son Terah had nearly equal claims to the divine heritage as did his grandfather Sargon.

Terah's grandmother and great-grandmother was Ora. His great-grandmother was Ninsun. His great-great-grandmother was Ninsun. His great-great-grandmother was Azura. His great-great-great-grandmother was Inanna. His great-great-great-great-grandmother was Mu'ak. And finally his great-great-great-great-great-grandmother was Ninsun, again! We can now see clearly how the matrilineal descent played a very important role in the line of the Patriarchs, in spite of the fact that the Bible overlooks the women entirely. We now also may understand better why it was to Terah that Enlil came when he became so enraged by the actions of Naram-Sin, the rogue son of Sargon (Serug) the Great. Enlil, speaking through Nahor as High Priest, elected Terah, the young king of the Gutians, to avenge him. Nahor, incidentally, was Terah's father, so the connection was, needless to say, close. While Terah did not succeed in Enlil's request, we have seen that Enlil proceeded to deal with his son Abraham instead.

On the Hamite side of the family, Inanna was also influential. Following the death of Nimrod, his heathen form of worship was continued by his wife, Queen Semiramis, which is another name for Inanna. She claimed that her husband had become the Sun god, and was to be worshipped. Some time after this, Queen Semiramis conceived through another "Sacred Marriage" ceremony and gave birth to a son whom she named Tammuz (Dumuzi). However, she went even farther than that and declared that Dumuzi was actually Nimrod reborn, and that he had been supernaturally conceived. However, even though Semiramis claimed to have given birth to a savior, it was she that was worshipped, and not her son. She was worshipped as the mother of the gods.

Many different ideas from the Babylonian religion have come down through the generations. One of the key doctrines is that of the mother-son relationship. As the Babylonian people were scattered throughout the world, they took with them the idea that Semiramis had miraculously conceived and given birth to Nimrod reincarnated. Thus, all through the world, men began to worship a divine mother and god-child, long before the birth of Christ. The woman appears in different ways, and is called by different names, but she is always the same person: Indrani in India, Cybelle in Asia, Fortuna (the boy) in Rome, Ceres in Greece, Shing Moo in China, Hertha in Germany, Sisa in Scandanavia. But the woman was really Semiramis, the queen of Babylon, who is Inanna the Sumerian goddess. Even Israel, when it fell into apostasy, worshipped Ashteroth, who was known to the Jews as the "queen of Heaven" as told in Jeremiah.[400]

Inanna had an affair with Asshur, the son of Shem, son of Noah. Asshur was an early resident and co-builder of the city of Nineveh, one of the oldest cities in the world. Nimrod is accredited with founding the city. It appears that Asshur, a son of Shem, became entranced by Nimrod, a grandson of Ham. For some reason, Shem may have disowned his older son, Asshur, because he became involved with the pagan Nimrod. In the genealogy of the descendants of Noah leading to Abraham, Shem lists his third son, Arphaxad, rather than Elam or Asshur, his first two sons. Perhaps Asshur had fallen away from the true faith and joined the pagan forces of Nimrod and his consort, Isis (Inanna). After the death of Asshur, he was immortalized by being worshipped as a god, a sign that this theory is correct. It was common for Inanna to immortalize persons with whom she had relations. She began her reign by building a splendid mausoleum in honor of Asshur (also called Ninus after the city he built) at Nineveh on the Euphrates plain. Inanna had had an affair with Asshur/Ninus so it was only appropriate for her to recognize him with a shrine after his death.

She then went full force on a building campaign and decided to have a large, immaculate city built for herself not far from Nineveh. This was the new city of Babylon where her husband, Nimrod, was King. It was marked out on horseback on the river bank of the Euphrates, and according to Diodorus, Semiramis (Inanna) employed about two million workmen she accumulated from all parts of her imperial realm to complete this task. The perimeter of the walls alone were 66 kilometers long and the width was so wide that 6 harnessed chariots could ride abreast along these walls. They were approximately 100 meters high, though some historians stated that their height was greatly exaggerated and were much less. The city was defended by 250 towers, and the Euphrates, which ran through the middle of the city, was crossed by a bridge 900 meters long that was lined with awesome quays for 30 kilometers. At each end of the bridge was built a fortified castle, and the queen's residence. They were linked by a subterranean passage under the river, which was diverted to carry this out.[401]

Inanna later traveled further into the land of Asia and built a vast park opposite Mount Bagistan, a number of ornate fountains at Ecbatana, and a reputation that far surpassed any other female warrior for the period of this time. She was said to have been responsible for many ancient cities on the banks of the Euphrates and the Tigris rivers, and also for erecting many of the most unique and wonderful monuments and sites in all of Asia. Several of these major extraordinary works in the Middle East were a bit extreme and astonishing for just one person, but became current in later ages. The builders, being unknown, were ascribed by popular tradition, and credited these feats to this mysterious queen. Besides conquering Media, she subdued Egypt with her husband, Nimrod, as well as a great part of Ethiopia. While she was in Egypt she consulted an oracle of Ammon - exploring foreknowledge of her future. Instead, the oracle gave her the prediction about the time of her unusual departure. The oracle replied that she would come to her end when her son, Ninyas, would conspire against her and try to take her life.[402]

When she returned to Bactra, she began making plans to invade India, and for several years she made elaborate preparations, resulting in the most grievous mistake of her notorious but flamboyant reign. She raised a gigantic army and succeeded in crossing the Indus, but her troops were soon put to flight and herself suffered an injury that nearly took her life. It was just too insidious of this strategy to match horse and chariots in battle with the size of ferocious, angry war-elephants. During the activity of battle, she was severely wounded in one arm by an arrow and a javelin that pierced through her back from the mighty King Stabrobates of India. She just scarcely managed to escape by crossing the Indus River, drawing her sword and destroying the bridge she had ordered assembled, since her enemies would not dare pursue her across the river.[403]

It was not long after her recovery that her son Ninyas (by Asshur/ Ninus of Neneveh), along with the eunuchs of the palace, plotted against her. Ninyas had always been a troublesome burden for the queen, as in her confession she mentions that she had done so much for him, and received nothing in return. "I was a good mother to him, as any sun-burned peasant who brings her babe into the vineyard on her back; and will you believe, he cared more for a rough word or a rude jest from the Great King than for my fondest caress, my smile, my tears. When I have pleaded with him, even to his own advantage, he has turned his back on me, and laughed outright. He loved the meanest dancing-girl out of the market better than the mother to whom he owed his life, his beauty, his favor with the Great King."[404] As the legend follows, Inanna reigned approximately 42 years and then turned the sovereignty of her rule over to her son Ninyas and clandestinely disappeared. Legends were told and flourished throughout the ages that she took flight towards heaven in the form of a dove from which the fabulous nature of this narrative is apparent. Inanna became affiliated with the Syrian goddess associated with the name of Astarte of Ascalon, Anaitis of Persia, or Ashtoreth of Canaan, which were handed down from the earlier renditions of the Semitic Ishtar of Babylon; originating from the earlier profile of the goddess Innana of Sumer - to whom the dove was sacred. [405]

Inanna was the instigator in forming the false religion aimed at supporting their rule and, of course, her suggestion fell upon open ears. The religion she invented was based primarily upon a corruption of the primeval astronomy formulated by Noah's righteous ancestors before the Flood. In the original, this system depicted, by means of constellations, the story of Satan's rebellion and the war in the heavens, his subversion of mankind, the fall of Adam and Eve, the promise of One to come who would suffer and die to relieve man from the curse of sin then be installed as Lord of Creation, and the final re-subjugation of the cosmos to God through Him. These eternal truths were corrupted by her into a mythic cycle whereby the great dragon is depicted as the rightful lord of the universe whose throne has been temporarily usurped by One whom we can recognize as the God of the Bible. The serpent creates man in his present miserable state, but promises that a child would one day be born of a divine mother - which child would supplant God and become a god himself, and return rulership of the earth to the serpent. These fables were based upon the then widely-known story of the constellations, and were introduced under the guise of revealing the hidden esoteric knowledge concealed in them (regardless of the fact that the original was quite straightforward).

Although this esotericism was the second element in Inanna/ Semiramis' cult, it only masked the actual goal which was the worship of the "heavenly host," which the Bible equates with Satan's army of fallen angels.[406] Satan was quite willing to receive worship "by proxy;" hence the third major element of the mystery religion was emperor-worship. This religion was propagated by a hierarchy of priests and priestesses, to whom were assigned the task of initiating the populace at large into it's ascending degrees of revelation, culminating at the highest level in both direct worship of Satan and demon-possession.

We may safely state that it was Inanna herself, with her husband, Nimrod (Menes, or Narmer in Egypt), who instituted the ancient rite in Egypt in which a Pharaoah would marry his own sister.

Of the gods of the Sumerian pantheon, only Inanna and Ninsun seem to have actually been born on earth. Perhaps because of this they weren't immortal after all. In any case, we know that Inanna finally died. According to my calculations, Inanna died in Egypt in 2065 BC, having lived well over 1200 years, longer than any of the Patriarchs. It is no wonder that she was considered divine.

Although not developed in this book, another goddess of Sumer was also instrumental in the process of infusing the "divine genes" into the family of the Patriarchs. I will simply post a chart to show this. It is not important to the case that I have made, but supports it. The bottom line is that the pantheon of gods, through the females, infiltrated the family of the Patriarchs from the earliest days after the Flood. The reader must weigh these facts as seen fit.

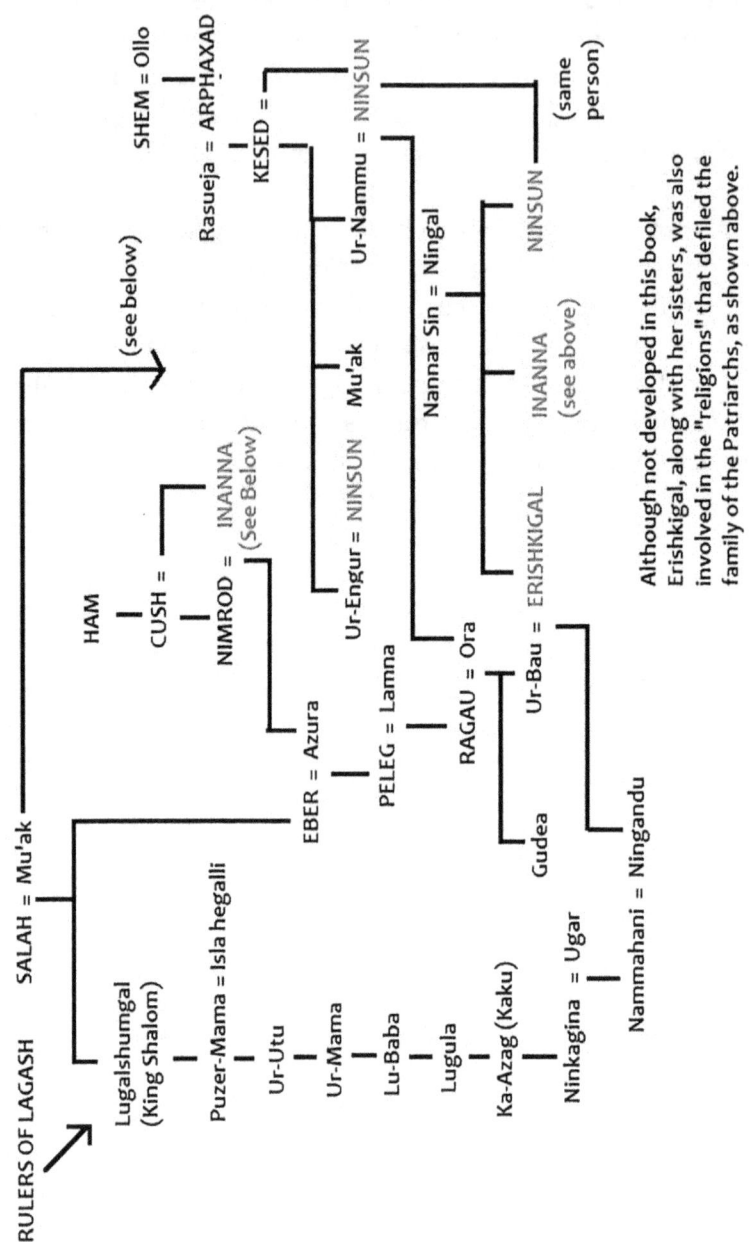

Fig. 61 Connections of the Goddesses to the Line of Shem

Epilogue

The Bible has proven to be an amazingly accurate record of ancient events. By comparing non-biblical records with the Biblical accounts, it is now possible to equate Biblical Patriarchs with non-biblical persons. The process began by locking the Bible to a date that was clearly defined from non-biblical sources. That date was the beginning of the reign of Soloman, who was shown, from non-biblical sources, to be a real king of Jerusalem. His reign began in 971 BC From that date the Bible allowed us to move backward, first to the Exodus (1447 BC), then the year that Jacob went to Egypt to buy grain (1877 BC), then Jacob's birth (2007 BC), then his father Isaac's birth (2067 BC) and then to Abraham, Isaac's father's birth (2167 BC).

Through this process two things were accomplished: first, we finally found a starting point for dealing with the history of the descendants of Noah. In theory, working backwards, we could place each Patriarch in his proper "sitz im leben." Second, by placing these Patriarchs in a particular time frame, we were enabled to see if history would verify that they were real people who fit the framework of the biblical record. As the process went forward, I have been able to show that, indeed, the Patriarchs began with Arphaxad, who was shown to be Igrish Halam, the first king of Ebla, the city he or his father founded when they left the mountains of Ararat after the waters of the Flood receded. Arphaxad's son, Cainan, was found to be Irkab-Damu, the second king of Ebla.

His son, Salah, was found to be Ar-Ennum, the third king of Ebla. His son, Eber, was found to be Ebrium, the fourth king of Ebla.

Ebrium was shown to be a very powerful leader of the sons of Shem. He lived at the time of Sargon the Great, a very powerful ruler who eventually conquered all of Sumer and Akkad, except for Ebla. Ebla was not destroyed. It was avoided. The reason it was avoided was because Eber, the King of Ebla, was shown to be the great-grandfather of Sargon himself. Eber essentially put a stop to his great-grandson's ambitions, and Sargon relented. Sargon was shown to be Serug of the Bible. This must have come as a shock to the reader, but as the story unfolded it became clear that he was, in fact, Sargon the Great.

At the same time that this secular rulership moved from Ebla into the plain of Sumer, an area that had been settled by the sons of Ham, there was a surprising acceptance, if reluctantly, of the over-lordship of the Shemites to the territory of Sumer. One by one the Shemites took over the rule of the city-states of Sumer. The family of Cush, a son of Ham, had gone against the will of Noah and had entered into Shemite territory. Noah had made it clear that certain lands were to be Hamite, Shemite, or Japhethite, but Ham's son, Cush, apparently didn't want to move that far away before starting his own empire.

The son of Cush, Nimrod, whose real name was Meshkiaggasher, the name Nimrod being a nickname for "the Rebel," became the point-man for Cush. He moved quickly to take over the central Sumerian plain, founding several cities. His son, whose name was Enmerkar, and Enmerkar's brother, Enshukeshdanna, the King of Aratta, land of the Gutian Empire, engaged in a sibling rivalry that managed to get written in stone, literally. This record proved that Aratta was the source of the ancient Gutian Kingdom that was to play a part hundreds of years later, bringing Terah, the father of Abraham, into Ur of the Kasidim, the city that was named after Kesed, a brother of Arphaxad, both being sons of Shem.

The history unfolded and showed that over time the descendants of Shem eventually eliminated the descendants of Ham. Even the great Nimrod was shown to have moved from Sumer to Egypt, where he formed the second greatest culture of mankind after the Flood. Over the next few hundred years a "jockeying" for positions occurred among the descendants of Shem, with a small segment of Hamites still in control in a key city-state, Uruk. However, even in Uruk, the son of Shem, whose name was Kesed, had been placed in what became a seminal position as the High Priest of the temple at Kullab, a "suburb" of Uruk. In that position, he became the "voice of god" in that his role was to communicate the will of the gods to the king.

Kesed never accepted the idea of a single god. Unlike his brother, Arphaxad, he delved deeper and deeper into the astrologically based faith in "gods" who were known to "exist" in the stars but who also "cohabited" with the people on earth. We found that in some strange way, the gods of Sumer did, in fact, exist on the earth. Kesed's allegiance was total, and he passed his knowledge along faithfully over several hundred years, eventually changing the faith in a single God into the faith in a pantheon of gods. His power must have been immense.

Kesed utilized his influence on both the secular and the religious levels. On the secular level, he enabled his sons Gilgamesh, Ur-Engur, Utu-Hegal, and Ur-Nammu to all become kings in Sumer. Their influence, politically, transformed Sumer. On the religious level his influence was more subtle, although not less powerful. He was a practical man, however, and the reign of Serug, whom the world knew as Sargon the Great, caused him to pause and "regroup," as it were. Serug was descended from Arphaxad, the brother of Kesed, so it was not important that Kesed be involved in any attempts to remove him, at least initially. However, on the death of Serug, his sons did not hold to the concept of a larger family in power, and they attempted to disrupt the hegemony that Kesed had spent literally hundreds of years to create. In the end, as the "voice of god," Kesed, working with his descendant High Priest Nahor, at Nippur, found it necessary to take out the sons of Serug, one at a time, with Naram-Sin being the most important, since Naram-Sin had decided to deify himself while still living!

Other descendants, such as Gudea, followed the plan and ruled effectively, and peacefully, with enormous building projects dedicated to the gods of the pantheon in Sumer. Kesed's sons followed, in due course, as kings of Uruk and then kings of Ur, controlling larger and larger portions of Sumer while also attempting to extend control even beyond Akkad into Canaan to the west and Elam in the east. By the middle of the 21st century BC, as Kesed neared his own death, one last remnant of the family of Ham reared its head. They were the descendants of the King of Aratta, Enshukeshdanna, who called themselves Gutians, who began to cause troubles in Sumer. After having been influential under their first king in Sumer, Enmerkar's (son of Nimrod) empire was quite successful in extending Gutian influence. It waned as time passed, but the continued influence of the Shemites finally reached a conclusion. After a "dynasty" of 120 years in Aratta, the Gutians moved south and west into Sumer to re-exert control over the land that their ancestor, Enmerkar, had held as far back as 2500 BC

The result was a minor skirmish which involved a young king of Guti named Terah, who was not, himself, of the line of Ham, but who had become a warrior and head of the army of Nimrod, who was a Hamite. Terah had only been assigned his role as a king of Guti for 40 days (this city-state, Aratta, did not believe in passing the reign from father to son), and he was not as experienced as his adversary. His adversary was Utu-Hegal, the son of Kesed. As the son of Kesed, he had the power behind him. Kesed was, after all, the "voice of god." As that voice, Kesed made it clear that Utu-Hegal would be the victor in this "skirmish" among related family members. Terah ran from the field of battle and hid in a small town. But the townsfolk had heard the "oracle" that Utu-Hegal would be the victor, so they captured Terah and held him until Utu-Hegal

arrived. Under normal circumstances, Terah would have been executed and his head placed on a pike to be displayed as a symbol of
the power of Utu-Hegal. However, that did not happen. Instead,
Terah was made the High Priest of the temple of Nannar at Ur. It
is only by understanding that this was a "family matter" that this
act of generosity can be understood. Terah was clearly a member
of the "royal family" and as such deserved a second chance. Both
Nimrod and Kesed made sure that this occurred.

Kesed finally died, but not before seeing that his oldest son,
Ur-Nammu, was placed on the throne of Ur on the death of Utu-
Hegal due to a drowning. Ur-Nammu became one of the most
influential rulers of his family line. He built temples to the gods
throughout Sumer, the most important of which was his Temple
of Nannar-Sin in Ur. He also made enormous improvements to
the life of the people, including establishing a code of conduct for
the people that was eventually copied by both Hammurabi and
Moses. However, Ur-Nammu became embroiled in a political
struggle with enemies from the west, in Canaan, and he engaged
in a war with other local kings that led to his death. While on the
battlefield, his chariot hit a rock, throwing him out of the carriage,
and he was subsequently trampled to death by the following chariots. The result was that Ur, while not attacked directly, devolved
quickly and lost its position as a powerful city-state. Even Nannar-
Sin, the god of Ur, moved his temple to Haran in northern Sumer.
Nannar took his chief priest, Terah, with him. Terah took his son
Abram as well.

When Abram was 75 years of age he received a "vision" or "call"
from Yahweh, whom he had learned was the "true God." He was
told to leave Haran and go into Canaan. He left Haran after his
father, Terah, had died and went into Canaan where he became a
great ruler, even though the Bible downplays his role. He communicated with pharaohs in Egypt and was, along with his large army,
one of five kings who held a battle in Canaan in which the enemy
was defeated. He was blessed by Melchisedek, the High Priest of

Jerusalem. The remainder of the life of Abraham, Isaac, and Jacob has already been told.

Finally, I have shown that it was the influence of Inanna and Ninsun, the two Sumerian goddesses, who influenced many of the events recorded in this book. Because the progression of rulership in Sumer was based upon a matrilineal succession, Inanna and Ninsun became the "matriarchs" of the family of Shem, beginning as early as the son of Arphaxad, namely Kesed, who married Ninsun, and then Salah's wife (a daughter of Kesed and Ninsun), and Eber's wife, whose mother was Inanna, and finally Ragau's wife, whose mother was Ninsun. The result of this enormous infusion of divine genetics into the family of the "Patriarchs" through the "Matriarchs" was both Sargon the Great and Terah, the father of Abraham, and eventually Abraham himself, the father of three religions. Each, in their own way, had a significant impact on the society in which they lived. Sargon's was purely secular while Terah's was purely religious. However, in the case of Terah, his son rebelled against the religion of Nimrod and Inanna, and instead was called to a faith in the true God, Yahweh. His faithfulness has resulted in the three largest religious institutions in the world today: Judaism, Christianity, and Islam.

In creating this book I have offered the "history" as it has been presented throughout time, both in the Bible and in ancient documents. The stories were presented as if there was a true interaction between the gods of Sumer and the descendants of Noah as I have identified them. Liberal scholars would discount these stories as "myths," with the clear implication that they could not have happened the way they are purported to have happened in the stories themselves. However, the only way in which the "myth" argument can be made is from pure prejudice. Once that prejudice is removed then history is allowed to speak for itself from first hand sources.

The fact that Ur-Nammu, the last great king of Ur, made a statement in stone that he was the older brother of Gilgamesh and that his mother was the goddess Ninsun is extremely important. It proves two important facts presented in this book: first, that the patriarchs lived very long lives (Ur-Nammu lived at least 550 years); and second, that there was definite interaction between humans and the Sumerian gods at the physical level. The details laid out in this book only make sense when both of these facts are conceded. However, once they are conceded, the stories then make complete sense and the flesh can be put back on the bones of these ancient figures. Their stories "make sense."

Appendix One

Ages of the Patriarchs and other Important Persons after Noah

Below I have organized the Patriarchs and other Important Persons by generation, showing their respective ages in each generation.

Name	Age
Generation 1:	
Noah	950
Generation 2:	
Shem	600
Japheth	885
Ham	Unk
Generation 3:	
Elam	386
Aram	400
Asshur	856

Arphaxad   535
Sumu-Abi   550
Cush   908

Generation 4:

Tudiya   650
Cainan   460
Kesed   500
Sumu-la-ilu 395
Nimrod   955

Generation 5:

Adamu   294
Salah   460
Gilgamesh   298
Ur-Engur   310
Utu-Hegal   537
Ur-Nammu   504
Zabium   209
Athothis   62

Generation 6:

Yangi   262
Eber   404
Ur-Lugal   278
Dungi   387
Shulgi   402
Abil-Sin   77
Kenkenes (Horus) Unk

Generation 7:

Suhlumu   238

Peleg   339
Utu-Kalamma 243
Bur-Sin   277
Amar-Sin   210
Shu-Sin   210
Ibbi-Sin   197

Generation 8:

Harharu   198
Ragau   339
Labasher   202
Gimil-Sin   234

Generation 9:

Mandaru   143
Serug   230
Ur-Baba   170
Ennundaranna 259
Ibi-Sin   209

Generation 10:

Imsu   120
Nachor   248
Meshede   245

Generation 11:

Harsu   unk.
Terah   205
Melamanna   201

Generation 12:

Didanu	82
Abraham	175
Haran	159
Nahor	172
Lugalkidul	187

Averages by Generation

1.	950	ending 2937 BC
2.	742	
3.	606	
4.	592	
5.	382	
6.	365	(Over 12 generations the average age fell 66 years per generation)
7.	245	
8.	243	
9.	205	
10.	204	
11.	203	
12.	155	ending on average 2125 BC (Abraham died 1992 BC)

The total sample consists of 59 persons, of whom 57 persons have been given an age. In all cases, the death year is known but in many cases, other than the Patriarchs, the birth years are estimated based on the previous generation birth year. In most cases, the difference between generational births was 20 to 50 years. While the higher end would be considered excessive today, apparently people had children later in life than we do today. The Biblical record supports this view.

Patriarchal Lifetimes after Abraham

Generation 1:

Ishmael	137
Achaim	149
Isaac	180

Generation 2:

Esau	147
Jacob	147

Generation 3:

Reuben	135
Simeon	120
Judah	129
Levi	137
Issachar	123
Zebulun	114
Joseph	110
Benjamin	125
Dan	125
Naphtali	139
Gad	130
Asher	120

Generation 4:

Kohath	133

Generation 5:

Abram	147

Generation 6:

Miriam	124
Aaron	122
Moses	120

Generation 7:

Eleazar	101

In this sample from Isaac to Moses we found the ages of 23 persons. Here are the averages by generation:

1. 155 (Isaac died 1887 BC)
2. 147
3. 126
4. 133 (Kohath only)
5. 147 (Abram only)
6. 122
7. 101 (Eleazer died 1299 BC)

During these 7 generations the average lifetime only fell 5.5 years per generation

In order to dispel the myth that somehow the average lifespan of a person continued to fall until it was considered that Jesus Himself was an "old man" when he was crucified, consider the following list. Incidentally, the average did fall, but that was because infant deaths were significant until the 20th century. As late as the 1940s in America, the average male lifespan was only 47 years. This number is low because infant deaths were included in the average. We also had gone through two world wars by the mid 40s, during which period millions of people died, either fighting or in the holocausts that followed. If one lived past puberty he had every expectation of living to be between 70 and 80 years.

Artaxerxes (Arsicas) II lived 94 years
Vologaeses IV Arcasid lived 94 years
Robert "The Pious" Capet II, King of France lived 88 years
Charlemagne lived 71 years
Seneca the Rhetoritician lived 92 years
Plato lived 82 years and committed suicide!
Athanasius of Alexandria lived 80 years

Admittedly many people died in their 40s, 50s, and 60s. However, in times past there were many wars. There was also famine, and drought. People worked with their hands, and accidents happened. Today with better medicines and more electronics we are able to avoid accidents and to enjoy longer lifespans. Today, the average person should expect to live to 80 years, with 70 years being relatively free from significant health problems.

Appendix Two

The Epic of Gilgamesh

Prologue – Gilgamesh, King in Uruk

A eulogy to wise and handsome Gilgamesh, King of Uruk (Uruk being the biblical Erech, known today as WArka), who built brick walls, a rampart and a temple for Anu, god of the firmament.

1 - The Coming of Enkidu

King Gilgamesh's strength and lust left him with no rivals, so the gods prevailed on the goddess Aruru to make him a brother, which she duly did. Thus Enkidu was created. Enkidu was brought up in the wild, eating grass in the hills. He was the strongest man in the world. He was discovered by a hill trapper who was so afraid of his strength that he sought advice from his father on what to do with the beast. The trapper's father instructed him to go to Gilgamesh and ask for his advice. Gilgamesh advised him to hire a harlot and introduce her to Enkidu. They duly did this and the harlot stripped before Enkidu, who was fascinated by her. She persuaded him to accompany her to see Gilgamesh in the city of Uruk.

Gilgamesh told his mother Ninsun of his dreams. She interpreted them as presaging the arrival of Enkidu in Uruk. The harlot encouraged the wild Enkidu to be more genteel in manner. He was warned of the power of Gilgamesh. Enkidu challenged Gilgamesh by preventing him from entering the house of a newly wedded bride according to the custom ordained by the gods of 'the king to be first and the husband to follow'. Gilgamesh threw him aside. Enkidu acknowledged Gilgamesh's strength, and they became friends.

2 - The Forest Journey

Enkidu regretted that he was losing his powers and becoming weak, so Gilgamesh had the idea of making a "shem" for himself by raising a monument of cedars to the gods. The trouble was, as Enkidu knew all too well, the cedars were guarded by a fearsome giant called Humbaba. Gilgamesh was not afraid of Humbaba, however Enkidu (having seen him before) was very concerned, as were the rest of the king's subjects. Ninsun, Gilgamesh's mother, pleaded to Shamash (the sun god) to protect them, and gave Enkidu an amulet. Gilgamesh was experiencing dreams that were worrying him, however Enkidu believed that they foretold victory - and indeed, as soon as the first cedars were felled, the great Humbaba was aroused and duly vanquished by the equal power of Gilgamesh and Enkidu. The god of the earth, Enlil, was not happy about this and threatened revenge on them both.

Fig. 62 Gilgamesh and Enkidu killing Humbaba

3 - Ishtar and Gilgamesh, and the Death of Enkidu

Having returned from the aforementioned adventure, Gilgamesh washed himself and put on his royal robes. He looked very handsome and was noticed by Ishtar, the goddess of love. She asked him to marry her and promised all sorts of things. Gilgamesh was not having any of this, and reminded Ishtar of how unfaithful she had been to a whole list of previous lovers. Ishtar fell into a rage and went up to high heaven to ask her father, Anu, for the Bull of Heaven with which to avenge Gilgamesh.

The fearsome Bull of Heaven rampaged the earth. With its first snort the earth cracked and a hundred young men fell down to their death. Early in the fight Enkidu was knocked down and got up immediately, but it was Gilgamesh who defeated the Bull. They cut out its heart and gave it to Shamash. Ishtar rose to the walls of Uruk and cursed Gilgamesh for killing the Bull of Heaven. When

313

Enkidu heard these words he tore off the Bull's right thigh and threw it at her. Enraged by this, she called together the dancing and singing girls, prostitutes and courtesans and set up lamentation over the thigh of the Bull of Heaven.

The smiths and armourers admired the build and body of the beautiful Bull of Heaven, and there were celebrations in the street as the crowd acknowledged the strength and might of Gilgamesh.

That night, however, Enkidu had a dream which he related the following day to Gilgamesh, in which the gods were meeting in council, and Enlil was declaring that, because of his involvement with the deaths of Humbaba and the Bull of Heaven, Enkidu must die.

With tears in his eyes, Enkidu prayed to Shamash, cursing the trapper; and the harlot who civilised him, and thus led to his downfall. Shamash, however, reminded him of the good times he had had, and Enkidu repented for his harsh words.

Enkidu told Gilgamesh of another of his dreams in which he was transformed into a bird and led to the palace of the Queen of DArkness. All the inhabitants of this dArk place were clothed like birds, and they were once rulers of earthly kingdoms. The servants were those who once had the stature of gods. The Queen of the Underworld was there, and the recorder of the gods who held the book of death. She looked up and enquired as to who had brought Enkidu here.

At this point Enkidu woke up. Despite Gilgamesh's prayers, his lingering illness worsened. Gilgamesh lamented greatly over his death, as did the people of Uruk who built a statue decorated with gold and lapis lazuli in his honour.

4 - The Search for Everlasting Life

Gilgamesh wept bitterly for his brother, whose demise reminded him of his greatest fear - death. He decided to find Utnapishtim (known as the Faraway, and also Noah), who lived in the land of Dilmun, in the garden of the sun. To him alone had the gods granted eternal life.

Our hero eventually arrived at the great mountains of Mashu, the gate of which was guarded by two man-scorpions. They warned him that no mortal man had ever done what he was to do. They opened the gate for him, and Gilgamesh walked in total dArkness for twelve leagues, after which he found himself in the garden of the gods, surrounded by wonderful gems and riches.

He came across Shamash, who warned him that he would not find what he was looking for. By the sea he encountered Siduri, goddess of wine, who looked on him as a thief and bolted her gate against him. He pleaded that he was the great hero King Gilgamesh. At first she didn't believe him, but later she relented, and warned him again that he would not find eternal life. Nevertheless, she told him that Utnapishtim (Noah) lived across the Ocean. Gilgamesh was carried across by the boatman Urshanabi, to whom he had to introduce himself in much the same way as he did with Siduri; and likewise on meeting Utnapishtim.

Utnapishtim (the Biblical Noah) reminded Gilgamesh that nothing on earth is permanent. With regard to how he came to enter the company of gods and possess everlasting life, he would tell Gilgamesh a secret:

5 - The Story of the Flood

Utnapishtim told a story of a city called, on the banks of the Euphrates. The gods considered the noise made by man in this city to be intolerable - so they agreed to exterminate mankind. Enlil was the main protagonist, but Ea, god of waters, warned Utnapishtim of their plan in a dream; telling him to tear down his house and build a boat, giving precise measurements; and to take into it the seed of all living creatures.

The boat was built and loaded, and the rain came. The storm raged fiercely for six days and nights. The great gods of heaven and hell wept. On the seventh day the storm subsided and Utnapishtim opened the hatch and saw water all around. The boat was grounded on the mountain of Nisir.

When it had been becalmed for seven days, he released a dove, who found no resting place and returned. A swallow was then released who found no perch, but the raven did not return.

Utnapishtim made a sacrifice and poured out a libation on the mountaintop. All of the gods were pleased except Enlil, who had intended to destroy all mankind. Ea calmed him down, and Enlil took Utnapishtim and his wife into the boat and made them kneel down on either side of him saying "In times past Utnapishtim was a mortal man; now he shall live at the mouth of rivers."

6 - The Return

Utnapishtim told Gilgamesh to prevail against sleep for six days and seven nights if he wished to gain eternal life. Gilgamesh, however, couldn't stay awake; and slept for seven days, waking up with his ever-present fear of death.

Utnapishtim banished the boatman Urshanabi; commanding him to take Gilgamesh, let him wash, and give him new clothes. With this done, they were about to launch off when Utnapishtim promised Gilgamesh a memento of the trip - a plant, like a rose with a prickle like a thorn, found at the bottom of the sea. This would restore lost youth.

Gilgamesh dived into the water to obtain this plant. Having travelled back twenty leagues, Gilgamesh and Urshanabi were attacked by a serpent and he lost the plant.

On returning to Uruk with Urshanabi, the hero was worn out. However he was able to engrave the story on a stone.

7 - The Death of Gilgamesh

Gilgamesh's destiny, decreed by Enlil (the father of the gods), was now fulfilled. The people of Uruk and his mother Ninsun mourned. The mourners weighed out their offerings to Ereshkigal, the Queen of Death; Namtar, the god of fate; and to all the gods of the dead. Gilgamesh lies in his tomb.

Appendix Three

A Sacred Marriage Hymn

The "Sacred Marriage" was accompanied, at least in later Sumerian times, by the recitation of explanatory hymns. This example, which seems to be typical of its kind and of the ritual texts of the period, is actually intended for the ritual involving the king Iddin-Dagan of Isin, who ruled about 50 years after the fall of Ur III, from 1975 BC to 1954 BC The "Sacred Marriage" that takes place is between the king, Iddin-Dagan, and Inanna, the goddess of Sumer. I have highlighted the parts that are relevant to the discussion. It should be noted that according to my research, as I have shown, Inanna was killed in Babylon in 2065 BC However, her religion lived on through surrogates. In fact, it flourished. This hymn is proof that the people were, through their "Sacred Marriage" rite, attempting to reproduce something that had actually taken place in the past. We may rest assured of this because the king himself participated in the "Sacred Marriage." The institution of this ceremony began with Inanna and Nimrod, and it passed on both with her and without her for centuries.

This translation is D. Reisman's.[407]

To [the one who comes forth from heaven, to the one who comes forth from heaven, I] would say ["Hail!"]

To the [hierod]ule who comes forth from heaven, I would say:
["Hail!"]
To the great [lady] of heaven, Inanna, I would say "Hail!"
To the holy torch who fills the heaven,
To the light, Inanna, to her who shines like daylight,
To the great lady of heaven, Inanna, I would say "Hail!"
(To) the hierodule, the awe-laden lady of the Anunna gods,
(To) the trustworthy one who fills heaven and earth with light,
To the eldest daughter of Su'en, Inanna, I would say: "Hail!"
Of her loftiness, of her greatness, of her reliability,
Of her coming forth radiantly at evening,
Of the holy torch which fills the heaven,
Of her stance in heaven, like the moon and the sun,
From above and below, all the lands know (of these things).
To the greatness of the hierodule of heaven,
To Innin I would sing.

   First **kirugu**.

Her coming forth is that of a hero

   Its antiphone.

In heaven she surely stands, the good wild cow of An.
On earth she is reliable, the lady of all the lands,
In the Abzu, in Eridu, she received the me,
Her father Enki presented them to her,
Lordship and kingship he placed in her hand.
With An she takes her seat upon the great throne,
With Enlil she determines the fates in her land,
Monthly, at the new moon, in order that the me might be perfected,
The gods of the land assemble themselves about her,
The Anunna gods kneel before her,
They come there with offerings and prayers,
They offer the prayers for all the lands.
My lady renders firm judgement of the land,

[Inanna (?)] gives firm decision [for] the land.
Her black-headed people walk before her.

Second kirugu.

They play the silver algar instrument before her,
They walk before the pure Inanna.
To the great lady of heaven, Inanna, I would say "Hail!"
The holy drum, the holy timpani, they play before her,
They walk before the pure Inanna.
To the great lady of heaven, Inanna, I would say "Hail!"
The holy harp, the holy, timpani, they play before her,
They walk before the pure Inanna.
To the eldest daughter of Su'en, Inanna, I would say "Hail!"

Third kirugu.

The male prostitutes comb their hair (?) before her,
They walk before the pure Inanna.
They decorate the napes of their necks with colored bands (?),
They walk before the pure Inanna.
They place upon their bodies the "cloak of divinity,"
They walk before the pure Inanna.
The righteous man and the first lady, the woman of the great wise women,
They walk before the pure Inanna.
The soothing harp which they had held, they place at their side,
They walk before the pure Inanna.
They gird themselves with the sword belt, the "arm of battle,"
They walk before the pure Inanna.
The spear, the "arm of battle," they grasp in their hands,
They walk before the pure Inanna.

Fourth kirugu.

Their right side they adorn with women's clothing,
They walk before the pure Inanna.
To the great lady of heaven, Inanna, I would say "Hail!"
Their left side they cover (?) with men's clothing,
They walk before the pure Inanna.
To the great lady of heaven, Inanna, I would say "Hail!"
With jump ropes and colored cords they compete before her,
They walk before the pure Inanna.
To the eldest daughter of Su'en, Inanna, I would say "Hail!"

Fifth kirugu.

The young men, carrying hoops, sing to her,
They walk before the pure Inanna.
The maidens, the sugia priestesses, coiffured,
They [walk] before the pure Inanna.
The sword, the double-edged axe, before her …
They walk before the pure Inanna.
The ascending kurgarra priests grasped the sword,
They walk before the pure Inanna.
The one who covers the sword with blood, he sprinkles blood,
They walk before the pure Inanna.
He pours out blood on the dais of the throne room.
The tigi drum, the sem drum, the ala instrument, they make loud noise.
The hierodule truly stands alone in the pure heaven.
All the lands, the black-headed people, the people numerous as sheep,
Upon them my lady looks in a friendly way from the midst of heaven.
They walk before the pure Inanna.
The lady of the evening, Inanna, is lofty.
The maiden Inanna I will praise.
The lady of the evening [is] as lofty as the horizon.

Sixth kirugu.

At evening, the radi[ant] star, [the Venus-star], the great light which [fills] the heaven,
The lady of the evening, the heroine, she surely comes forth from heaven.
The people in all the lands, they raise their glance to her.
The men purify themselves, the women cleanse themselves,
The ox tosses his head in his yoke,
The sheep stir up dust in their pen,
The numerous beasts of Šakan, the creatures of the steppe,
The quadrupeds of the broad steppe,
The orchards and gardens, the plots, the green reeds,
The fish of the deep, the birds [of] heaven,
They hasten to lie by my lady.
The living creatures, the numerous people, they bend the knee before her.
The matriarchs who have been summoned,
They prepare great quantities of food and drink for my lady.
My lady refreshes herself in the land.
There is play in the land, which is made festive,
The young man makes love to his spouse.
Upon them my lady looks in a friendly way from the midst of heaven.
They walk before the pure Inanna.
The lady of the evening, Inanna, [is] lofty.
The maiden Inanna I will praise.
The lady of the [eve]ning is as lofty as the horizon.

Seventh kirugu.

Good in advice, the joy of An, the ornament, the ornament of the broad heaven.
She comes forth like the moon at night,
She comes forth like bright daylight in the heat of noon.
When good food has been placed in the storehouse of the land,

When all the lands, the black-headed people, the people have assembled,
When abundance has been placed in the storehouse of the land,
(The assembled people) lying on the roofs, lying on the walls,
They come to her with …, they bring their matters before her,
Then she knows the matter, she recognises evil,
She renders an evil judgement to the evil, she destroys the wicked,
She looks favorably upon the just, she determines a good fate for them.
Upon them my lady looks in a friendly way from the midst of heaven.
They walk before the pure Inanna.
The lady who reaches unto heaven is as lofty as the horizon.

Eighth kirugu.

The good lady, the joy of An, a heroine, she surely comes forth from heaven.
In the … of heaven, she bears the ornament.
She consults with An in his lofty place.
From among youths and heroes, she lone is surely summoned.

Its antiphone.

She is mighty, she is trustworthy, she is great, she is exceeding in youthfulness.

sabatuk

the lady, the amazement of the land, the solitary star, the Venus-star,
the lady who reaches unto heaven, the heroine, she comes forth from heaven.
All the lands fear her …
The people, the faithful black-headed people, bow before her,
The young man on the road makes his way to her,
The ox raises his head in his yoke to her,

The farmer ... [...]
In the steppe, both laments and songs are [sung] in their ...,
The ox [...] to its yoke in the land.
Everything is made abundant for her (Inanna) in the storehouse of the land.
They hasten to the pure Inanna.
They prepare well for my lady, (even) to the midst of heaven.
In the pure places of the steppe, at its good places,
On the roof, the high roof, on the roof of the Badurra,
On the "platforms of mankind,"
They make offerings to her of heaped up incense, like sweet-smelling cedar,
Fine sheep, long-haired sheep, (and) fat sheep they offer to her,
They purify the earth for the hierodule, they celebrate her in song.
Ghee, dates, cheese, fruits of all kinds,
They fill the table of the land with first fruits for her,
They pour dArk beer for her,
They pour light beer for her.
DArk beer, emmer beer,
Emmer beer for my lady,
The sabub vat and the lamsari vat make a bubbling noise for her.
Mixing honey with ghee,
[Mixing] ... [wi]th ghee,
They make gug bread in date syrup for her.
Beer at dawn, flour, flour in honey,
They pour out honey and wine for her at sunrise.
God and man go to her with food and drink.
They feed the hierodule in the pure clean place.
Upon them my lady looks in a friendly way from the midst of heaven.
They walk before the pure Inanna.
The lady who reaches unto heaven is as lofty as the horizon.

Ninth kirugu.

In the palace, "the house of counsel for the land," "the shackle of all the foreign lands,"
When the black-headed people, the people, have assembled in "the house of the river of ordeal,"
They set up a throne for the lady of the palace [Inanna].
The king, the god, sits with her, inside.
For the one who determines the fate of all the lands,
Who oversees the true first day,
Who perfects the me on the day of the disappearance of the moon,
On the New Year's day, the day of ritual,
They set up a bed for my lady.
They cleanse rushes with sweet-smelling cedar oil,
They arrange them (the rushes) for my lady, for their (Inanna and the king) bed,
They arrange the cover on the outside of the bed.
So that they (Inanna and the king) might rest comfortably on "the cover which rejoices the heart,"
My lady bathes (her) pure lap,
She bathes for the lap of the king.
She bathes for the lap of Iddin-Dagan,
The pure Inanna washes with soap,
She sprinkles cedar oil on the ground,
The king approaches (her) pure lap proudly,
He approaches the lap of Inanna proudly,
Ama'ušumgalanna lies down beside her,
He caresses her pure lap.
When the lady has stretched out on the bed, in (his) pure lap,
When the pure Inanna has stretched out on the bed, in (his) pure lap,
She makes love with him on her bed,
(She says) to Iddin-Dagan: "You are surely my beloved."
To pile up offerings, to perform laving rites,
To heap up incense, to burn juniper resin (?),
To bear food offerings, to bear bowls,
He (the king) orders them (the people) to enter her Egalmah.

He embraces his beloved consort,
He embraces the pure Inanna.
From (her) side of the throne, she comes forth like daylight,
The king, like the sun, fills (his) side next to her.
He arranges abundance, lushness, and plenty before her.
The loud instrument, which drowns out the south storm,
The algar instrument of sweet sound, the ornament of the palace,
The stringed instrument, the source of the joy of mankind,
(With these) the musicians play her a song which rejoices the heart.
The king stretches forth his hand in eating and drinking.
Ama'ušumgalanna stretches forth his hand in eating and drinking.
The palace is festive, the king is joyous,
The people spend the day in great joy.
May he spend long life on the radiant throne!
Proudly (?) he sits on the dais of kingship.
He utters praises of heaven and earth to my lady.
"You are the hierodule born with the heaven and the earth."
In the pure clean place they celebrate the hierodule in song,
(She is) the joy of the black-headed people, the ornament of the assembly,
Inanna, the eldest daughter of Su'en.
Lady of the evening, your praise is sweet.
Upon them my lady looks in a friendly way from the midst of heaven,
They walk before the pure Inanna.
The lady who reaches unto heaven, Inanna, is lofty.

    Tenth kirugu

Mighty, trustworthy, great, lofty and great,
Exceeding in youthfulness.

    Its antiphone

A "song of heroism" of Ninsianna.[408]

Index

Bibliography

Against Apion, Flavius Josephus

The American journal of Semitic languages and literatures, University of Chicago. Dept. of Semitic Languages and Literatures.

Ancient Mesopotamian Temple Building In Historical Texts And Building Inscriptions, Bruce Satterfield ,Brigham Young University – Idaho. (http://emp.byui.edu/SatterfieldB/Papers/MesopotamiaTempleBuilding.htm).

Antiquities of the Jews, Flavius Josephus.

Antiquity, "A Mesopotamian Trilogy," article by M.E.L.Mallowen, 12 (50), June, 1939.

Apocrypha and Pseudepigrapha of the Old Testament-in English, . R. H. Charles, Oxford University Press, Ely House, London,1913, 1968.

The Archaeology of the Bible Lands, Magnus Magnusson, BC

The Babylonian Empire, A. T. Olmstead, 1919, (http://www.jstor.org/pss/528561).

The Bible and the ancient Near East: collected essays , Jimmy Jack McBee Roberts, 2004.

The Bible in its World: The Bible and Archaeology Today, Kenneth A. Kitchen, Exeter: The Paternoster Press, 1977.

The Book of Genesis: chapters 1-17, Victor P. Hamilton, 1990.

The Book of Genesis, S. R. Driver, Kessinger Publishing Co., 1891.

Book of Jasher, (http://www.ccel.org/a/anonymous/jasher)

Book of Jubilees, (http://www.pseudepigrapha.com/jubilees)

A Brief Introduction to the Old Testament, Michael D. Coogan, Oxfrod University Press, 2009.

Bulletin of the American Schools of Oriental Research 208, Frank Moore Cross, "An Interpretation of the Nora Stone," 1972.

The Cave of Treasures, (http://www.sacred-texts.com/chr/BCt/BCt06.htm).

Civilization Past and Prestent, 11th ed., Palmira, Brummett, et. Al., Pearson Longrman Publishers, 2007.

The Cradle of Agriculture? New Evidence Moves the World's First Farmers into Turkey, Reagan Duplisea, (http://www.discover-ingarchaeology.com/ articles/ 060100-turkeyfarm.shtml).

Daily life in ancient Mesopotamia Karen Rhea Nemet-Nejat . 1998.

EBLA: Its Impact on Bible Records, Clifford Wilson, M.A., B.D., Ph.D., (http://www.icr.org/article/ebla-its-impact-bible-records/).

Eblaitica: essays on the Ebla archives and Eblaite language, Robert R. Stieglitz, edited by Cyrus Herzl Gordon, Gary Rendsburg, Nathan H. Winter, 2002.

Encyclopedia Brittanica, (http://www.britannica.com)

Epic of Gilgamesh, (http://www.wsu.edu/~dee/Meso/Gilg.htm)

Fasti Hellenici-the Civil and Literary Chronology of Greece from the Earliest Accounts to the LVth. Olympiad, Henry Fynes Clinton, Burt Franklin, New York, 1834, 1965.

Flying Serpents and Dragons: The Story of Mankind's Reptilian Past, R. A. Boulay, 1999.

Gilgamesh, John Gardner and John Maier, Alfred A. Knopf, Inc., New York, 1984.

History of Ancient Egypt, George Rawlinson. Harvard College Library, 1881.

A History of the Pharaohs, Arthur Weigall, E. P. Dutton, 1927.

Hutchinson's story of the nations, containing the Egyptians, the Chinese, India, the Babylonian nation, the Hittites, the Assyrians, the Phoenicians and the Carthaginians, the Phrygians, the Lydians, and other nations of Asia Minor, http://www.archive.org/stream/hutchinsonsstory00londuoft/hutchinsonsstory00londuoft_djvu.txt

Innovation in diplomatic practice, Jan Melissen, 1999, ISBN 0-312-21592-4.

The International Standard Bible Encyclopedia, Geoffrey W. Bromiley.

Israel Exploration Journal 3, J. Liver, "The Chronology of Tyre at the Beginning of the First Millennium BC," 1953.

Lanuage and Diplomacy, S. Abu Jaber, (http://www.diplomacy.edu/Books/language_and_diplomacy/texts/pdf/abujaber.pdf)

Manetho, W. G. Waddell, University of Toronto, 1940.

Mesopotamian Origins, E. A. Speiser, Philadelphia, PA, University of Philadelphia Press, 1930.

The Mysterious Numbers of the Hebrew Kings, E. R. Thiele, 3rd ed.; Grand Rapids: Zondervan/Kregel, 1983.

Nature: international journal of science, Sir Normon Lockyer, Volume 55, 1897.

New Light on the Most Ancient East, V. G. Childe, London, UK, Kegan Paul, 1935.

The New Testament in the Original Greek, with an introduction by Philip Schaff, Brooke Foss Westcott and Fenton John Anthony Hort, Harper & Brothers, Franklin Square, New York, 1891.

Pausanias. Description of Greece" , ed. W.H.S.Jones, Litt.D., & H.A. Ormerod, 1918.

Reinventing Jesus: What the Da Vinci Code and Other Novel Speculations Don't Tell You, Grand Rapids, Mich: Kregel Publications.

Royal Archives of Tell Mardikh-Ebla' in *Biblical Archaeology*

Royal Inscriptions of Sumer and Akkad, "Inscription of Entemena #7", George A. Barton, New Haven, Conn. 1929.

The Second Cainan, Jared L. Olar, (http://graceandknowledge.faithweb.com/cainan.html)

The Septuagint with Apocrypha: Greek and English, Sir Lancelot C. L. Brenton, Hendrickson Publishers, 1851, 2001.

Studies in the Chronology of the Divided Monarch of Israel, William H. Barnes, Atlanta, GA: Scholars Press, 1991.

The Sumerians: their history, culture and character, Samuel Noah Kramer, 1965.

The Wars of Gods and Men, Zechariah Sitchin, 1985

What Happened in History, V. G Childe, Pelican Books, 1948.

Who were the Babylonians?, Bill T. Arnold, 2004.

Endnotes

1   Chap. XIII
2   Chap. XIV
3   George W. Norris, father of the author
4   Komoszewski, J. Ed; Wallace, Daniel J. (2006). *Reinventing Jesus: What the Da Vinci Code and Other Novel Speculations Don't Tell You*, Grand Rapids, Mich: Kregel Publications. p. 70.
5   https://www.metmuseum.org/toah/hd/akka/hd_akka.htm
6   Palmira, Brummett, et. Al. *Civilization Past and Prestent*, 11th ed., Pearson Longrman Publishers, 2007, p. 10
7   Flavius Josephus, *Against Apion* i:17,18.
8   *Ibid* i:18.
9   2 Samuel 05:11, 1 Kings 05:01, 1 Chronicles 14:01
10 1 Kings 9:13, Amos 1:9 [Michael D. Coogan, *A Brief Introduction to the Old Testament*, (Oxfrod University Press, 2009), 213-214.
11 2 Chronicles 8:16,17.
12 *Against Apion* i:17.
13 1 Kings 5:1, 12.
14 Flavius Josephus, *Antiquities of the Jews*, Book VIII, Chapter II, Section 7.
15 E. R. Thiele, (1983) *The Mysterious Numbers of the Hebrew Kings*, 3rd ed.; (Grand Rapids: Zondervan/Kregel) pg. 78.
16 J. Liver, "The Chronology of Tyre at the Beginning of the First Millennium BC," *Israel Exploration Journal* 3 (1953) 113-120. Also Frank Moore Cross, "An Interpretation of

the Nora Stone," *Bulletin of the American Schools of Oriental Research* 208 (1972) 17, n. 11. Also William H. Barnes, *Studies in the Chronology of the Divided Monarch of Israel* (Atlanta, GA: Scholars Press, 1991) 29-55.

17   1 Kings 6:1

18   *Ibid.* 6:37

19   Exodus 12:40-41

20   *Ibid.* 47:8-9

21   *Ibid.* 47:8

22   *Ibid.* 25:26

23   *Ibid.* 25:26

24   *Ibid.* 21:4

25   *Ibid.* 21:1

26   Zechariah Sitchin, *The Wars of Gods and Men*, (Avon Books, 1985), 291.

27   http://history-world.org/ur.htm.

28   Genesis 11:10-26.

29   Flavius Josephus, *Antiquities of the Jews*, Book III, 9.

30   http://www.pantheon.org/articles/g/gilgamesh.html.

31   http://www.earth-history.com/Sumer/ur-nammu-praise-poem.htm.

32   Genesis 8:4.

33   http://www.accuracyingenesis.com/adam.html.

34   Reagan Duplisea, *The Cradle of Agriculture? New Evidence Moves the World's First Farmers into Turkey,* http://www.discoveringarchaeology.com/ articles/ 060100-turkey-farm.shtml.

35   https://www.worldhistory.org/elam/

36   S. R. Driver, *The Book of Genesis*, (Kessinger Publishing Co., 1891), 128.

37   First observed by E. A. Speiser excavating at Tepe Gawra in 1927 and reported in *Annual of the American Schools of Oriental Research*, 9, 1929, 22ff.

38   V. G. Childe, *What Happened in History*, (Pelican Books, 1948), 81.

39   _____, *New Light on the Most Ancient East*, (Lon-

don, UK, Kegan Paul, 1935), 133, 136, and 145-146.

40   *The Book of Jubilees*, 9:2-6.

41   M. I. I. Mallowen, "A Mesopotamian Trilogy," *Antiquity*, 12 (50), June, 1939, 161.

42   E. A. Speiser, *Mesopotamian Origins*, Philadelphia, PA, (University of Philadelphia Press, 1930).

43   Campbell Thompson, *Man*, 23, 1923, 81.

44   http://www.wsu.edu/~dee/MESO/GILG.HTM (*Epic of Gilgamesh*).

45   *Hutchinson's story of the nations, containing the Egyptians, the Chinese, India, the Babylonian nation, the Hittites, the Assyrians, the Phoenicians and the Carthaginians, the Phrygians, the Lydians, and other nations of Asia Minor*, http://www.archive.org/stream/hutchinsonsstory00londuoft/hutchinsonsstory00londuoft_djvu.txt.

46   Shushan was the ancient capital of Elam whose inhabitants were called Susanchites.

47   *Book of Jubilees*, 8:1 (http://www.pseudepigrapha.com/jubilees/8.htm).

48   http://www.britannica.com/facts/5/262960/descent-as-discussed-in-Elam-ancient-kingdom-Iran.

49   http://www.interfaith.org/articles/torah_torah_torah/torah6.php.

50   Genesis 22.22.

51   The *Royal Archives of Tell Mardikh-Ebla'* in Biblical Archaeology, Vol. 39, May 1976, p. 44-52.

52   Robert R. Stieglitz, *Eblaitica: essays on the Ebla archives and Eblaite language*, Volume 4, page 222, edited by Cyrus Herzl Gordon, Gary Rendsburg, Nathan H. Winter, 2002.

53   *Ibid.*, pg 216

54   *Ibid.*, pg. 216-217

55   *Ibid.*, pg. 209

56   *Ibid.*, pg 59

57   *Ibid.*, pg 59; article written in *Eblaitica* by Michael C. Astour.

58   Geoffrey W. Bromiley, *The International Standard Bible*

Encyclopedia, pg 755.

59   http://www.angelfire.com/ego/et_deo/ancient_sumeria.
wps.htm.

60   https://text-message.blogs.archives.gov/2020/07/07/the-
royal-archives-of-ebla-reference-and-processing-archi-
vists-4000-years-ago/

61   Extracted from Kenneth A. Kitchen, *The Bible in its
World: The Bible and Archaeology Today*. (Exeter: The
Paternoster Press, 1977), 168.

62   http://history-world.org/ebla.htm.

63   https://text-message.blogs.archives.gov/2020/07/07/the-
royal-archives-of-ebla-reference-and-processing-archi-
vists-4000-years-ago/

64   Pettinato, Giovanni (Johns Hopkins University Press,
1991) *Ebla, a new look at history* p.135.

65   Paolo Matthiae; Licia Romano (2010). <u>*6 ICAANE*</u>.
p. 482. <u>ISBN</u> <u>9783447061759</u>.

66   https://www.cambridge.org/core/books/archaeolo-
gy-of-elam/elam-and-awan/47A79A486A39B08672C-
B8A6E8F47CBE7

67   http://www.historyfiles.co.uk/KingListsMiddEast/Easter-
nElam.htm.

68   http://autocww.colorado.edu/~toldy3/E64ContentFiles/
HistoryMidEastAsiaAustralasia/Elam.html.

69   https://www.historytoday.com/archive/puzzle-pro-
to-elamite

70   http://en.wikipedia.org/wiki/Proto-Elamite.

71   *Ibid.*

72   http://www.historyfiles.co.uk/KingListsMiddEast/Easter-
nElam.htm.

73   *Ibid.*

74   *Book of Jasher*, chapter 7 verse 15 (http://www.ccel.org/a/
anonymous/jasher/7.htm).

75   The first three kings of Awan were also kings of Mesopotamia. This is more evidence that the three kings were
Arphaxad, Cainan, and Salah. These three also ruled

parts of northern Mesopotamia.

76 https://dbpedia.org/page/Awan_(ancient_city)

77 *Ibid.*

78 *Ibid.*

79 *Ibid.*

80 https://www.britannica.com/topic/Damu-ancient-god

81 Kamel S. Abu Jaber, *Lanuage and Diplomacy*, pg. 52, (http://www.diplomacy.edu/Books/language_and_diplomacy/texts/pdf/abujaber.pdf).

82 Jan Melissen, *Innovation in diplomatic practice*, (MacMillan Press Ltd.,1999, ISBN 0-312-21592-4), 3.

83 https://www.historyfiles.co.uk/KingListsMiddEast/MesopotamiaHamazi.htm

84 http://www.historyfiles.co.uk/KingListsMiddEast/MesopotamiaHamazi.htm

85 *Ibid.*

86 *Book of Jubilees,* 8:1-6.

87 https://www.britannica.com/topic/Book-of-Jubilees

88 Jared L. Olar, *The Second Cainan*, (http://graceandknowledge.faithweb.com/cainan.html).

89 For those interested in this biblical problem here are some sources for research:

1. Sir Lancelot C. L. Brenton, *The Septuagint with Apocrypha: Greek and English,* (Hendrickson Publishers, 1851, 2001), pp. 12-13, 530, 1134.

2. R. H. Charles, The *Apocrypha and Pseudepigrapha of the Old Testament-in English,* (Oxford University Press, Ely House, London, 1913, 1968), vol. II, p.25.

3. Henry Fynes Clinton, *Fasti Hellenici-the Civil and Literary Chronology of Greece from the Earliest Accounts to the LVth. Olympiad,* (Burt Franklin, New York, vol. I, 1834, 1965), pp. 288-289.

4. Brooke Foss Westcott and Fenton John Anthony Hort, *The New Testament in the Original Greek, with an introduction by Philip Schaff,* (Harper & Brothers, Franklin Square, New York, 1891), pp. xxvii-xxviii, 124-125.

90   https://www.assyriologie.uni-muenchen.de/personen/
      professoren/sallaberger/publ_sallaberger/wasa_2014_pre-
      sargonic_mari.pdf

91   *Viollet, Pierre-Louis (2007) [2005]. Water Engineering
      in Ancient Civilizations: 5,000 Years of History. IAHR
      Monographs. 7. Translated by Holly, Forrest M. CRC
      Press. ISBN 978-9-078-04605-9. Pg. 36.*

92   Ibid.

93   Pettinato 1986:72–4; Klengel 1992:27; Archi, in Gordon
      and Rendsburg 1990:115–24

94   https://www.britannica.com/place/Emar

95   *Ibid.*

96   http://historel.tripod.com/orient/01mesop.htm.

97   https://thebiography.us/en/enshakushanna

98   Kenneth A. Kitchen, *The Bible in its World: The Bible and
      Archaeology Today.* (Exeter: The Paternoster Press, 1977),
      168.

99   *www.biblicalstudies.org.uk/pdf/biiw/chapter3.pdf.*

100   Kenneth A. Kitchen, The *Bible in its World: The Bible
      and Archaeology Today.* (Exeter: The Paternoster Press,
      1977),168.

101   http://www.britannica.com/EBChecked/topic/499121/
      Resheph#ref290852.

102   http://history-world.org/ebla.htm.

103   Kenneth A. Kitchen, *The Bible in its World: The Bible and
      Archaeology Today.* (Exeter: The Paternoster Press, 1977),
      168.

104   Kenneth A. Kitchen, *The Bible in its World: The Bible and
      Archaeology Today.* Exeter: The Paternoster Press, 1977.
      Pbk. pp.168.

105   Flavius Josephus, *Antiquities of the Jews,* 6:4.

106   Zechariah Sitchin, *The Wars of Gods and Men,* (Avon
      Books, 1985), pg. 295.

107   https://www.britannica.com/place/Nippur

108   Jean-Jacques Glassner, *Mesopotamian Chronicles,* (Brill
      Academic, 2005).

109 https://www.britannica.com/place/Nippur

110 *Ibid.*

111 *Book of Jubilees,* 8:6

112 http://www.ridingthebeast.com/resources/two-baby-lons/n/nebrod.html.

113 http://www.historyfiles.co.uk/KingListsMiddEast/SyriaE-bla.htm.

114 https://www.worldhistory.org/Sargon_of_Akkad/

115 Kenneth A. Kitchen, *The Bible in its World: The Bible and Archaeology Today.* (Exeter: The Paternoster Press, 1977), 168.

116 *Ibid.*

117 *Ibid.*

118 Incidentally, Tudiya and Asshur are the ancestors of the Hyksos Pharaohs of Egypt from about 1650 BC for a couple of centuries. The Hyksos, then, were Amoritic invaders.

119 Kenneth A. Kitchen, *The Bible in its World: The Bible and Archaeology Today,* (Exeter: The Paternoster Press, 1977), 168.

120 https://www.britannica.com/topic/lugal

121 R. A. Boulay , *Flying Serpents and Dragons,* 1990, Editorial Comments By Roberto Solàrion, 1997, ch. 16 (http://www.apollonius.net/boulay16e.html).

122 http://www.formerthings.com/ebla_tablets.htm.

123 http://unexplainedmysteriesoftheworld.com/archives/the-mystery-of-the-ebla-tablets.

124 Clifford Wilson, M.A., B.D., Ph.D. , *EBLA: Its Impact on Bible Records,* (http://www.icr.org/article/ebla-its-im-pact-bible-records/)

125 *Ibid.*

126 Magnus Magnusson, BC - *The Archaeology of the Bible Lands,* (London, The Bodley Head/British Broadcasting Corporation, 1977), 156.

127 http://www.oocities.com/encyclopedia_damascena/an-cientsyria/ebla.htm.

128   http://history-world.org/ebla.htm.

129   *www.biblicalstudies.org.uk/pdf/biiw/chapter3.pdf.*

130   Kenneth A. Kitchen, *The Bible in its World: The Bible and Archaeology Today.* (Exeter: The Paternoster Press, 1977), 168.

131   https://thebiography.us/en/ibbi-sipish

132   *Ibid.*

133   Genesis 10:25.

134   Flavius Josephus, *Antiquities of the Jews,* 6:4.

135   *The Cave of Treasures,* (http://www.sacred-texts.com/chr/BCt/BCt06.htm).

136   *Book of Jubiliees,* 10:18-34.

137   This will be shown subsequently to be the case.

138   *Book of Jubilees* 11:1-6.

139   http://www.sacred-texts.com/chr/bct/bct07.htm.

140   https://www.google.com/books/edition/The_Sumerian_World/qSOYAAAAQBAJ?hl=en&gbpv=1&dq=mesanne-pada++meskalamdug&pg=PR23&printsec=frontcover

141   https://peoplepill.com/people/meskalamdug

142   http://en.wikipedia.org/wiki/Sumerian_King_List.

143   http://mysticways.wiki.zoho.com/The-Sumerian-Pantheon.html.

144   http://en.wikipedia.org/wiki/Talk%3AUr.

145   http://en.wikipedia.org/wiki/Lugalbanda.

146   *Book of Jubilees,* 11:1-2.

147   http://www.biblesearchers.com/ancients/Patriarch/abram1.shtml.

148   *Book of Jubilees* 8:3, compare with *Book of Enoch* 8:1.

149   http://en.wikipedia.org/wiki/Epic_of_Gilgamesh.

150   http://www.atlastours.net/iraq/ur.html.

151   http://www.aina.org/news/20050125100240.htm.

152   *The American journal of Semitic languages and literatures,* (University of Chicago. Dept. of Semitic Languages and Literatures, Volume 35, pg. 69.

153   *Ibid.,* pg. 70

154   *Ibid.*

155   http://history-world.org/sumerian_floor_story.htm.

156   http://net.bible.org/dictionary.php?dict=dictionaries&word=Babylon.

157   Hilprecht, *Old Babylon*, Ins., vol 1, part ii, pp. 17, 18.

158   http://www.angelfire.com/nt/Gilgamesh/urIII.html.

159   http://www.britannica.com/EBChecked/topic/620912/Utu-khegal.

160   http://www.angelfire.com/nt/Gilgamesh/urIII.html.

161   *Ibid.*

162   see page 76 above ("And then the lands were at peace.").

163   http://www.biblesearchers.com/ancients/Patriarch/abram1.shtml.

164   http://faculty.mdc.edu/jmcnair/joe2pages/Mesopotamia%20Kings%20List.htm.

165   http://www.angelfire.com/nt/Gilgamesh/urIII.html.

166   http://www.jstor.org/pss/528561, A. T. Olmstead, *The Babylonian Empire*, 1919, pg 65.

167   Samuel Noah Kramer, *The Sumerians: their history, culture and character*, 1965, pg 62-63.

168   http://en.wikipedia.org/wiki/Gutian_people.

169   http://en.wikipedia.org/wiki/Enmebaragesi (this article says he lived around 2500 BC).

170   http://www.britannica.com/EBChecked/topic/188533/Enmebaragesi (this article says he lived around 2700 BC).

171   http://en.wikipedia.org/wiki/Enmebaragesi.

172   *Ibid.*

173   Pritchard pp.44-47; Kramer 1963 pp. 187-190.

174   http://www.third-millennium-library.com/readinghall/GalleryofHistory/Ancient-People/MESILIM.html

175   *Ibid.*

176   *Ibid.*

177   *Ibid.*

178   http://www.crystalinks.com/sumerhistory.html.

179   George A. Barton, "*Inscription of Entemena #7*", The *Royal Inscriptions of Sumer and Akkad* (New Haven, Conn. 1929) pp. 61, 63 & 65.

180   http://en.wikipedia.org/wiki/Lugal-zage-si.

181   *Ibid.*

182   http://www.crystalinks.com/sumerhistory.html.

183   http://en.wikipedia.org/wiki/Lugal-zage-si.

184   http://en.wikipedia.org/wiki/Sargon_of_Akkad.

185   http://en.wikipedia.org/wiki/Gilgamesh.

186   Sumerian administrative documents dated in the reigns of the kings of the .. edited by David Wilhelm Myhrman, 1910, page 29.

187   Zechariah Sitchin, *The Wars of Gods and Men*, (Avon Books, 1985), pg. 272.

188   Bill T. Arnold, *Who were the Babylonians?*, 2004, page 29.

189   http://realhistoryww.com/world_history/ancient/Sumer_Iraq_3.htm.

190   http://www.swartzentrover.com/cotor/bible/timelines/Babylon/Ur.htm.

191   http://en.wikipedia.org/wiki/Epic_of_Gilgamesh.

192   http://www.swartzentrover.com/cotor/bible/timelines/Babylon/Ur.htm.

193   *Book of Jubilees* 11:3.

194   http://www.angelfire.com/nt/Gilgamesh/urIII.html.

195   Genesis 14:5-12.

196   Zechariah Sitchin, *The Wars of Gods and Men*, (Avon Books, 1985), pg. 276

197   *Ibid.*

198   *Ibid.*, pgs. 309-315.

199   *Ibid.*, pgs. 309-342.

200   http://home.swipnet.se/~w-63448/mesbro.htm.

201   http://www.earth-history.com/Sumer/ur-nammu-death.htm.

202   http://faculty.mdc.edu/jmcnair/joe2pages/Mesopotamia%20Kings%20List.htm.

203   Sir Normon Lockyer, *Nature: international journal of science*, Volume 55, 1897, pg.244. Nin-Kagina has been confused as a daughter, but this record proves that he was the son of Ka-Azag, or Ka-Azaggid in this old book.

204 http://www.third-millennium-library.com/readinghall/ GalleryofHistory/Ancient-People/GUDEA.html.

205 Bruce Satterfield , *Ancient Mesopotamian Temple Building In Historical Texts And Building Inscriptions,* (Brigham Young University, Idaho), http://emp.byui.edu/SATTER-FIELDB/Papers/MesopotamiaTempleBuilding.htm.

206 http://en.wikipedia.org/wiki/Shar-Kali-Sharri.

207 http://www.third-millennium-library.com/readinghall/ GalleryofHistory/Ancient-People/GUDEA.html.

208 *Ibid.*

209 *Ibid.*

210 Sanderson Beck, *Sumer, Babylon, and Hittites,* http:// www.san.beck.org/EC3-Sumer.html.

211 Waddell 1929, p.379.

212 http://history-world.org/akkadians.htm.

213 http://www.crystalinks.com/sumerhistory.html.

214 http://history-world.org/akkadians.htm.

215 http://en.wikipedia.org/wiki/Gutian_dynasty_of_Sumer.

216 *Ibid.*

217 http://www.bibliotecapleyades.net/merovingians/ merovingios_08.htm.

218 http://en.wikipedia.org/wiki/Gudea.

219 http://www.third-millennium-library.com/readinghall/ GalleryofHistory/Ancient-People/GUDEA.html.

220 http://www.sacred-texts.com/chr/BCt/BCt07.htm.

221 *Book of Jubilees* 11:5-6.

222 *Book of the Cave of Treasure"* (http://www.sacred-texts. com/chr/BCt/BCt07.htm).

223 *Book of Jubilees* 11:6-8.

224 http://www.hyperhistory.net/apwh/bios/b1sargon.htm.

225 http://www.angelfire.com/ego/et_deo/ancient_sumeria. wps.htm.

226 Karen Rhea Nemet-Nejat, *Daily Life in Ancient Mesopotamia.* (Greenwood Press, 1998), page 22.

227 Ur-Bau was survived by two daughters; one married her uncle, Gudea (who succeeded Ur-Bau as King of Lagash),

and was the mother of Ur-Ningirsh, the father of Ugme; and the other daughter married Urgar, a Semitic prince, and was the mother of Nammakhni, last King of Lagash's Second Dynasty.

228 *Book of Jubilees* : 11:1-5

229 so-called by Prince Turgi/Terah in memory of his late middle son.

230 *Eblaitica: Essays on the Ebla Archives and Eblaite Language,* Volume 4, edited by Cyrus Herzl Gordon, Gary Rendsburg, Nathan H. Winter, pg 65.

231 Jimmy Jack McBee Roberts, *The Bible and the Ancient Near East:Collected Essays,* (Eisenbrausns, 2004), page 65.

232 http://www.bibliotecapleyades.net/serpents_dragons/boulay16e.htm.

233 http://sites.google.com/site/collesseum/sargon.

234 http://web.me.com/kbolman/Sumeria_3,000_BCE/8_The_Cup_Bearer_Who_Became_King.html.

235 http://www.bibliotecapleyades.net/serpents_dragons/boulay16e.htm.

236 R. A. Boulay, *Flying Serpents and Dragons: The Story of Mankind's Reptilian Past,* (The Book Tree, 1999), pg 184.

237 http://www.bibliotecapleyades.net/serpents_dragons/boulay16e.htm.

238 http://historel.tripod.com/orient/01mesop.htm.

239 http://www.mailstar.net/gordon.html .

240 http://home.swipnet.se/~w-63448/mesbro.htm.

241 http://en.wikipedia.org/wiki/Naram-Suen_of_Akkad.

242 http://www.al-azim.com/falak/komet.html.

243 Some scholars believe that the large conical objects are phallic symbols.

244 http://www.sacred-texts.com/chr/BCt/BCt07.htm.

245 Genesis 24:10.

246 *Ibid.* 11:24-26.

247 http://www.crystalinks.com/sumerhistory.html.

248 http://en.wikipedia.org/wiki/Ngushur.

249 http://en.wikipedia.org/wiki/History_of_Sumer.

250   *Ibid.*

251   http://www.crystalinks.com/sumerhistory.html.

252   Flavius Josephus, *Antiquities of the Jews*, 1:6.

253   http://en.wikipedia.org/wiki/Cush_%28Bible%29.

254   Jeremiah 13:23.

255   http://en.wikipedia.org/wiki/Cush_%28Bible%29.

256   http://www.angelfire.com/ego/et_deo/ancient_sumeria. wps.htm.

257   *Book of Jasher*, 7:44-46.

258   http://www.angelfire.com/ego/et_deo/ancient_sumeria. wps.htm.

259   Genesis 10:8-10.

260   *Ibid.* 11:1-9.

261   *Ibid.* 10:8-10.

262   http://en.wikipedia.org/wiki/Mesh-ki-ang-gasher.

263   http://www.christiananswers.net/dictionary/nimrod.html.

264   http://en.wikipedia.org/wiki/Mesh-ki-ang-gasher.

265   http://en.wikipedia.org/wiki/Enmerkar.

266   http://en.wikipedia.org/wiki/Mesh-ki-ang-gasher.

267   Genesis 6; see later where I discuss the interaction of the "gods" with the sons of Noah.

268   John Gardner and John Maier, *Gilgamesh,* (Alfred A. Knopf, Inc. New York, 1984), Tablet I, Lines 4-6, 22-25.

269   *Cave of Treasures,* 27:6-11.

270   Her name was Ne'elatama'uk; she was the daughter of Methusaleh and his wife Edna. She was one of the wives who entered the Ark prior to the Flood.

271   Genesis 11:1-2.

272   *Ibid.* 10:32.

273   http://en.wikipedia.org/wiki/Euphrates.

274   Genesis 11:9.

275   *Ibid.* 10:9-12.

276   *Ibid.* 10:11.

277   Victor P. Hamilton, *The Book of Genesis: Chapters 1-17*, (Eisenbrauns, 1990), pg 337.

278   http://en.wikipedia.org/wiki/Nimrud.

279   Waddell 1929, p.379.

280   http://www.cgca.net/coglinks/wcglit/hoehcompendium/hhc1ch3.htm.

281   http://www.mnsu.edu/emuseum/prehistory/egypt/history/people/menes.html.

282   http://en.wikipedia.org/wiki/Menes.

283   Flavius Josephus, *Antiquities of the Jews,* VIII, Ch. 6, Sect. 2.

284   http://en.wikipedia.org/wiki/Ian_Shaw_%28Egyptologist%29.

285   http://en.wikipedia.org/wiki/Egyptian_chronology.

286   Rev. Alexander Hislop, *The Two Babylons*, 2007, pg. 293.

287   http://www.biblebelievers.org.au/2bab038.htm.

288   http://en.wikipedia.org/wiki/Menes.

289   http://www.thepharaohs.net/ancient-egypt/pharaoh/menes-aha.

290   http://www.touregypt.net/featurestories/narmer.htm.

291   http://www.mnsu.edu/emuseum/prehistory/egypt/history/people/menes.html

292   *Ibid.*

293   *Ibid.*

294   *Ibid.*

295   E. A. Wallis Budge, *The Mummy: A Handbook of Egyptian Funerary Archaeology*, (Cambridge University Press, 2010), pg 25.

296   http://www.essaysbyekowa.com/Nimrod.htm.

297   *Book of Jasher* 7:23-31.

298   *Cave of Treasures* pgs. 144 and 145.

299   *Book of Jubilees* 10:21.

300   *Book of Jasher* 11:6.

301   George Rawlinson, *History of Ancient Egypt*, (Harvard College Library, 1881), vol. II, p. 26.

302   W. G. Waddell, *Manetho*, (London ,W. Heinemann, 1940), p. 215.

303   Genesis 10:8.

304   Arthur Weigall, *A History of the Pharaohs*, (Thornton

Butterworth, 1927),Vol. I, pg 111.

305 http://www.annomundi.com/history/samotheans.htm.

306 http://www.cgca.net/coglinks/wcglit/hoehcompendium/
hhc1ch3.htm.

307 http://en.wikipedia.org/wiki/Hor-Aha.

308 *Ibid.*

309 http://coeurdeleon.org/?p=198.

310 http://salmun.cwahi.net/histry/gen/cwh_v1/cwh_v1.htm.

311 http://coeurdeleon.org/?p=198.

312 *Ibid.*

313 http://www.ancientegyptonline.co.uk/Djer.html.

314 *Ibid.*

315 http://www.ancient-egypt-history.com/2010/05/egyptian-
First-dynasty-hor-aha-till-qaa.html.

316 http://www.touregypt.net/featurestories/earlydyn2.htm.

317 *Ibid.*

318 http://www.ancient-egypt-history.com/2010/05/egyptian-
First-dynasty-hor-aha-till-qaa.html.

319 *Ibid.*

320 http://www-etcsl.orient.ox.ac.uk/section1/tr1823.htm.

321 http://en.wikipedia.org/wiki/Sumerian_King_List.

322 http://www.jrank.org/cultures/pages/5332/Enmerkar.
html.

323 http://www.accuracyingenesis.com/babel.html.

324 Genesis 11:9.

325 Carleton S. Coon, *The Mediterranean World: (4) - The
Irano-Afghan Race*, 1939, p.415.

326 S. N. Kramer, *Ancient Sumer and Iran: Gleanings from
Sumerian Literature*, (Bulletin of the Asia Institute, 1,
1987), (Izady 1995).

327 http://rbedrosian.com/Memyth.htm.

328 http://www.xs4all.nl/~nippur/Aratta.html.

329 http://www.third-millennium-library.com/readinghall/
GalleryofHistory/Ancient-People/MESILIM.html.

330 http://realhistoryww.com/world_history/ancient/Misc/
Sumer/LUGALBANDA_IN_THE_MOUNTAIN_CAVE.

htm.

331   Zechariah Sitchin, *The Wars of Gods and Men*, (Avon Books, 1985), pg 243.

332   *Lugalbanda in the Mountain Cave.*

333   *Ibid.*

334   *Ibid.*

335   http://www.historyfiles.co.uk/KingListsMiddEast/Meso-potamiaUruk.htm.

336   Tore Kjeilen, "Yazidism". *Encyclopaedia.* LookLex. (http://i-cias.com/e.o/uyazidism.htm). "Malak Taus filled 7 jars of tears through 7,000 years. His tears were used to extinguish the fire in hell. Therefore, there is no hell in Yazidism."

337   http://www.britannica.com/EBChecked/topic/295507/Islam.

338   Kjeilen, Tore. *Yazidism. Encyclopaedia.* LookLex. http://i-cias.com/e.o/uyazidism.htm.

339   Zechariah Sitchin, *The Wars of Gods and Men*, (Avon Books, 1985), pg 296.

340   *Book of Jasher* 7:49.

341   *Book of Jasher* 7:49,51.

342   R. A. Boulay, *Flying Serpents and Dragons: The Story of Mankind's Reptilian Past*, (Thhe Book Tree, 1999), pg 193.

343   http://www.vnnforum.com/archive/index.php/t-48126.html.

344   http://www.biblesearchers.com/ancients/Patriarch/abram1.shtml.

345   *Ibid.*

346   According to the dating scheme that I have developed Noah and Shem had already died. Therefore, this is mythological and almost certainly not historic.

347   http://mb-soft.com/believe/txh/abraham.htm.

348   Zechariah Sitchin, *The Wars of Gods and Men*, (Avon Books, 1985), pg 297.

349   http://www.ask.com/wiki/Nannar.

350   *Book of the Cave of Treasures*, section 13.

351   *Book of Jubilees*, 11:15-23.

352   *Ibid.*, 11:1-14

353   http://en.wikipedia.org/wiki/Nimrod.

354   Genesis 12:1.

355   *Ibid.* 11:31.

356   *Ibid.*, 11:32

357   Ralph Ellis, *Jesus, Last of the Pharaohs*, (Edfu Books, 1998), pgs. 33-40.

358   Genesis 12:9.

359   http://en.wikipedia.org/wiki/Negev.

360   Genesis 12:10-20.

361   *Ibid.*, 12:6.

362   Flavius Josephus, *Antiquities of the Jews*, 1-8.

363   http://www.jewishvirtuallibrary.org/jsource/biography/abraham.html.

364   Zechariah Sitchin, *The Wars of Gods and Men*, (Avon Books, 1985), pg 296.

365   Genesis 16:1-4.

366   *Ibid.*, 21:1-7.

367   *Ibid.*, 22:1-8.

368   *Ibid.*, 12:5-9.

369   *Ibid.*, 12:10.

370   http://en.wikipedia.org/wiki/Ninth_dynasty_of_Egypt.

371   http://en.wikipedia.org/wiki/Herakleopolis_Magna.

372   http://en.wikipedia.org/wiki/Neferkare,_ninth_dynasty.

373   *Ibid.*

374   *Ibid.*

375   http://en.wikipedia.org/wiki/Thebes,_Egypt.

376   http://en.wikipedia.org/wiki/Intef_I.

377   http://en.wikipedia.org/wiki/Intef_II.

378   Genesis 16:1-35.

379   Ralph Ellis, *Jesus, Last of the Pharaohs*, (Edfu Books, 1998), pg 20.

380   http://www.livius.org/pha-phd/pharaoh/pharaoh.htm.

381   *Ibid.*

382   Kim S.B. Ryholt, *The Political Situation in Egypt during the*

Second Intermediate Period, (CNI Publications, [Museum Tusculanum Press: 1997]), p.128.

383 http://www.livius.org/pha-phd/pharaoh/pharaoh.htm.

384 Kim Ryholt, *The Political Situation in Egypt during the Second Intermediate Period c.1800-1550 BC* , (Museum Tuscalanum Press. 1997), p.125; and *Kings of the Second Inermediate Period,* (University College London); scroll down to the 15th dynasty.

385 http://en.wikipedia.org/wiki/Nehesy.

386 Kim Ryholt, *The Political Situation in Egypt during the Second Intermediate Period,* (CNI Publications, Copenhagen: Museum Tusculanum Press, 1997), pp.252-254, 366-376.

387 *Epic of Gilgamesh*

388 *Ibid.*

389 http://en.wikipedia.org/wiki/Inanna.

390 http://en.wikipedia.org/wiki/Ishtar.

391 http://en.wikipedia.org/wiki/Astarte.

392 http://en.wikipedia.org/wiki/Semiramis.

393 http://en.wikipedia.org/wiki/Inanna.

394 http://worldsofimagination.com/Twenty%20worlds%20 Atlantis%20Arabia%20Gods.htm.

395 http://en.wikipedia.org/wiki/Inanna.

396 Zehariah Sitchin, *The Wars of Gods and Men,* (Avon Books, 1985), pg. 240.

397 Zechariah Sitchin, *The Earth Chronicles,* Five Books (Harper Books, 1976 through Avon Books, 1993).

398 Genesis 6:1-2.

399 see Appendix 3.

400 Jeremiah 44:17-19.

401 http://www.earth-history.com/Babylon/legend-semiramis.htm.

402 http://atlantisonline.smfforfree2.com/index.php?topic=1007.0.

403 http://www.syria-wide.com/index.php?option=com_content&view=article&id=70&Itemid=86.

404 George John Whyte-Melville, *Sarchedon: A Legend of the*

Great Queen, (Chapman and Hall, 1871), pg. 139.

405   George John Whyte-Melville, Herbert Maxwell (Sir.), *The works of G.J. Whyte-Melville*, (Morrison and Gibb, Limited, 1898) Volume 15, pg 286.

406   Genesis 6:1-6.

407   D. Reisman, "Iddin-Dagan's Sacred Marriage Hymn", (*Journal of Cuneiform Studies*, Vol. 25, No. 4, Oct. 1973), pp. 185-202.

408   stevewatson.info/writings/Sumer/S18.NeoSumerDocs.doc.